THE FOUNDATIONS OF SCOTLAND

DAVID I AND MALCOLM IV

The initial letter of the charter granted by Malcolm IV to the Abbey of Kelso

THE FOUNDATIONS

OF

SCOTLAND

BY

AGNES MURE MACKENZIE

M.A., D.Litt.

Author of

Robert Bruce King of Scots, The Rise of the Stewarts,
The Scotland of Queen Mary and
The Passing of the Stewarts

W. & R. CHAMBERS, LTD.

38 SOHO SQUARE, LONDON, W. 1; AND EDINBURGH

1938

First Published 1938

Printed in Great Britain by T. and A. CONSTABLE LTD
at the University Press, Edinburgh.

UT SCOTIA SERVETUR

Then said I unto them, Ye see the evil case that we are in, how Jerusalem lieth waste, and the gates thereof are burned with fire: come and let us build up the wall of Jerusalem, that we be no more a reproach. And I told them of the hand of my God which was good upon me; as also of the king's words that he had spoken unto me. And they said, Let us rise up and build. So they strengthened their hands for this good work. But when Sanballat the Horonite, and Tobiah the servant, the Ammonite, and Geshem the Arabian, heard it, they laughed us to scorn, and despised us, and said, What is this thing that ye do? . . . Then answered I them, and said unto them, The God of heaven, he will prosper us; therefore we his servants will arise and build: but ye have no portion, nor right, nor memorial, in Jerusalem.

Nehemiah, II.

Εἷς οἰωνὸς ἄριστος ἀμύνεσθαι περὶ πάτρης.

Hector in Iliad XII. Engraved on a snuff-box of Sir Walter Scott's.

The best omen is that one is fighting for one's country.

GENERAL PREFACE

HISTORY is more than a study of things past. It is a study of the roots of the present, of the seeds of the future. No man can guide present or future who forgets it, and one major cause of Scotland's unhappy present is that, though her sense of the past is still keen and vivid, she recalls it only confusedly and in part. If she is to shape her future worthily, that past must be recalled and understood, not as a series of highly coloured stories but as a consecutive process of event.

These volumes are an attempt to understand it, to study the growth of Scotland as a nation and as a part in the larger whole of Europe. I have tried in special to consider those problems that in succession have presented themselves to the men responsible for governing Scotland, because every native reader of these books is himself responsible for governing Scotland, or will be when he reaches voting age. And I have also tried, consistently, to deal with things, people, actions, and desires, not with forms of words. It is easy to think in those, but there is no deadlier habit of the mind. We have seen often enough in our own time how men fighting for the word *Freedom* can end as slaves. Men must fight not for freedom but to be free men, not for prosperity but for a prosperous

country : and to know what a free man is they must
know what a man is—not a sound or a pattern of black
marks on paper but a curious three-dimensional
complex creature that works and eats and suffers and
rejoices, loves certain things and hates others, and can
act in some accordance with these loves and hatreds.
History was never made by the alphabet, in any per-
mutation or combination, but by what men were and
valued and believed, did or refrained from doing or
failed to do.

I have tried to put back again into the picture certain
elements that for the last two hundred years have
frequently been, for practical reasons, omitted from
the official teaching of the subject, thus considerably
distorting the common impression. I have also tried,
in dealing with various conflicts, to give the aims of
the opposing parties not in the formulae used by their
descendants but as in their own contemporary statements, and as far as possible in their own words.
Thus instead of merely praising those crucial documents, the two Covenants, or merely denouncing
them, I have printed their text, which appears to be
unfamiliar to most Scots. I have quoted freely the
operative phrases from a good many others, and given
a careful précis of others again which do not lend
themselves to quotation in fragments but are too
voluminous to quote *in extenso*, such as the Treaty of
Northampton, the Confession of Faith of the 1560
Reformers, the Articles of Perth, or the Treaty of
Union. The results may startle the reader now and

then by contradicting inculcated prepossessions, but in dealing with any sort of national, and still more perhaps with international conflict, the method is that which appears to me most just. I have desired to be just : but I do not claim to be indifferent. No historian can very well be that, unless he is so detached from human feeling as not to care if his country is saved or hurt : and if he should attain that impartial height he will find it hard to comprehend his subject, for history has never been made by indifferent men, but by those who cared with vigour for something or other, if it was only their own material comfort. Moreover, to quote the prose of a great poet, undeservedly neglected in our day—of Robert Browning in *A Soul's Tragedy* :

My friend, as you, with a quickened eyesight, go on discovering much good on the worse side, remember that the same process should proportionably magnify and demonstrate to you the much more good on the better side . . . . God has His archangels and consorts with them : though He made too, and intimately sees what is good in, the worm.

Let us assume there is good on every side in any political conflict, for that is almost invariably true. But let us also, if Scotland is to prosper, remember that good may be the foe of better.

This volume covers a period much neglected. There is in fact much sound and scholarly work on Scots pre-history and the Scots Dark Ages—work whose volume and value increase with every year : but the eleventh, twelfth, and thirteenth centuries, one of the vital times in the history of Europe, are

almost ignored, even by our historians themselves.
Yet centuries went to make the Scotland of Bruce,
and we have some record at least of twelve of them :
and many things that are a part of their story are part,
no less, of our own Scotland today, and may throw
some light on enduring and difficult problems behind
the pages of this morning's paper.

I am indebted to many writers and editors, whose
names appear in the Bibliography, and in special to
Mr Alan Orr Anderson for his monumental collection
of source-material from Scottish, Irish, English, and
Scandinavian records ; to Professor Galbraith of the
University of Edinburgh for his kindness in reading
the book in manuscript and giving me some valuable
criticism ; to the Duke of Roxburghe and the National
Library of Scotland for permission to reproduce the
famous portraits from the Kelso Charter ; to Sir John
Lorne MacLeod, G.B.E. for the kind loan of important out-of-print books ; and to Mr John Mackay
for the end-paper map and genealogy, and for the seal
which decorates the jacket.

North Sea, off Hanstholm,
    August, 1938.

CHRONOLOGY

B.C.
55. *Caesar in Britain.*
27. *Augustus Emperor.*

A.D.
43. *Aulus Plautius in Britain.*
78. *Agricola in Britain.*
81. Agricola reaches the Forth.
84. Mons Graupius.
120. Hadrian's Wall.
140. Antonine Wall.
190. *c.* Frontier withdrawn.
208. Severus in Caledonia.
280. *c. Saxons attacking Britain.*
306. Pictish raids on Britannia.
324. *Christianity the official religion of the Empire.*
368. Picts raid as far as London.
376. *The Goths enter the Empire.*
378. *Adrianople.*
397. *c.* St Ninian founds Candida Casa.
410. *Fall of Rome.*
432. Death of St Ninian.
450. *c.* Jutes, Angles, and Saxons in Britannia.
451. *Council of Chalcedon.*
476. *Fall of Western Empire.*
481. *Franks in Gaul.*
500. *c.* Fergus King of Scots.
524. *Death of Boethius.*
528. *St Benedict founds Monte Cassino.*
529. *Code of Justinian.*
547. Ide founds Bernicia.
563. Arrival of St Columba.
569. *Birth of Mohammed.*

A.D.

590. *Gregory I Pope.*
597. Death of Columba. *Augustine in Kent.*
613. *c.* Cumbria cut off from Cambria.
622. *The Hegira.*
635. Aidan in Lindisfarne.
637. *Moslems take Jerusalem.*
664. Synod of Whitby.
686. Nectansmere.
711. *Moors in Spain.*
732. *Islam checked at Tours.*
735. *Death of Bede.*
787. *Vikings appear in England.*
794. Norse in the Isles.
800. *Charlemagne Emperor.*
802. *Accession of Ecgberht.*
841. *Norse settlement in France.*
843. *Partition of Verdun.* Union of Picts and Scots.
874. *Settlement of Iceland.*
875. *c.* Norse earldom of Orkney.
876. *Rollo in France.*
887. *France and Germany separate.*
901. *Death of Alfred.*
910. *Foundation of Cluny.*
919. *Henry the Fowler Emperor.*
962. *c.* Edinburgh annexed.
987. *Capets on French throne.*
999. *Sylvester II Pope.*
1013. *Danish Conquest of England.*
1018. Carham. South-east Lowlands annexed.
1034. Accession of Duncan I. South-west Lowlands under Scots Crown.
1035. *Death of Cnut.*
1040. Death of Duncan I. Accession of Maelbeatha.
1042. *Accession of Edward the Confessor.*
1056. *Norman Conquest of Apulia.*
1057. Death of Maelbeatha. Accession and death of Lulach. Accession of Malcolm III.
1066. *Norman Conquest of England.*

A.D.

A.D.

1199. *Death of Richard I. Accession of John.*

1204. *England loses northern French fiefs.*

1213. *England a fief of the Pope.*

1214. *Bouvines.* Death of William I. Accession of Alexander II.

1215. *Magna Charta.*

1216. *Death of John. Accession of Henry III.*

1222. Argyle recovered.

1225. Scots Church reconstituted. *Birth of St Thomas Aquinas.*

1235. *c. Roman de la Rose.*

1237. Northumbrian controversy settled by Treaty of York.

1238. Robert Bruce named heir to Scotland.

1240. *c. Birth of Cimabue.*

1249. Death of Alexander II. Accession of Alexander III.

1250. *Death of Frederick II.*

1263. Largs.

1265. *Birth of Dante.*

1266. Treaty of Perth : Hebrides ceded by Norway.

1270. *Death of St Louis. End of Last Crusade.*

1272. *Death of Henry III. Accession of Edward I of England.*

1274. Birth of Robert Bruce (Robert I).

1281. Alliance with Norway.

1284. Death of Prince Alexander.

1286. Death of Alexander III. Accession of Margaret.

1290. Treaty of Birgham. Death of Margaret.

1296. Opening of Three Hundred Years' War.

CONTENTS

xv

The natural loue of zour natiue cuntre suld be inseparablye rutit in zour hartis. . . . Al pepil ar disnaturalit fra there gud nature quhilkis in necessite enforsis them nocht, at there pouer, to purchas and til auance the public weil of ther natiue cuntre.

The Compleynt of Scotland.

CHAPTER I

THE DISTANT ISLAND

TO A.D 80

'They had no compass in those days, only the North Star and their nerve.'

H. M. Tomlinson, *All Hands*.

EVEN now when anyone who has turned thirty has seen the map of Europe change shape and colour, we are apt to think of what we call a country as a space of land inherently defined. This way of thought is easier, of course, to people whose country is nowadays clearly bounded by some great natural feature, plain to sight : and most of our own marches are traced by the sea. Yet for many centuries after our story begins, there was no such country as our present Scotland. It was something like five hundred years, in fact—a time as from now to the death of James the Second outside the vanished town of Roxburgh—before even a little kingdom of the Scots filled a mere fraction of what to-day is Scotland. Twelve hundred—a longer time by a good deal than from Charlemagne to ourselves—had to go by before Scotland covered the ground she holds to-day. It is not yet seven hundred years since Largs. Indeed, it is only since 1482 that the shape of Scotland has been what it is now. As for the nation inhabiting the country, a single Scottish nation is hardly formed yet. Less than a couple of

3

hundred years ago, the kingdom of Scotland, though older than most in Europe, was still composed of two quite different nations, united, certainly, by a common Crown, a common central machine of government, but more unlike than modern France and England—different in language, costume, administration, in mode of life and largely in standards of value. If we go back another nine hundred years, we find *five* nations under separate rulers, each with its individual language and culture, and some of them differing much more widely in race than Highlands and Lowlands in 1745.

These things must be remembered, for comprehension. Yet it is worth our while to remember also that if we take a time roughly midway between Kenneth MacAlpin and Culloden Muir, we find this odd congeries of little nations was yet capable of more than a formal union. French, Gaelic, English, possibly yet some Welsh, a trifle of Flemish, a trifle again of Norse, and the international Latin of the scholar might be heard in the camp that lay to the south of Stirling on the Midsummer Eve of the year 1314 : yet the troops who marched from the wood and knelt to pray with their faces against the sunrise of the morrow, and having prayed, went forward then for Scotland, were united by a common national will. And we know what happened before that midsummer noon. The ebb and flow of that will to unity is an element that we need to watch in reading, for it has always been a crucial factor. Not the only one : there was unity at Flodden. None the less, but for unity, Bannockburn would have been lost, and Scotland been erased from the map of the world.

We need not go back to the time when the North Sea was merely a low-lying river-basin, whose main stream was a confluence of the Thames and Rhine. Let us think of an island beyond the shores of the world, roughly six hundred miles from end to end, with many others lying to the west of it, ranging from one a third of its own size to mere rocks thrust from the shifting of the ocean. What we must look for is first the growth of a kingdom, and then of a nation co-terminous with that kingdom, filling the northern third of the main island, and most of the smaller ones that lie to the west.

Before man touched that land, it had seen great changes, passed from a tropical country to one deep covered in enduring ice, risen and fallen above the height of the sea. When first it came to be inhabited, at a time before it was actually an island, more than half its north part was covered by dense forest, full of beasts—the boar, the wolf, the lynx and the wild ox, the reindeer and the elk : but under a climate now grown damp and mild, the trees were beginning to go, to turn into peat. Yet still its surface was difficult to cross : it was filled for its major part with great steep hills, their passes blocked by forests, bogs, and rivers. For thousands of years the beasts were unquestioned lords.

Then slowly the southern districts of the island began at last to be inhabited by a primitive race of men, using rough stone tools. It was long, however, before man reached the northern, for few 'Palaeolithic' remains are found in Scotland. But by and by man

> adventured first to sea
> His fragile raft,

and coastwise intercourse became possible, and was easier, given fine weather, than internal. Small colonies of fishers and of hunters began to settle on the more northern coasts—few yet, however, for there they could find but little of the flint that counted then as iron counts now. Professor Gordon Childe is of the opinion that what brought them first was the early routes of trade, carrying the valued amber from the Baltic to the shores of what now are Spain and Southern France : their remains at least show a culture which seems connected with that of those countries and of what is now Southern England, and the Professor is of the opinion that their rank and file came from this last, and their ' officer class ' from Spain, and possibly also from Sardinia.

Their culture was of the type called Neolithic. They used stone implements yet, but finely, even delicately fashioned : they were skilled hunters, surprising seamen, had become herds, and practised a rudimentary agriculture. They built houses, had something of art (though less advanced than that of some Palaeoliths) and they were capable of organisation, not only for defence but for creation, making great structures like the Standing Stones at Callernish or Stennis, and burying their dead in great monumental cairns. It is clear that they had some elements of religion. In short, they were not tool-using animals, but men, with a culture higher than that of some races now living : and they spread along the coasts and into the more accessible sheltered valleys of the north parts of the still nameless island, and came to the lesser islands of the West, for the amber trade-route seems to have run by these rather than by the strong tides of the Straits of Dover.

These shadowy people are part of modern Scotland, though not part of the five small states that united to make her. They are called by a variety of names, Turanian, Silurian, Iberian. All three beg a number of very complex questions, to which better scholars than the present author give answers often very positive, but in fiery contradiction one with another. The certain fact about this race, at least, is that it was not of what is called the Aryan group of peoples. It was short, stocky, powerful, and probably dark, with a certain Mongol cast about the eyes. Some say that it survives as a community in the present Basques, whose strange complex speech, unlike any other in Europe, is a development of its ancient language. Undoubtedly, though in the island we are discussing it was conquered before any history began, and ceased to exist as a nation (if it ever had been what we can call a nation), it was not by any means extirpated. ' Pockets ' of it survive to the present day in the West and the Isles, and it is a very conspicuous element in Ireland, especially Southern Ireland, and in Wales : in this last, it is possibly stronger than the Celtic. Mixed stocks (and all our descents are very mixed) throw back to it often in individual members.[1]

To this first race was later added another, known from their pottery as the Beaker-people. These came from the Low Countries to the North-east, and were strong in what is nowadays Aberdeenshire, where apparently they survived as a separate strain. It is possible, or very probable, that they and also their language and their culture may have provided some distinctive elements in the nation that we know by a derivative of its Latin name, *Picti*. They may have been Celts, or not : it seems more probable that they were not. They understood the use of bronze for weapons.

While Neolithic culture still held the island, much of our history, as commonly happens, was proceeding in places several hundred miles off. That continual pressure of the East on the West that shows since the dimmest history began drove other races across what we now call Europe. The Aryan division of the so-called White race of mankind was spreading steadily westward from its home, the Asian country north-west

---

[1] The writer knows two (unrelated) pairs of sisters, Scots and English, in which one of each is conspicuously of this type in colouring and build, though not in feature, while the other is a completely typical ' Nordic,' brilliantly fair. The Scots pair have four brothers, of whom one belongs to the Iberian type (his army nickname was ' the Gurkha '), two are markedly ' Nordic ' and the fourth resembles his ' Iberian ' brother and sister in build and feature but the ' Nordics ' in colour.

of the Indus. The first wave it sent over Europe was that of the Celts. Some two and a half millennia before Christ—or a few centuries or so each way—they were filling what we know as Central Europe, driving west, or subjugating and enslaving, the races of the Neolithic culture, whose stone weapons were no match for their fine bronze. Still one people drove on another— Celts who used iron on Celts who still used bronze, Teuton on Celt as Asia poured out its hordes beyond the marches of the Levantine and Mediterranean cultures, that already were very ancient civilisations. By the time that the great Greek tragedies were written, when Rome was becoming mistress of Italy—the fourth century before Christ—bronze-using Celts had reached as far as the Orkneys : they may have worked north from the southern part of the island, or come overseas from the Weser and the Rhine. They were a tall race, apparently fair : ethnologists call them Goidels (our Gaidhel, Gael) and their language is the original of Scots and Irish Gaelic and of Manx. They are to-day the dominant racial stock of Ireland and of Scotland north of Forth.

Following these came another Celtic race, iron-using. They were identical with the Gauls who gave the infant Roman republic so much of trouble and humiliation. By 200 B.C., when Rome was at death-grips with Carthage for the control of the Western Mediterranean, they had pressed northward over much of this island, and had settlements at Taymouth and on the Moray Firth. They did not, however, penetrate the great hills, and their race does not touch the North of Scotland, the West above Clyde, or Ireland, although the influence of their crafts was felt there. Their speech was akin to that of the Gauls : [1] its descendants are the Cymric languages, Welsh, Brézonec, Cornish. It was sprung from the same older speech as that of the Goidels, but had had time to develop differences. One conspicuous one is that the sound *qu-* in the primitive Celtic speech becomes a *q* or hard *c* sound in the one and *p* in the other : Goidelic *mac*, son, is Cymric *(m)ap* ; Goidelic *ceann*, head, is Cymric *pen* : and the two tongues are labelled by Professor Rhys as Q-Celtic and P-Celtic respectively. This people nowadays forms the major stock of South-west Scotland between the Clyde and Solway, of Cumberland, Wales (much mixed with the Iberian), of Cornwall, and of a great part of France. They are called now Brythons, which approximates to their own name for themselves.

These peoples were by no means savages. They were organised on a tribal or clan system, they had a considerably developed culture, and worked metals and pottery into a beauty of form that suggests a sensitive care for the graces of life. They were capable of considerable feats of engineering, and both were lively and accomplished fighters.

The above description of prehistoric events is that

---

[1] Gaul, Gallia, is *(G)wlad*, the Home-land. *(G)uladh*, which with the Norse suffix *-ster* becomes Ulster, is a form of the same word.

generally accepted : but it has been challenged.
Professor Kuno Meyer and his school, represented in
Scotland by Professor Watson, consider that no Gaels
ever came to Scotland until, much later, they arrived
from Ireland. The point is of no great practical
importance. They did come, before we have much
' history,' and they filled the districts enumerated
above. It is more important to remember henceforth
that all these descriptions of movements of early races
are of necessity broadly generalised. The period
covered by the next seven chapters is that from
Agricola to Malcolm III—a time longer than that from
Malcolm III to ourselves. That age was one of fluid
political changes, of shifting boundaries and constant
migration, and gave scope for much interchange of
culture and language. Language is very little guide
to race. Many Scots whose mother-tongue is Gaelic
or English are of a racial stock that is mainly Norse :
many Welsh or Irish, born to a Celtic language, are of
a stock anterior to the Celtic. And during so long a
time, languages change, intermingle, and take on new
elements. If Malcolm said the Lord's Prayer with his
English wife, in her own tongue, its opening would go
thus :

Fader ure, þu þæt eart on heofenum, sie þin nama gehalgod.

Yet for half the time that separates us from him,
English has had the printing-press to fix it.

This first millennium is vague and distant. Yet we
must remember that each of its thousand years had

as many days in it as a year has now, and each of these
days had as many hours as this one.

During the long slow process that has been sketched,
the island lies over the margin of written history. The
Straits of Gibraltar were the End of the World. Yet
men sailed at times beyond the End of the World, and
brought back stories of its cloudy marches. So early
as 1200 years before Christ, about the time when the
Judges judged Israel, the Phœnician colonists of the
Mediterranean traded for tin to what may have been
this island. By 600 B.C., when Sappho was making
her songs and Jeremiah crying his prophecies, the
Phocaean colony of Massilia, that we call Marseilles,
was probably doing so. About a hundred years later,
when Greece was fighting Persia, and Rome by
tradition was driving out her kings, one Himilco set
out from Carthage on a voyage, and he reached the
islands of the Albiones, which may have been called
for something like our *Alba*. Then at last, about
350 B.C., when Rome was bidding for the mastery of
central Italy and the Greek culture was reaping its
last great harvest, the islands come clear through the
mist, if but for a moment. Pytheas sailed from
Massilia through the Straits, and followed the coast
right up to the Arctic Circle. He brought back with
him a story of great islands, with a promontory Orcus
on their north : and the isles are called αἱ νῆσοι
πρεταννικαί, the Pretannic Isles, which appear in the
Welsh tongue as Ynys Prydain, and in Latin as Insulae
Britannicae.

We know that after that there was trade with Gaul, and with the Mediterranean by sea : the islands were acknowledged to be there, not a mere sailor's story after dinner. But they were known, for another three hundred years, as the Europe of 1500 knew the Americas. The first clear sight—and that only a brief glimpse, though it came through a most intelligent pair of eyes—does not come until the year 55 B.C., when Caesar brought a Roman force from Gaul to the coast of the island he knew as Britannia, and found its tides extremely disconcerting. Caesar was man-about-town who had turned great soldier, not a professor of ethnology : he did not go far and he did not stay for long, and much of his information was simple hearsay. He reports a culture akin to that of Gaul in the southern part, but a good deal more primitive inland : some of his statements are contradicted, however, by the evidence of archaeology.

Caesar went back, and added Gaul to the dominions of Rome, made himself master of the world, and died. For another century Britannia was again outside history. Then Rome invaded, this time to stay for nearly four hundred years : and this time, though not for half a man's lifetime after their landing in Britain, her soldiers were to look on what now is Scotland.

CHAPTER II

THE ROMAN AND THE PICT

THREE HUNDRED AND FIFTY-TWO YEARS : 80–432

' Ecce Caesar . . . qui subiegit Gallias.'
Roman Soldiers' Song.

WHEN Pytheas sailed to the Isles of the Pretannoi, Rome was not young, but she was still apparently unimportant. She was a small city-state who had wrested from the Etruscans the control of what now is Central Italy, and beaten back certain waves of Celtic invasion. By a generation after Pytheas—by 272 B.C., that is to say—she was mistress of Italy. A century and a quarter after that, she was ruler of the Western Mediterranean. A century more, and the Mediterranean was a Roman lake, and Rome's march was on the Rhine and the English Channel. For four hundred years thereafter, the history of Western civilisation is the history of the Roman Empire, of a single state covering what now are Spain, Portugal, England, France, Italy, Belgium, Switzerland, the lands from the Adriatic to the Danube, Greece and the Balkan States to the Danube again, Asia Minor, Mesopotamia, the Levant, Egypt, and the north coast of Africa for a depth of a hundred to three hundred miles. All of this state to the west of the

14

Adriatic formed for practical purposes a single nation, centrally organised (though with a wise measure of local devolution) in a common political life, with a common official language, educational system, a culture common to all the upper classes, a common (though very tolerant) state religion, and a far better system of communications than anywhere between about 400 and the second half of the nineteenth century. And during much of this four hundred years (a time as from ourselves to James the Fifth) peace was as normal to most of Western Europe as war has been since. There was intermittent fighting on the Marches : there were occasional local insurrections or armed *coups d'état* : but peace, a peace firmly policed, and for free men, comfortably organised, was a thing that the average man could take for granted. That age of peace, the longest peace, and the widest, the world has known, nurtured the infancy of the Christian Church, whose cradle was girt by the shields of the frontier legions.

Augustus, counted the first Emperor, was the man who crystallised this mighty system : and some thirty years after he gathered the power in his hands ' the Angel of the Lord came unto Mary,' and her Son was born in a little Syrian town that once had been the City of King David . . . born to be King of Peace and to bring a sword, to reign above emperors from the Roman gallows, and make the weak things of the world confound the mighty. The first Gentile to profess faith in Our Lord, the first man to acclaim Him crucified, the

first man to die in these islands for the Faith, were
Roman soldiers : and it was not unfitting.

Augustus organised, and bounded, the Empire.
Rome deliberately abandoned the policy of conquest
and expansion she had held for something like four
hundred years. There were, however, some temporary
and local returns to it, and in one of them, under the
fourth Emperor, Claudius, Aulus Plautius in 43 crossed
to Britannia, and set about the conquest of the island.
He and Ostorius Scapula pushed northward. There
was fierce resistance at first, under Caradog, whom they
knew as Caractacus, but by 51 he had been betrayed to
their hands, and was sent to Rome, and Ostorius
granted a triumph.[1] Within twenty years, the years
when St Paul was going about his journeys, the south
of the island was made a Roman province, and the
legions pushed on in a moving wall to the north.
But the province was exploited and mishandled :
Tacitus gives a grim picture of the conditions. In 61
it rose bloodily, led by the queen of a south-eastern
tribe : even a legion, marching south, was massacred.
The revolt was put down, and in 78 Cnaeus Julius
Agricola, a fine soldier and a most admirable type of
colonial administrator, was sent to establish good
government, which he did. He settled Roman rule
over the south of Britannia, west to the Silurian March,

---

[1] Caradog and his family were in Rome at the same time as
St Paul. It is said that when he returned he brought four Christian
missionaries, one being an Italian, Arwystli, who may be the
Aristobulus of Romans xvi. 10 : the Greek Martyrology refers to
this man as a Bishop of the Britons.

the border of Wales, and north past the frontier town of Eboracum. (Caer-efrog, Eorwic, York.) Then he moved against the clan of the Brigantes, that filled what we now call Northumberland.

Next year he came to the river Taus or Tanaus, among *ignotas gentes*, unknown peoples, and possibly looked upon what now is Scotland, for that river may be either of the Tynes. In 81, before the death of St John Evangelist, he had certainly made a post beside the Tweed, at Trimontium underneath the triple Eildons, and pushed west through the great hill mass that looks over the Clyde to Tinto and the hills of the South-west. In the same year he marked out a new frontier, the northmost boundary of the far-flung Empire, by a line of fortified posts, *praesidia*, from Boderia to Clota, Forth to Clyde. And in this manner was our Southern Scotland brought into the Roman Empire, for a little.

Now the natural course for Agricola thereafter was to continue the process of the last forty years, and push north through what his ships had just proved an island [1] until the whole of it was in Roman hands. The obvious, however, did not happen, for at this point he encountered a new people. His son-in-law, Cornelius Tacitus, was a great man of letters, and wrote of this campaign from eye-witness accounts,

---

[1] They sighted Thule on their circumnavigation. It may have been the Shetlands, but Ptolemy's map suggests it was the Lews : the Lews, seen from the coast of Wester Ross, may well have looked like the last land of the world.

and at last our country comes clearly into daylight : and the first thing recorded in its history is successful resistance to a strong invasion. Agricola could push the march no further, and although for more than three centuries to come Rome held the southern part of Britannia, when this northern frontier moved it was to fall back.

Agricola did advance beyond the Forth, in 83 and again in 84 : but in the latter year the tribes of the North, of Caledonia, were organised by Calgacus to resist him. Tacitus gives the Caledonian leader a speech to his troops that Wallace might have made : good Roman as he was, he could see clearly the case against ' Imperial expansion.'

Auferre, trucidare, rapere, falsis nominibus imperium : atque ubi solitudinem faciunt, pacem appellant.[1]

Calgacus had Wallace's luck. Agricola pushed on, apparently into the hills, to a place his son-in-law calls Mons Graupius : he may have crossed Forth above Stirling (where there is a Roman paved ford) and gone up the Teith or the Earn, or even the Tay. There Calgacus met him. The long Celtic cutting sword, like the pike against the handier bill at Flodden, was outmatched by the short thrusting *gladius*. But as happened to many more of our invaders, Agricola won the battle but lost the campaign. He could not press effectually forward, and Domitian recalled him shortly after.

[1] ' Loot, massacre, rape, they call by the lying name of a government : where they make a wilderness, they call that peace.'

There was no further serious attempt to push north, and in 115 the frontier was actually withdrawn, to a new line from Segedunum to the Ituna—from the Tyne to the Solway. The clans still gave trouble, and in 119 there was a rising in which the Ninth Legion was completely wiped out. The Emperor Hadrian came in person next year to settle the matter. He had already, in his three years' rule, reversed Trajan's expansionist policy on the Danube. Now he applied the change to Caledonia, making this new retired line a permanent march, defined by 80 Roman miles of rampart, with a garrison of 11,000 men.[1] Now the Wall ran through the land of the Brigantes, and in 138 Lollius Urbicus, commanding for Antoninus Pius, drove their clan out of Roman territory. The result was a rising. He pushed beyond the Wall, and in 142 the March was defined again, at Agricola's old line from Forth to Clyde, by a great turf vallum and fosse. For the second time the land between the walls became a portion of the Empire, briefly.

Soon after 180 the clans from the north had broken through this further, Antonine, wall, and in a few years, before 190, the frontier again was withdrawn to Hadrian's Wall.[2] It seems that the Caledonians by this time were learning the lesson of union. They had been defeated because they would not unite.

[1] It is about this time we have the first map of Britannia, by the Alexandrian scientist Ptolemy. He gives seventeen tribes in Caledonia, which he calls Albion.

[2] The great fortified camp at Trimontium (Newstead) shows traces of five separate occupations.

Tacitus says candidly

Nec aliud adversus validissimas gentes pro nobis utilius quam quod in commune non consulunt . . . ita singuli pugnant, universi vincuntur.[1]

The comment can be applied to most of our history, and the exceptions more than prove the rule, for united Scotland has beaten colossal odds. Now the clans organised in confederacies. About 200, Dio Cassius speaks of them as forming two groups, the Maeatae between the Walls, and the Caledonii to the north of them. (The long-standing division, north and south of Forth, thus appears very early.) They rose formidably. Rome decided to make an end, and in 208 the Emperor Septimus Severus drew troops from all over the Empire and led them as far, it would seem, as the Moray Firth. He was a sick man, and it brought him to death, but that was all he gained by the expedition. His forts benorth the vallum went back to forest : he strengthened Hadrian's, the southern, wall, and was about to go north again, when he died.

Caledonia then slips into mist for a while. The third century was an anxious time for the Empire, with civil disturbances by emperor-making soldiers, and the barbarians pressing on the frontier. The south of Britannia, however, was fairly quiet. The Roman civilisation had taken root there. There were ninety-odd towns, over thirty being of some size,

[1] ' Nothing is of more service to us against the strongest tribes than the fact that they have no common policy . . . thus they fight singly and are collectively beaten.'

each a miniature republic on the Mediterranean pattern, with all the apparatus of civilisation, and a good deal more of its comforts, in many ways, than anything till this present century. Agriculture and mining were well developed, and transport, both passenger and goods, was well organised and easy. It was a snug and comfortable country, so Romanised that even in the small farms, well to the north, there is no trace of Celtic art, and the workmen's casual scrawlings are in Latin. But it was rather like the American Colonies of the mid-eighteenth century, the days of the Iroquois League. In the south was a country tamed into urban comfort : in the north the sentries challenged on the Wall, one to another, across its eighty miles, in a permanent state of siege, with the chance of violent attack at any moment.

All through the middle of that third century the soldiers were in charge of politics. So early as 37 they had made an Emperor : but in the fifty years after 235, they made a couple of dozen. After 284 Diocletian attempted to check this state of affairs, and reorganised the administrative system, making Britannia a diocese of the Prefecture of Gaul . . . and in 287 the diocese made an Emperor of her own, Carausius or Carawn, the British admiral of the Roman Channel Fleet. He was murdered, and his murderer seized the power, and in 296 was put down by Constantius Chlorus, and Britain was held for another hundred years. But already, during this brief separation, the Teutonic pirates made raids on the East Coast.

None the less, most of the fourth century was quiet
in South Britain—a fact which made it a useful re-
cruiting-ground. (Indeed, some quarter of the Roman
army was said to consist of British troops at this time :
and Dugal Dalgetty had begun his campaigns, for
Caledonians were enlisted also.) Christianity spread.
At the Council of Arles in 314 British bishops were
present. There were others at Nicaea in 325, the
year after Christianity had become the State religion,[1]
and at Rimini in 359. But the Saxon pirates were
threatening the coast, and a special department of
defence, whose head was the Count of the Saxon Shore
(*Comes Litoris Saxonici per Britanniam*), was created to
deal with them, while always, as elsewhere in this
century, there was a sense of unease beyond the
Marches, like wolves wandering round a warm closed
house in the night.

We know little of Caledonia between Severus and
about 360, but there seem to have been new com-
binations of tribes, for in 297 the enemies of the Britons
are said to be the Hiberni and the Picti. The Hiberni,
of course, are men of Hibernia, Ireland. A reference
in 310 fixes the others : it is to ' the Caledonians and
other Picts.' In fact the name, or some variant of it,
was used for several centuries thereafter for the
majority (a decreasing majority) of the inhabitants of
Caledonia, the people who had occupied the country
from the beginning of more or less historic times, as

[1] The fact is a commentary on the system of transport and
communication, for Nicaea is in Asia Minor.

distinct from the incoming Scots, Angles, Britons and
Northmen. There has been much dispute about the
Picts, based too often on a forgetting of the fact that
countries full of loosely organised tribes with fluid
boundaries may in the course of a time several centuries
long produce some varied mixtures of races and
cultures.

Most of what has been said of the Picts is probably
true . . . in part, and at some time of their long story.
(We have to remember that some sort of Pictish nation
existed for at least six hundred years.) It has been said
that they were a pre-Celtic people, because the Kings
of Picts were succeeded as a rule not by their sons, but
by the sons of their mothers, their sisters, or their
aunts : and this is certainly not a Celtic custom.
Others declare that they were indubitably Celtic : and
archaeological evidence suggests a culture with strong
resemblances to known Celtic features.[1] That culture
was far above the savage level : the Roman colonists
whose houses they sacked were vituperative, naturally :
but if we are to accept Dio Cassius's description, we
must also believe that there was no water in the
Highland hills : his authority is equally good for both.
In fact, we know that they tilled the soil and possessed
flocks and herds, that they were capable of building

[1] On the strength of what survives of their language—that is to
say, of a number of proper names—Skene considers it to have been
Goidelic Celtic. Stokes, Loth, MacBain, D'Arbois, and Mayer
think it to have been a form of Brython-Celtic. Professor Rhys is
of the opinion that it was not only non-Celtic but non-Aryan. The
proper names have in fact certain similarities to Brythonic, but with
elements, as *pit* and *foder* or *fodel*, which are not found in Wales.

immense hill forts and many towers of a kind well
adapted for defence, showing considerable engineering
capacity, and not found elsewhere. They made cloth,
dyed and patterned. They did fine carving in bone,
and they produced metal-work of a consummate and
delicate skill which has never been surpassed. The
general character of their 'remains' (which are
plentiful throughout Pictavia) is Late Celtic, but with
highly individual features, as in the stone brochs and
some types of ornament.[1] The general inference from
ethnology and archaeology and such common-sense
as the mere word *Pict* does not banish, is that the people
who came, for whatever reason, to be called Picts were
simply the inhabitants of Caledonia generally, who by
the late third century were a mixed race, with Celtic,
probably, for its strongest factor, and possibly a Celtic
ruling class : and that racially, culturally, and linguisti-
cally, some of their characteristics were derived from
the infusion of two older races, the ' Beaker-people '
of the North-east and the descendants of the Neolithic
Iberians : there may even have been a Teutonic
infusion as well, of immigrants from over the North
Sea. It may be added that the proportion of the
different ingredients would no doubt vary, and perhaps
very widely, from district to district through an area
that once covered the whole of Scotland north of
Forth, and from time to time through a range of

[1] Their Christian monuments from the fifth to the tenth century
show a peculiar and definite group of motifs, so constant that they
seem to be ideographic, though archaeologists have not found
the key.

centuries as long as that which separates us from Bruce.

In fact, the mystery, as so often happens, is not so much in the thing as in the name. Its simplest explanation, of course, is that they painted themselves, at least for war,[1] and the Romans therefore called them the Painted People, *Picti*. That may indeed be a mere translation of *Breatann*, for *brith* (Gaelic *breac*) is *particoloured*, or *speckled*. The Gaelic word for a Pict is *Cruthen*, which may be cognate with *cruth*, form, pattern:[2] and it is simply the early Q-Celtic form for the P-Celtic *Pryden*, Briton, which is later borrowed a second time as *Breatann* or *Britt*. On the other hand, *Picti* may simply be a rationalisation, based on the habit of painting, of some native name—a parallel with the lower-deck use of the *Angry Cat* for the *Henri IV* or the *Billy Ruffian* for the *Bellerophon*. There were Pictones in Gaul and a district Pictavia (Richard Cœur de Lion witnessed the Treaty of Falaise as *Comes Pictaviae*, Count of Poitou), and the Norsemen, who were not in contact with Latin, called a Pict *Pettr*. The Welsh called them *Ffichti*, and the Saxon word is *Peohtas*, which comes into Scots as *Pecht*. One observes that Tacitus, the first to mention the inhabitants of the district north of Forth, calls

[1] This is another non-Celtic custom . . . but the Christian Angles had to be checked by the Church from adopting the practice, so it is not impossible that the heathen Celts did so, along with their succession law, from an older people.

[2] *Rex Pictaviae* and *Rex Pictorum* appear in Gaelic as *Righ Cruithinigh* and *Righ Cruithentuach*.

them simply *Britanni*, though he mentions one tribe, the Boresti, of whom no more is heard, and implies the existence of others. It seems probable that whatever word turned into *Pictus* may have been the name of a tribe, and was subsequently used, as *Scot* was later, for the confederation of which it was part, and to which it supplied the ruling dynasty . . . for while early Caledonia was a mosaic of apparently independent tribes, Pictavia, in historic times, is generally one kingdom, occasionally dividing in two.

The mid fourth century brought very serious danger to the Empire. Her stately structure had been weakened by the disorganisation of dissension, by too urbanised a life, by over-taxation. She began to seem weak to her enemies without. In 355 the Franks and Alemanni, Teutonic peoples from across the Rhine, raided Gaul and took no less than forty towns. Julian, who was then Caesar (the Emperor's appointed heir, like the Gaelic tanist), drove them back, but soon there was similar trouble in Britain. The Picts were over the Wall—Hadrian's Wall : and with them came allies, the already very sadly familiar Saxons, a Teutonic tribe from south or south-east of Jutland, and along with them the Scoti, Gaels from Ireland. By 368 they were raiding as far as Londinium, the greatest trading city in all Britannia, rich by three centuries odd of Roman commerce . . . a longer time than any of the Dominions have been British.

Valentinian, now Emperor, sent an able Spanish

general, Theodosius, to deal with the situation. He did so, and to such effect that he reclaimed the lost district between the Walls, and brought it a third time into the Roman Empire.[1] This was the last push north. Before men who fought in it had left the service, the whole Empire west of Greece had been broken to pieces, and her culture was plunging into barbarism.

Far in Asia, the huge mass of the Huns was moving westward, destroying all that lay before them like locusts. They crossed the Volga and they crossed the Don. They drove before them the Goths, in the country between the Dnieper and the Danube. In 376 the Western Goths, Visigoths, came over the Danube that was the Roman march, though peaceably yet, as suppliants for shelter. Then they rose in arms, and at Adrianople in 378 defeated and killed the Emperor who had received them. Adrianople is about 1800 miles from Edinburgh : but that battle is a landmark in British history.

Then there was civil war in the West as well. In 383 Maximus, the British-born *Vicarius Britanniarum* —the Governor of the Britains—made a bid for the imperial dignity. He nearly won it, but in 388 was defeated and killed by the son, and namesake, of Theodosius. This younger Theodosius became the last strong Emperor. He reunited the Empire

---

[1] He is commonly said to have called it Valentia. Professor Cunningham, however, has shown some cause for considering that the district so called may have been a part of Wales.

Domitian had divided in two, and was the last to hold both East and West.

Theodosius died in 395, leaving the Empire to two useless sons. The Picts had been through the Wall in Maximus's time, and he had driven them back. Now in 396 they came again. And in that year the Goths under Alaric marched through Macedonia and Thessaly, sacked Argos, Corinth, Sparta, put Athens to ransom. They were held by a half-surrender for a little, but in 401 rose and marched on Italy. Troops were withdrawn from Britannia to deal with them. Alaric was pushed back, and the troops returned again to cope with the Picts : but in 405 Radagaisus was across the Apennines with a flood of 200,000 Vandals, Suevi, and Burgundians, and in 406 Gaul also was invaded. Next year, Britannia was evacuated by the garrison. The Picts took the northern districts and breached the Wall. The unhappy provincials, with the end of the world crashing down on their settled living, cried for help to Rome : and Rome gave them—their freedom.

In 410 the Goths sacked the Eternal City. Though the name of the Empire was to last in the West for a man's lifetime yet, west of Greece only patches of the thing remained, storm-beaten isles in a barbarian sea, where men like Aëtius or Boniface made heroic stands in North Gaul or Africa. The Huns, behind it all, pressed steadily on. In 445 Attila, Scourge of God, was King from the Volga to the Rhine and Baltic, and moving west. In the extremity, in 451 what was left of the Empire allied with her invaders, and under Aëtius beat back the Huns at Châlons, in one of the major battles of the world. But Aëtius was murdered for his pains. Rome was sacked again four years later by the Vandals, and in 476 Odoacer deposed the puppet Emperor, and reigned in Italy. All of the Empire from Dalmatia westward, save for North Gaul and part of Spain, was gone : and their hour was at hand.

Britain was left a prey to Picts, Scots, and Saxons. There was some attempt to organise a resistance, and cloudy figures stand out in that desperate time—Cunedd or Kenneth, son of Coel Hen,[1] a chief of what now is Ayrshire or thereabouts ; Owain ap Maxim, son of Maximus ; Emrys Wledig—Aurelius Ambrosianus ; Uthyr ; and Arthur, who was to become a legend that all Western Europe had a hand in the making. But we know little of that long losing war, although the defence went on, without hope, for generation after generation, each watching the front move a little further inland. The soldiers had gone : the orderly world they guarded had gone also, and for many centuries : but behind them—he did not die for a score of years after the thunderbolt news of the sack of Rome—they left beside the Solway a Roman bishop, who did what the legions could not in Caledonia and whose work there was to endure for longer than theirs.

This was the son of a chief of the Novantae, whose

---

[1] Coel the Old—Old King Cole, in fact. Kyle is supposed to take its name from him.

country was in what we call Galloway. His name was Nenn, or with the affectionate diminutive, Nennan, which in Latin gives Nennius or Ninianus. Now in Roman Britannia there was already a well-established Church. There were martyrs in the persecution of 304, and since 324 Christianity had been the State religion all over the Empire. Apparently, even much earlier than that, the Faith had spread to some extent over the Marches. Tertullian early in the third century speaks of *Britannorum inaccessa Romanis loca, Christo vero subdita*—places of the Britons, out of reach of the Romans, conquered by the true Christ. Who their apostles were, we shall never know : but Ninian's father, apparently, was a Christian.

The saint was born about 362, in what was then independent territory. Before he was ten, Theodosius had recovered the district between the Walls, and it may have been as a hostage that the boy was sent to Rome for his education. There he received orders and eventually the episcopate : and he decided to return to his own people.

Three of the great Doctors of the Church, St Ambrose, St Jerome, and St Augustine, were then men in middle age. In Gaul, St Hilary was lately dead, and the leadership of the Gallican Church had devolved on St Martin, Abbot-Bishop of Caesarodunum, which is Tours. The long connection of Touraine with Scotland goes back before either Scotland or France existed, for the cradle of organised Scots Christianity is St Martin's abbey, still by the

Loire near Tours. The Church in Gaul derived from the East rather than from Italy. Potinus, apostle of Gaul, was a pupil of St Polycarp of Smyrna, and St Hilary had been for long in Phrygia. Now St Martin, a soldier of noble family, a great administrator as well as saint, scholar, and founder of the first Christian hospital in the West, had brought into Gaul an institution new in the Western Church. Long before Christianity, men had withdrawn themselves to solitary contemplation of God. After Christianity came there had been Christian hermits. In the early fourth century St Pachomius had drawn many of these together to live in groups, under a rule of poverty, chastity, and obedience, combining organised prayer with study and manual labour. The new institution was to save civilisation, and Christianity with it.

St Martin brought it into the Western Church, in the country of the Pictones, Poitou, Poictou, or Pictavia. His community became famous : he was forced to leave nis first small house at Ligugé and found another, Magnum Monasterium, Mòr Muinntir, Marmoutier, close to Tours, of which city he became the bishop. Ninian went there to study the system, and became Martin's enthusiastic disciple. The names of his own foundations witness loving remembrance. His own first was to be known as *Muinntir Mòr*, but he called it himself after Martin's first at Ligugé. Logotegiacum, the Latin name of that, is Celtic *leuk* (Gaelic *geal*, shining white) and *tigh*, a house. Ninian's was *Candida Casa*, and its daughter-house in Wales *Ty Gwynn*, the Bright House.

About 397 Ninian returned to his country. The Empire, though troubled and threatened and invaded, was still apparently part of the nature of things. He settled at Whithorn, in a Roman province, and there built an abbey on the lines of St Martin's. By the time its garden was in decent order, the Goths were marching into Italy, and when Ninian died in 432, the Empire had lost Spain, Gaul, and Britain, and Rome itself had been sacked. Brave men, though, worked in the chaos; and he was one. He established at Whithorn a great monastic school that for generations was a focus of scholarship and missionary enterprise, and probably, too, a shelter for scholars fleeing from invaded Gaul. Its influence was felt outside Caledonia. Many great Irish saints were trained there —St Tighernac and St Kiaran, founder of the great school of Clonmacnoise; SS. Finian and Kevin; St Finnbarr of Moville, the teacher of St Columba and founder of Dornoch Cathedral; and Caranoc, who baptised the Briton St Patrick. It is worth remark that some of the scholars were women.

St Ninian did not stay for disciples to come. He set out on journeys among the heathen Picts, through that wild country. It is commonly said that he did not cross the Grampians. Mr Black Scott, however, has pointed out that Bede, who is the authority for that statement, was going by Ptolemy's map: and Ptolemy's map turns Scotland at right angles to its real axial line.

The Mull of Galloway is its northmost point, and *Dorsum Britanniae, Druim Albann,* Bede's *ardua et horrentia montium iuga,* the long ridge of watershed, runs east and west instead of north and south. Bede's Southern Picts, to whom Ninian went as apostle, are really those *east* of the Grampians. He went, in fact, by the natural route, by Cathures (Glasgow), Stirling, and so by Strathmore and the Lowlands of the North-east, where modern archaeological research has tracked his footprints. In the early Celtic Church, churches bore the name of their founders : and prehistoric churches dedicated to St Ninian are found as far as the Shetlands—some so old they were out of use in the sixth century. He is in fact one of the major founders of that Celtic Church whose monks (for all the Celtic clergy were monks : there were no seculars) were to spread in time from Iceland to the Danube.

He died in 432, before the final overthrow of the Empire : and his work among the Picts was carried on, not only by his own pupils but by St Palladius, a Roman bishop, sent first, by tradition, to the Irish, who would not hear him, so that he came to Caledonia, and died at Fordun in Angus, leaving his charge to his pupils St Serf and St Ternan. Banchory-Ternan is St Ternan's *bangor,* or monastic school. St Serf, at Culross, was the master of St Kentigern, who revived St Ninian's work in the South-west, but under another rule than the Kings of the Picts.

c

CHAPTER III

THE BRITON

A HUNDRED AND EIGHTY-ONE YEARS : 432–613

' In illo tempore Saxones invalescebant in multitudine et cres-
cebant in Britannia. . . . Tunc Arthur pugnabat contra illos in
illis diebus cum regibus Brittonum.'

Nennius, c. 800, *Historia Brittonum*.

FOR centuries after the death of St Ninian the general
history of all this island reflects in miniature the
history of Europe in that age of the Wandering of the
Nations. We see a chaos of little shifting states, of
invasions of one by another, and of new races entering
from without. To make the tale clear is not an easy
matter, and possibly the most lucid method of handling
is to trace the growth of the small independent states
into which what is now Scotland became divided in
the centuries that followed the Roman withdrawal.
By the end of four hundred years after Ninian's death
there were five of these. The Caledonia or Pictavia
of Roman times was divided in three, Norse, Pictish,
and Irish. The old district between the Walls, that
included the modern South Scotland, was divided in
two, the western half being part of the territory of a
Welsh state, the eastern half part of an English.

All five contributed elements to our Scotland.

34

Later on, Norman-French, a race considerably mixed
itself, and even a strain of Flemish were to be added :
and the process of mingling was made more complete
by the racial intermarriages natural in a small country
where all these races had one sovereign, one court,
and where the racial and class distinctions did not, as
in neighbouring England, coincide. It is partly this
complexity of race that produces the combination of
toughness and adaptability which makes the Scot the
supreme coloniser, the brilliant administrator of all
countries but his own. It may also be responsible for
some of the strange antinomies of the national temperament, the combination, not only in the race but in
individuals, of dour reticence and a violent forthright-
ness, of dry humour in the article of passion, and of—
according to a man's quality—strength with deep
tenderness or violence with sentimentality. No doubt,
too, it makes for a subconscious conflict that may lock
and paralyse the individual, even drive him mad (our
insanity-rate is high) or, healed and transcended, make
for a rich integrity of living, a power of linking varied
parts to a whole : it is significant, and a healthy sign,
that Scotland has always mistrusted specialism.
Whence comes the national turn for deductive logic,
for the carrying of abstract principles into action, is
hard to say. We share it, like so many other things,
with France, and like France suffer for it now and then.

Other qualities may perhaps have taken their rise
from men for centuries in a state of siege, as for
instance the extreme self-consciousness and sensitive-

ness to contacts that may show as a magnificent courtesy or as a surly and angular awkwardness. And perhaps the oddest combination of all derives from this double factor—the long siege borne by the nation as a whole and the conflict of elements within that nation : one of the races most addicted in history to an internecine strife within its borders is, once outside them, notoriously cohesive. If there were a St George's Society in Paris or Edinburgh, it would be surprising. If in Susanville, Oklahoma (where are two Scots and a man with a Scots aunt) there were not a St Andrew's Club, it would be more so. It would seem that an awareness of other countries brings to mind the union rather than the diverseness . . . which is a further reason why for Scotland an insular habit of mind is a special danger.

Through the fifth century, all over Europe, the Teutonic and Gothic races were in flux. Its second half saw a Vandal kingdom in Africa, a Visigothic in Spain (that lasted for two centuries and a half before the advancing Moslems rolled it up), a Swabian west of it, and a Frankish in Gaul, which, unlike the other small Teuton states of the North, was officially Christian almost from its beginning.[1] Other Teuton races were invading Britain. The Jutes, the Angles, and the Saxons, from about the ' stalk ' of Denmark and the

[1] Chlodovech (Clovis), its founder and first of the Merovings, was baptised in 496 by St Rémy. It was then twenty years since the fall of the Western Empire, and ten since he had wrested Northern Gaul from its last Romano-Gallic governor Syagrius.

lands to the west of it, came overseas. For a couple
of generations already they had made raids as allies
of the Picts, or as mercenaries in British pay had
fought them. Now they came as colonists, and began
to settle and carve out small states. By 500 the Jutes
had founded one in Kent; the Saxons four, besouth
or astride the Thames—Wessex, Sussex, Middlesex,
and Essex; and the Angles had settled on both sides
of the Wash, and were spreading northward along the
coast beyond the Humber; while all three, with continual reinforcements from overseas, drove inland,
sacking and plundering and enslaving. The unfortunate Romano-British, as has been said, attempted
to organise and withstand them, and did so with more
success than is commonly realised, for their resistance
endured for centuries—much longer than that of the
Anglo-Saxons to the Scandinavians who in turn invaded
and twice conquered them.

The tradition of Roman civilisation had remained;
for a while the organisation of the Imperial Church,
that had survived the broken temporal framework,
held the British to the Continent. Towards the
middle of the fifth century St Germanus of Auxerre
and St Lupus of Troyes arrived to combat the Pelagian
heresy, which began in Britain about the time when
St Ninian made his missionary journeys. Even in the
middle of the sixth century the British gentry commonly spoke Latin, and Latin names are found alongside Celtic, in the same family. But all through the
fifth century and the sixth, the relics of the long Roman

civilisation were steadily crumbling as their marches were driven in.

We know extremely little of that time, and what we do know is mainly the invaders' side of it. We know that their movement was northward and westward. They begin to touch the history of Scotland when about 547 an Anglian chief, Ide, established a fortress at Bamborough, about seventeen miles south of Tweed-mouth and well up the coast of the district between the Walls—over forty miles north of Hadrian's, in fact. He carried his power from the Tees along to the Forth, forming a little state called the land of the Beornicas, Bernicia, with its town Beornicawic at the mouth of Tweed.[1] Bernicia, when fully grown, came to include what is now the counties of Durham and Northumberland, Berwick, Roxburgh, Selkirk, Peebles, and the three Lothians : and in time it joined with its neighbour Deira, which is roughly Yorkshire, to make up the kingdom of Northumbria. There will be more to say of it presently.

As for the British, by the time of Ide, they still held about two-thirds of Roman Britain. By the end of the sixth century this had shrunk to something less than half of it. The British seem to have formed a group of small chiefships, at times united under a common war-leader, and conscious, in face of the invaders, of a common race, for they called themselves Cymru, the Fellow-countrymen. (Their invading

---

[1] This is one derivation. But it may come from Bryneich, the Country of the Braes.

enemies called them Wealhas, the Foreigners, or
Wælisces, the Foreign.[1]) Their country still ran from
the Clyde to the English Channel, but steadily it was
growing less and less, and the fifth and sixth and seventh
centuries were ages of a constant losing struggle to
save not merely freedom but a civilisation that itself
was breaking up under their feet.

It is the common tale of that age in Europe. Yet
these ages of despair could produce saints. Benedict,
who gave form and definition to the monasticism that
was to save the seeds of civilisation, was a lad of twenty
in Italy in 500. Gregory of Tours, holding fast the
relics of shattered civilisation, lived through much of
the sixth century. It was in one of the worst of the
violent and pointless Merovingian reigns, the night-
mare epic of Brunhild and Fredegund, that the kindly
and learned Venantius Fortunatus wrote some of the
noblest of the Latin hymns, still sung to-day to
immemorial tunes—the lovely *Salve festa dies* pro-
cessionals for Easter and Pentecost, full of the sense
of spring weather, and the splendid battle-pieces of
the Passion, *Pange lingua*, *Fidelis Crux*, and *Vexilla
Regis*. Far west, in the comparative peace of Ireland,
there were many such men. There were some among
the Britons, as for instance St Dafyd in what now is
Wales. One belonged to the northmost of the British
chiefships, in what now is Clydesdale. This was
Cyndyrn, called Mwyngu, the Courteous or Amiable,
or, as we know him, Kentigern or Mungo. There is

---

[1] Pronounced something like *Wālīshes*. It became *Welsh*.

a tradition that his father was Owain, son of Urien, and his mother Thenog (Thenew or Enoch), daughter of Lot, a kinglet of still British Lothian. He seems to have been brought up by St Serf at Culross, and then to have taken orders and become the Bishop of Cathures (Glasgow), where he founded a monastery. Then Marken, the king of that district, drove him out. He preached for a time about Caerleol (Carlisle), where there are still nine churches bearing his name, but his enemies still pursued him, and he sought shelter with St Dafyd in Mynyw or Menevia. He carried on his missionary work, founding Llanelwy, by another Clyde, in what now is North Wales. Then Marken's successor, Rydderch Hael, Roderick the Generous, called him back, and in 573 he returned to Clydesdale, leaving Asaf in charge of his Welsh foundation, later on St Asaph's. Little more is known definitely, but that he settled once more in his old see at Glasgow, and lived there in the love of king and people. About 584 another saint, Columba from the little Irish colony that the Dalriad Scots had established north of Clyde, paid him a visit beside the Molendinar Burn, where they talked as friends and exchanged their crosiers. He lived, it would seem, till about the year 612, and the Northern Britons held fast in his time.

There was soon, however, to be a tale of defeat. Further south, the invaders had driven steadily west, and in Kentigern's lifetime, in 577, they had reached the west coast of Southern Britannia, for in that year Ceawlin, King of the West Saxons, had defeated the

British at Deorham, between Bath and Bristol, pushed his lands to the estuary of the Severn, and cut off 'West Wales' (that is, the south-western peninsula of England) from the British country to the north of it. Just after Kentigern's time, a similar movement broke that also in two, and permanently. Æthelfrith, King of Bernicia, had married a sister of the King of Deira, and about 590 he drove out his brother-in-law and made the two kingdoms into one, that we know as Northumbria, which ran from the Humber to the Forth, and inland as far as the summit of the Pennines and the head-waters of Tweed. In 613, or it may have been 616, he defeated the Britons heavily at Chester, and drove a corridor to the Irish Sea, dividing Cambria—Wales, more or less—from Cumbria, which is also, though less correctly, called Strathclyde.

The latter name, though more commonly used, is misleading. It suggests to the mind both a more limited area and also a part of the extant kingdom of Scotland : we should think rather of a separate state, astride what is now the Scottish frontier and then was merely a river like another, and stretching from the mouth of the Clyde to a long way south of its source— to a shifting line then somewhere between the Ribble and the Mersey. Looking forward, we still find, two hundred years later, a march running eastward from as far south as the top of Morecambe Bay. That is, so late as the year 800, this state of Cumbria, part of which was in time to be part of Scotland, included the modern counties of Renfrew, Ayr, Lanark, Dumfries, both Galloways, Cumberland, Westmorland, and part of Lancashire. Although it continued to shrink, its existence as a separate political unit endured for a couple of centuries after that, until the early part of the eleventh century. Naturally, however, as the buffer state between the rising powers of the Scots and English and a near neighbour of the fighting Picts, it had a stormy career, and was generally under the suzerainty of one or the other. It was not, however, until 1018 that the greater part of what then was left of it was to pass for good under the Scottish Crown, and become what are nowadays the South-western Lowlands.

CHAPTER IV

THE SCOT

A HUNDRED AND THREE YEARS : 500–603

' The Scottes . . . com out of Irlond, þat ys þe propre contray of
Scottes, and wiþ love other wiþ strengþe made ham a place faste
by þe Pictes, in þe norþ side of þat arm of þe se þat brekeþ into þe
lond in þe west side.'
Ralph Higden, *Polychronicon*. Trevisa's version, *c.* 1385.

PICTAVIA, Cumbria, Northumbria . . . and we have
mentioned already a fourth state. As the Britons of
the district between the Walls were being driven back
by the Anglian invaders from the east, so a similar
process, on a much smaller scale, was going on above
Antonine's Wall, but on the west, and a little kingdom
of Scots was growing up. It was, in fact, somewhat
older than Bernicia : that is to say that when, as we
have just seen, the battle of Chester divided Cumbria
from Cambria, this Scotia was rather more than a
century old. The ' English ' may ' have been in Scotland before the Scots,' as a recent popular historian
puts it : it is unlikely that we shall ever determine
the precise date of the first landings. Certainly,
however, an English state including what now is
Scottish territory does not appear until some time
after Ide's foundation of Bamborough in 547, while

43

the little Scottish state on the opposite coast was founded somewhere about the year 500, when three brothers, Fergus, Erc, and Loarn, princes of Dalaraidhe or Dalriada, the District of the Uplands (now the Glens of Antrim), founded an independent principality in what is now Argyllshire. There seem to have been settlers there from an earlier time, and there may have been others also in Galloway, which certainly had a Gaelic (or perhaps Irish Pictish) settlement later. Antrim, one may remember, is the extreme north-east corner of Ireland, its coast within fifteen miles of the Mull of Kintyre.[1]

These Scots were Gaelic Celts, of the race dominant in Ireland, and their arrival is a landmark in our history. Their connection with Pictavia was already long-standing. In the fourth century they had joined with the Picts to raid Britannia : and since the time of St Ninian there had been a constant intercourse between the Irish Church and the Pictish and British ones. St Patrick, the chief apostle of the Irish and a younger contemporary of St Ninian (he died in 461), was a Briton, possibly born near Dumbarton,[2] whose father was a Christian Roman official. A Scots raid

---

[1] Argyle is Arraghael, Oirer Gaidheal, the Coast of the Gael. There is a very constant connection of Antrim with Scotland. In the early thirteenth century King John of England, then Lord of Ireland, gave it to Alan of Galloway, Constable of Scotland. About 1550 it was seized by Scots MacDonalds under Somhairle Buidhe. James VI made this man's son Earl of Antrim, and it was his son in turn who sent Colkitto to Montrose.

[2] This has been questioned : at the present stage of the conflict the matter seems open.

under Niall of the Nine Hostages carried him off. He became a slave, escaped, became a priest (part of his training was at Marmoutier), and just about the time of Ninian's death, about 430, went back again to Ireland. He was a most successful missionary, for the Irish held their scholars in high repute, and Patrick early won them to his side : the most famous poet of the time was his friend. Other missionaries came also, from Gaul and Britain, and we have mentioned already the influence of Candida Casa. The increasingly desperate state of affairs in Europe sent an increasing number of scholars to Ireland for refuge, and there they found an honourable welcome.

By the sixth century, Ireland was paying her debt. Her monastic schools were the intellectual centre of all Christian Europe. Again and again we hear that some great figure ' sojourned in Ireland for the love of God and learning.' Nor did she merely receive and shelter such men. Ireland herself sent missionaries through the turmoil of Europe, winning the incoming heathen to the Cross and quickening the hoarded relics of scholarship in the monasteries that had survived the Empire. Irish MSS. are found as far off as Carinthia. In the sixth century St Columbanus and his disciples alone founded over a hundred monastic settlements, including houses as far, and as famous, as Jumièges in France, St Gall in Switzerland, and Bobbio in Lombardy : and the MS. of the Life of St Columba, written at Iona by Adamnan his successor, was found at Reichenau on the shores of

Lake Constance.[1] This intellectual primacy of Ireland lasted for the best part of four centuries : so late as 825, when the Norse invasions had begun to break it, an Irish scholar was one of the founders of what was to become the University of Pavia. It was only to be expected that an actual Irish colony, so near as fifteen miles from the Irish coast, should share this outpouring of the mind and spirit.

In fact, the great figure of our sixth-century history is an Irish abbot. He was not the first of the Irish mission saints to work in Caledonia or the adjacent country. St Darerca, or as she is more commonly called, St Modwenna, who died about 517, founded several churches in Northern Cumbria : the two Kirkmaidens in Galloway are hers. About 545 St Brendan of Clonfert sent a mission to his fellow-countrymen in Caledonian Dalriada, and he himself lived for a time in the Garvelloch Isles, where his pupils included St Machutus or Malo, who was one of the great mission-saints of France. St Oran, who died in 548, had founded a church of some sort on a small island off Mull, Hy or Ioua, that we call Iona. A few years after his death, the island received the most famous of its abbots, St Columba, whose work gave new life to the Christianity of Britain at large.

He was born about 521, of the Northern branch of the Irish royal house, the Hy Niall : his father was

---

[1] The service of such houses to literature and philosophy may be gauged from the fact that the library at Bobbio included texts of Aristotle, Demosthenes, Cicero, Vergil, Juvenal, and Martial.

grandson of Niall of the Nine Hostages, his uncle the first Christian King of Ireland, his mother a princess of Leinster, and he all his life had a princely status, a princely gift of rule. He was trained for the priesthood by St Finnbarr of Moville, who himself had been a pupil of Candida Casa, and grew up learned, fiery, and lovable, with the impetuous strength and the gentleness, the flaming courage and sweet courtesy that so often have endowed the great mission-saints. We know that he was a man of noble presence, with a voice of great beauty and uncommon ' carry.'

For a while after ordination he worked in Ireland, founding various houses, including the famous Durrow. Then in some manner that is not very clear (tradition says through the copying, without leave, of St Finnbarr's Psalter) he was involved in a quarrel with Dermot, High King of Ireland. Dermot came of the other branch of the dynasty. The families took sides, and the quarrel spread, and brought about the battle of Cooldrevny. Columba, exiled or self-exiled as penance, made his way to the Dalriada overseas, arriving there about 563.

He found the colony in evil case. Comgall, its king, his father's second cousin, had been defeated and killed by Bruidhe, King of Picts, and Conall, Comgall's son, had been forced to become in some sort Bruidhe's vassal. Conall welcomed his kinsman and his followers, and gave him St Oran's island of Iona. There the saint founded, or refounded, the abbey that for generations was the religious centre of what are now

Scotland and Northern and Midland England. Iona, like all the Irish foundations, followed the primary pattern of Candida Casa and of its mother-house of Marmoutier : it was both a school of learning and a centre of mission-work. The latter was set on foot almost from the beginning. Columba had scarcely been there a couple of years before he carried his warfare of the Cross to the court of Conall's suzerain King Bruidhe, who was still a heathen. Bruidhe's seat was on the Ness, and thither Columba went, up the Great Glen, accompanied by two Pictish abbots, St Comgall, Abbot of Bangor in Down, and St Cainneach (Kenneth), Abbot of Kilkenny. They seem to have served him as interpreters, which suggests a certain difference at least between the Pictish tongue and Columba's Gaelic. The Celtic races do not seem at any time to have met Christianity with persecution : but naturally Columba had to face the opposition of the Pictish priests. He succeeded, however, in converting the King, and Christianity became the official religion of all Pictavia, as of the British and Scottish states : the Anglo-Saxons, north and south alike, were heathen until after Columba's death.

Columba, like St Ninian and St Patrick—like all the saints of the Gaelic Church, in fact—was not only a missionary but a teacher of missionaries. His disciples brought new life to the old foundations of St Ninian in Caledonia, and made new ones. St Machar carried the Cross to Aberdeen, St Cormac the Navigator to the Orkneys, St Moluag among the Isles : and St

Donnan and St Devenick are also of that generation. All worked on the pattern laid down by St Ninian, establishing monasteries and conducting their mission-work from them as bases.

Columba's reputation spread beyond the boundaries of his actual work. He was consulted by Riderch, King of Strathclyde, and about 584 he visited St Kentigern at Glasgow, and was received by him as an honoured guest. Pope Gregory I sent him a gift to Iona, the cross called the Great Jewel, and Columba returned to him a Latin poem. During at least the last twenty years of his life, Columba was recognised as the local head of the Church through all the country to the north of Forth. Within a generation, Iona was the spiritual capital not only of the Scots and the Western Picts but of the Eastern Picts and the Cumbrians, and in a couple more of almost all the various Anglian kingdoms.

As might be expected from his character, his birth, and his ecclesiastical position, Columba's political influence was immense, on both sides of the water. When King Conall died, in 571, Columba already had sufficient power to secure the monarchy to the King's cousin Aidan instead of to his son : and Aidan, with Columba playing the part of Bishop Kennedy to James II or Bishop Elphinstone to James IV, did much to consolidate his kingdom. In 575 the saint, with a train described as twenty bishops, forty priests, fifty deacons, and thirty novices, took a prominent part in the great convention at Drumceatt in Ireland,

D

which defined the position of the two Dalriadas : his
objects are given by a contemporary as the release from
imprisonment of a Prince of Ossory, ' the keeping of
the poets in Ireland,' and ' the making of peace between
the men of Ireland and Scotland regarding Dalriada.' [1]
The usual statement is that the point in dispute was
the independence of Caledonian Dalriada.   In fact
the contemporary account makes clear that the issue
between Aidan and the King of Ireland was *Irish*
Dalriada, which was claimed by both.   The actual
judgment (pronounced by St Colman, as Columba was
in a sense party to the dispute) was according to one
authority, that the Irish Dalriada should pay taxes to
the King of Scots, but do military service under the
King of Ireland, ' because military service goes with
the soil ' :   according to another (but much later) both
went to the King of Ireland, but the men of Irish
Dalriada were bound to provide quarters and transport
for any people of Scottish Dalriada who should visit
their country.

Thereafter, the political connection of Alba, Caledonian Dalriada, with its parent country grew weaker,
and the colony turned rather to its immediate neigh-

----

[1] The poets were about to be expelled as an intolerable burden :
there were 1200 professed and certified poets, and every *ollam* or
as we might say, Doctor of Poetry had a right to thirty followers,
every *anrad* or Master of Poetry to fifteen : and no doubt each of
them thought as well of himself as accepted authors generally do.
And as satire was extremely popular, they had the means for very
extensive blackmail.   Columba managed to check the various abuses
and to organise the bards in a corporate body, a kind of university,
where secular history and the 280 forms of Gaelic verse should be
adequately taught.

bours the Picts, though not always peaceably. In time the descendants of its dynasty were to reign over what is now Scotland, which takes her name from the Latin one for this state. Until the mid ninth century *Scotia* always, and until the end of the tenth it generally, means Ireland, and *Scotus* is an Irishman : and even so late as the twelfth century the conservative Bishop of Caithness was grumbling that *Albania . . . nunc corrupte Scotia appellatur*, Alba is now corruptly called Scotland.

Columba's work both in and from Iona went on for a full generation : he died before the altar of his church on his way to say the midnight offices of Sunday the 9th of June 597. In that year Augustine came to Canterbury . . . and Mohammed was a man of twenty-eight.

Soon after the saint's death King Aidan came into collison with the Anglian invaders on the east. Under Æthelfrith, the King of Northumbria, they were pressing heavily on the northern Britons, whose unhappy case has already been described. Aidan's mother had been a British princess : he allied with the King of Cumbria against the Angles, and with ill success. In 603, when he was an old man of seventy, he and the British fought a pitched battle against the Angles at Degsastane (which may be Dawstane near Jedburgh) and were heavily defeated. None the less, Æthelfrith's onward push was checked, and he turned his attention rather to the South, where, as we have seen, he was to be more successful, for his victory at

Chester in 613 cut Cambria off for good from Cumbria. Aidan reigned for some six years more in comparative peace, and left his throne to his son Eochaid Buidhe : and before the latter's reign had come to an end, the Church of his kingdom of Scotia was to achieve the spiritual conquest of Northumbria.

CHAPTER V

THE ANGLE

EIGHTY-TWO YEARS : 603-685

'Beraþ linde forþ,
bord for breostum and byrnhomas,
scire healmas in sceðena gemong.
Fyllan folctogan fagum sweordum,
fæge frumgaras.'   *Judith*, c. 700.

'Bear forth among the foe the linden-wood,
The shield, the coat of mail, and the bright helm.
The chiefs went down among the reddened swords,
The captains, for their doom was come on them.'

WE must turn now to another element in the complex political group that was to be Scotland—to the rising Anglian state whose northern part was to be, though not yet for over four hundred years, incorporated in the Scottish kingdom. At Aidan's death the east coast of what had been Roman Britannia from the Wash northward to at least the Tweed had been Anglian territory for a generation: and the wave of invasion was rolling west to the hills. Its history, of course, had been closely involved with that of the unfortunate British. We have already seen how the Angles had come overseas and had founded a group of small independent states, including Deira and Bernicia (see p. 38). It has also been told how Æthelfrith, Ide's grandson, united these to form Northumbria, and greatly extended his kingdom, defeating the Scots and

53

the British at Degsastane, and the British again, with permanent results, at Chester.

He made further wars upon his other march, and in 617 was defeated and killed by the King of East Anglia. The Northumbrian throne passed to Eadwine, the brother-in-law he had ousted from Deira. Eadwine proved himself a highly successful raider, extending his kingdom to the Forth on one side, the Humber and Trent on the other, with a limb stretching across to Ribble-mouth; further north it reached the head-waters of the Tweed.

The Anglo-Saxon states had already been struggling among themselves for supremacy: their union, in fact, was clearly inevitable, for their race differed little, and their language less than Aberdeen and Devon speech to-day, while their culture was practically identical. Already a King of Sussex, a King of Wessex, and a King of Kent had successively attained a degree of power that enabled each to call himself *Bretwalda*, which may mean either Broad-ruler or Ruler of Britain.[1] This vague hegemony now was won by Eadwine, and in fact, until nearly the end of this seventh century, Northumbria was the leading state in the group to which the Angles were to give their name. By the ninth century, though the Saxon Wessex had become supreme among them, Saxon and Angle alike, even in Saxon writings, are Angelþeod, the race

---

[1] *Britain*, of course, means the Roman ' diocese,' not the whole island. After the Roman conquest of the South, the non-Roman part is always Caledonia.

of the English, and their country the Angles' Land, Englaland, England.

Under Eadwine, Christianity reached Northumbria. It came first from the South. The old British Church had attempted no mission-work among the invaders, but in 597, the year of St Columba's death, Pope Gregory had sent Augustine to Kent. The Jutes of Kent, through their close connection with Gaul, were the most civilised of the Teutonic states in Britain, and Æthelberht of Kent, who was then Bretwalda, had married a Frankish Christian princess, Bercta. Kent became christianised, and the Kentish Church, whose seat was at Canterbury, was directly the daughter of Rome—not only, as were the Irish and Pictish Churches, in touch with the old Imperial ecclesiastical organisation, that had survived the Empire, but part of it.

The influence of Canterbury spread north. In 625 Paulinus came thence to Eadwine : and Eadwine was not only Æthelberht's son-in-law, but had spent part of his exile at the Christian court of North Wales. He listened readily, and was baptised : but the new faith spread slowly in Northumbria, and soon had a set-back. Penda, the heathen King of Mercia,[1] allied with Cadwallon of North Wales in 633, and killed Eadwine at the battle of Hæþfelþ, supposed to be

[1] 'The Mark' or boundary—the Middle Kingdom, which ran roughly from the Humber and the Ribble to the march of Essex and the Middle Thames. Its population was mainly Angle, as the Saxons came but little above the Thames.

Hatfield near Doncaster. Paulinus fled, and the rise of Penda to chief power in England seemed to drive back the new faith to the South.

It returned from the North instead, and very soon. Æthelfrith's sons had fled at their father's death and his old northern enemies gave them shelter. Eanfrith, the eldest, married a Pictish princess, and their son Talorcan became King of Picts, inheriting, Pictish fashion, through his mother. Oswald and Oswiu were bred at the monastic school of Iona, and grew up as Christians, in much more than name. In 634 Oswald returned to Northumbria, and avenged the uncle who had driven him out by defeating Cadwallon at what came to be called the Heofenfelþ, the Heavenfield, for his victory was won beneath the Sign of the Cross. The battle gave him the throne, and at once he set to work to reorganise, and christianise, his kingdom. He called from Iona the wise and learned St Aidan, who was consecrated bishop before he left, and gave him Lindisfarne, Holy Isle, for his see. (Paulinus's had been York, which was in Deira.) There Aidan founded an abbey: following the usual practice of the Gaelic Church, he established first a monastery school, and then used it as base for missionary tours, in which the King himself was not only his guard but the interpreter of Aidan's Gaelic. Both Bishop and King were saints and able men: in no long time Northumbria had been re-Christianised, and to such effect that for the next hundred years it was the intellectual centre of England, rivalling Iona and the great Irish schools, and sending scholars to the Continent, where the intellectual tide was then running low. The best of the Old English poetry (and some of it is very noble stuff) is Northumbrian, and the Gospels of Lindisfarne reveal how the Gaelic influence was creating a fine convention of decorative art.

Aidan had many and valuable pupils. His foundations included Melrose, where St Boisil (Boswell) trained the greater St Cuthbert. St Hild, the Northumbrian Deborah, Eadwine's great-niece, who became Abbess of Whitby, was Aidan's disciple, and hers in turn included Caedmon, the first great name in the roll of English poets, and St John of Beverley, a pioneer in the training of the deaf. St Ebba, Oswald's half-sister, became Abbess of Coldinghame : and it was from Lindisfarne that St Chad went forth as apostle of the Mercians, while in the sunset of the Northumbrian power the great scholar Bede, who died in 735, was famous throughout Europe.

Oswald's brilliant reign, however, lasted briefly. In 642 Penda attacked again, and defeated and slew him at the Maserfield. This left Penda the most powerful sovereign in ' Britain.' Bernicia and Deira, which Oswald had united, were separated once more, Penda ruling the former, while Deira was still held by Oswald's brother Oswiu. Aidan lived until 651, and continued his missionary work, extending it into heathen Mercia : the first Mercian bishop was Diuma the Scot, sent with Oswiu's daughter, who married Penda's son. Penda himself was not converted but ceased to be hostile, and the stout old pagan is recorded by Bede as having despised bad Christians, 'who did not obey the God in whom they believed.'

In 655 the balance changed again. There was war once more, and Oswiu killed Penda at the Winwæd. The battle is of great importance, as it made Christianity supreme in England. Oswiu reunited the two Northumbrian states, and made Northumbria once more the dominant power south of Forth. His long reign lasted till 671, and during it the Gaelic Church spread through Mercia. St Aidan's successor Finan was sent from Iona, where he had been ordained. Diuma's first Angle successor was trained there, and when Finan died in 661, the Gaelic Church was supreme in England from the Forth to the Thames: above Thames it was only in East Anglia that there was any administrative connection with Canterbury.

The increasing contact of the two ecclesiastical organisations brought them into conflict, however— a conflict to be settled, for the time being, at the famous Synod of Whitby in 664. The situation is rather frequently misunderstood or misstated: and as various important issues really do turn upon it, while others, actually irrelevant, are made to do so, it is worth while to describe it in some detail.

The greater part of England by 660 was officially Christian from the Forth to the Channel. The Church in East Anglia, Kent, and the Saxon kingdoms besouth the Thames had been founded by missionaries from the Continent, and was from the beginning within the ambit of that organisation which had grown up

under, and paralleling, the civil organisation of the
Roman Empire, and, surviving that, was still centred
on Rome : it formed one organised body, transcending
the shifting and fluid political units, in incessant
change since the downfall of the Empire. North and
west of it, however, were two other bodies. Both were,
most definitely, part of the Catholic Church, at one
with it theologically and acknowledging the *seniority*
of the See of Peter. They were in no sense heretical,
and only in the most narrow sense schismatic : [1] St
Columba, in fact, had exchanged gifts with Pope
Gregory the Great, who was no man to countenance
unorthodoxy. The political and military events of
the last three centuries had, however, cut off the Celtic
Churches from the administrative machinery of which
Rome now claimed to be the ruling head.

Of these two bodies much the more important was
what is, untidily, called the Celtic Church and would be
more precisely described as the Gaelic one, for there
were *two* Celtic Churches, whose condition, and origin,
differed very widely, and whose contact by now was
slight and incidental. The Cymric or British Church
was the remnant of that of the Roman Occupation.
It was the Church of Cambria, and also of West Wales,

---

[1] The Continental missionaries complained in forcible terms of
various usages, and later, laxities, of the Gaelic Church : but they
never suggest it was heretical in belief. Late in the eleventh
century St Margaret, initiating measures for its reform, is recorded
by the Englishman Turgot (a scholarly priest who apparently
agreed) as stating definitely that it was not in any way heretical in
doctrine. Her proposed reforms were all in matters of discipline
or ceremonial.

the Cornish peninsula. By this time we hear very
little of it : it had ceased from missionary enterprise,
and the centuries of losing external and frequent civil
war had left their mark. Its importance for mediaeval
history is practically confined to Wales. The Gaelic
Church—that of Ireland, Scotia, Pictavia, and most
of England—was much more important, both then
and in relation to later times. To understand our
mediaeval history it is needful to grasp its peculiar
position, the more as for propagandist purposes quite
fantastic statements are often made about it.

It was the church, primarily, of Ireland and Pictavia
—that is, of districts never, or only in small part and
very briefly, within the Roman Empire—and was
founded just when the Imperial organisation was
breaking up. These facts very greatly affected its
history. But it was founded from the Empire, and had
done an enormous amount of missionary work over
much of the (Western) Empire's territory, drawn
innumerable scholars from that area. As result, its
relation to Rome was precisely that of the Episcopal
Church of America to that of Scotland. If Columba
had gone to Rome, he would have received, and given,
communion there. If Aidan had gone, he could have
ordained a Roman layman to the priesthood. They
and their Roman congregations would have held the
same theological beliefs, and their accustomed ceremonial practice would have differed no more than
that of St John's, Princes Street, differs from Old St
Paul's, and much less than that of St Giles from the

average parish kirk in a Highland clachan. But although they acknowledged the Pope as the Senior Bishop of Christendom, they did not consider that the seniority involved supremacy of jurisdiction, and in certain other points, important though not fundamental, there were differences, for the Gaelic Church had grown up so remote from that of the Empire as to develop some peculiar uses. It was not so remote, of course, as it may seem : there was constant coming and going of missionaries and scholars. And the forms are not so peculiar as one might gather from the works of certain popular historians. We hear it said, for instance, that ' they administered the sacred ordinance of communion in a way totally different from the Romish ritual, not at the altar but in a corner of the church ' : and this absurdity is gravely copied by other scholars from the eminent gentleman who was first responsible for it. His source is a statement that the Culdees (the later monks of the Columbite Order) said *suum officium in angulo ecclesiae*, said their office in a corner of the church. But a monk's office is not the Mass but the breviary ' hours,' which to-day are often, in fact, said in a train : they do not involve any use of the altar, and though their customary place in church would be the choir, in the roughly built little chapels of the Isles they may well at times have been said out of line with the door, as concession to the climate and human frailty. In the lives of the Celtic saints there are constant references to the altar and to the Sacrament of the Altar. There were, however, some authentic peculiarities in the Mass of the Gaelic Church : it was said only on Sundays and holy days ; more than one priest might take part in the consecration ; and as in the modern Reformed Episcopal Churches, Communion was given in both kinds ; while as in the early Spanish or the modern Greek, the broken Bread was laid out in symbolic patterns : but the fundamental doctrine was identical with that of Rome, and the difference was only in ceremonial.

The major and most important difference was administrative—the peculiar position of the bishop. The nature of bishops has much to do with Scottish history, both as it was made and even more as it is written : and a great deal of confusion has been caused by an ignoring of the primary point that there are two aspects of a bishop's office—the sacramental and the administrative. The former means that he can perform all the offices of a priest, and two more : it is he alone who can admit to full lay membership of the Church and to the priesthood—can confirm and ordain. This sacramental right, conferred by his valid ordination as bishop, is the essence of his office, and it is clear that in this point the Gaelic Church conformed to the universal Catholic pattern.[1] The other side of the office is the administrative : and although, as Ignatius (d. 110) makes clear, the sacramental side has been constant since the Primitive Church, the adminis-

[1] An Irish Latin rhyme about Columba at Drumceatt shows him accompanied by bishops, priests, and deacons. Adamnan shows him doing honour to Bishop Cronan as to his superior, and in another story makes it clear that only a bishop could ordain a priest.

trative has varied, and varies, very widely, with time and even with locality. And the place of the Gaelic bishop in this aspect differed greatly from the general Roman pattern, though there are several parallels for it elsewhere. The reason is rather interesting. The Continental Church had grown up in an Empire organised in cities, and therefore it had so organised itself. The bishop was the ecclesiastical head of the district about a city. In Gaeldom, however, the social unit was not territorial but tribal—not an area but a society or group : and the Church was organised in societies rather than districts, partly because men's minds worked on these lines, largely because the general conditions made the monastery the centre of its structure. In the Roman Church the secular priest came long before the monk. In the Gaelic there were no secular clergy at all, no parish priests under a diocesan bishop whose charge was a defined *territory* : all were monks, attached to a monastic *community* under an abbot. Now, at first the abbot might be priest or bishop : St Ninian and St Patrick had both been the latter. Later, in the Church of the Dalriad Scots and their spiritual children the Picts, Northumbrians, and Mercians, it was a rule that he had to be a priest, because their monasticism looked back to Columba, and Columba, in his saintly humility, had refused the episcopate as being unworthy of it. Therefore, for *administrative* purposes, the head of the unit was a priest-abbot, or an abbess, and not a bishop. The bishop had no administrative function as such. But he had to be there, for only he could ordain the priest-abbot who was his administrative superior. So a bishop-monk was so to speak part of the staff of the larger monasteries, under the Abbot's rule in general matters, but with the right to ordain which the Abbot had not. This status was of course unusual: but it is not without Continental parallels. The rule that one monk, not the Abbot, should be a bishop obtained, in France, at the great royal abbey of St Denis, and at Tours, the cradle of Western monasticism ; in Italy at Monte Cassino, the very house of St Benedict himself, who gave that monasticism form and definition ; and in Germany at the great house of Fulda, where in fact it lasted till 1752.

The differences between the Gaelic and the Continental Churches were bound to cause disputes as these came in close contact. The first serious clash was, however, on a very minor matter. The Gaelic Church observed all the customary fasts and feasts of the Church's Year: but they still calculated the fall of Easter, which depends on the moon, by an astronomical formula which Rome had in 463 abandoned as inaccurate. In two hundred years the inaccuracy had increased : the Roman and the Gaelic Easter were several days apart, with disturbing results at the Northumbrian court, for while the Angle Oswiu feasted Easter his Saxon queen was still keeping the fast of Lent. A synod was called at Whitby to settle matters. The Gaelic side was represented by Colman, Bishop of Lindisfarne, new come from Iona and handicapped by an ignorance of English ; by St Chad of Essex ; and by St Hild, in whose abbey

of Whitby they were meeting. On the other side the
leaders were St Wilfrid, a brilliant Bernician of noble
blood, trained at Lindisfarne and Rome; a Scot, Ronan;
and the Irish-trained Agilbert, later Bishop of Paris:
those for the change had thus the advantage of having
known both churches at first hand. Proceedings were
marked by considerable acerbity, increased by the fact
that someone raised a fresh point. The Gaelic men
were tonsured by shaving the front of the head, the Con-
tinentals shaved the crown : and the difference roused
as fiery a run of objection as there would be if a modern
Free Kirk minister should preach in white linen
instead of black Russell cord.

In the upshot, Oswiu conformed, and so did St
Hild. Lindisfarne split. St Colman went back to
Iona, with some of his monks, and the Abbot of
Melrose succeeded to his place. The new uses, in
fact, won their way in time. The Southern Irish,
more in touch with Continental scholarship, had in
fact adopted the Roman Easter already, and in a
generation or two the Gaelic Church in general was
to do so. The Cymric did not follow till 768, and its
Cornish branch indeed held out for much longer.

The actual points at issue were very trifling, not
touching even the larger of the by no means fundamental differences. Yet the Synod of Whitby is of
great importance, for it marks the initial posing of a
question that was to dominate the next six centuries
of the history of a kingdom then still non-existent.
Was Scotland to become a part of Europe, or was she

E

to be an appendage of Ireland ? Was her culture to be continental or insular ? Much indignant ink has been spilt on the solution : but it was a Scotland very much part of Europe that beat back Edward II, Edward III, and Henry VIII, while on the other hand, in 1707 our country was nothing if not insular.

Oswiu died in 671, with the Northumbrian power supreme in England. For a time his son Ecgfrith continued that power and extended it, making successful war on the Picts and the Mercians, and even on Ireland: he seems also to have won part of Cumbria, on both sides of the Solway. In 685, however, he over-reached himself, and Northumbria fell from its ascendancy. Much against the advice of the great St Cuthbert, he sought to push his march beyond the Forth. Bruidhe, King of Picts, led him on by strategic retreats beyond the Tay, and on the 20th May 685, at Nectansmere, which may be Dunnichen in Angus, turned on him, killed him, and utterly routed his army.

It ended Northumbrian supremacy. In the North, the Britons of Cumbria were again independent. The Picts recovered the territory Ecgfrith had annexed, and seem to have made a bid for some Northumbrian : they certainly raided into Bernicia, as the Northumbrian bishop had to flee from Abercorn. In the South, Mercia and Wessex were left as rivals, each to hold power in turn. Northumbria never recovered her lost position, and in time, when Scotland and England, in the modern sense of the words, came into being, she was divided between the two of them.

CHAPTER VI

THE NORTHMAN

A HUNDRED AND FIFTY-EIGHT YEARS: 685–843

'A furore Normannorum, libera nos, Domine.'
Ninth-century litany.

THE heading of this chapter is something of an anachronism. The chapter itself covers over a century and a half, and it was not until two-thirds through that time that the Norsemen made their appearance in our country and founded the fifth and last of the little states whose union produced the modern kingdom of Scotland—the last to be founded and the last to be incorporated, for it was to endure for over four hundred years, a longer time than Great Britain has now existed.

The century after Nectansmere, however, may be passed over briefly. To those who lived in it, it was as long as any other century, and more important : but to the modern historian it is, so far as our country is concerned, a cloudy time : we know no more than the outlines. It was full of violent action, certainly, but looked at from a point twelve hundred years later, it appears almost static, for there were no great or enduring political changes.

67

Nectansmere is one of the most important battles in British history, for had its result chanced to go otherwise, the Northumbrian power might have run to the Moray Firth, and the kingdom of Scotland never have existed. After it, during the eighth century, the chief powers in the island were Pictavia in the north and Mercia in the south. For a generation after the battle there were vague and intermittent wars : but the chief point historically is the closer contact of the Gaelic Church with the Continental, with its cultural consequences. The influence of the latter church increased in Northumbria, where it won a base for further extension northward.   After Ecgfrith's death the kingdom was ruled by Ealdfrith, an illegitimate son of Oswiu : he was a scholar, had studied in Ireland, knew Latin, and could write Gaelic verse.   And the spirit of Canterbury in his time was changing. The Continental Church in the seventh century had shared the decadence of Continental learning: but in 668 Pope Vitalian sent to Kent as Archbishop the Greek Theodore of Tarsus; and Theodore, who had studied at Athens, had an attitude to scholarship that was much nearer that of the Gaelic Church than was that general in Europe at the time. He made the schools of Canterbury famous, and his friend and pupil, Benedict Biscop, carried their influence north to Wearmouth and Jarrow, and pushed further the rapprochement of the churches. At the same time Theodore himself and the African Hadrian gave the southern church a more definite organisation, on territorial lines : they set about dividing the country into *scriftscires*, shrift-shires, areas small enough for a single priest to act as confessor and spiritual director : the germs of the parish system were in being, and a secular clergy had begun to function.

Theodore's work took effect further north. In 703 the Pictish throne went to Nectan MacDerile, and in 710 Nectan called a general synod, to discuss the questions that had been raised at Whitby. According to Bede (in whose lifetime the meeting took place) ' many learned men of the Picts ' debated the matter with the southern missionaries. Nectan agreed with the latter, adopted the Roman computation of Easter, induced his clergy to wear the Roman tonsure, and chose St Peter as patron of the Picts. In 716 Iona (*non sine pulvere*) came into line, and the influence of the new movement was strengthened by the work of St Boniface (Curitan, a Celt) who worked from Restennet in Angus, founding churches at Invergowrie and elsewhere in the north-eastern districts.

There are vague wars in this time : we know of a battle somewhere about Clackmannan in 711 where the Saxons (sic : ? Northumbrians ?) overcame the Picts, and one the same year at an unidentifiable place, where the Scots overcame the Britons : and there were civil wars also among the Picts and Scots. In 723 Selbach, King of Scots, became a monk, and next year Nectan followed his example. There was more civil war, but towards the end of that decade Angus

MacFergus, Angus I, King of Picts,[1] put down his rivals in a vigorous war, and for a generation held the supreme power in the north of the island as Ardrigh or High King. He made Dalaraidhe tributary to him, taking Dunadd, its capital, in 736, and achieving its complete conquest in 741 at Druimcathmail. He allied with Northumbria and with Mercia, whose king, Æthelbald, was in 736 calling himself Rex Britanniae.

Northumbria had been recovering somewhat, and about 720 was pushing into Galloway, where an Anglian bishop was placed at Candida Casa. By 756 she held Cunningham and Kyle. Angus I also had been at war with the British, and in 750 they defeated and killed his brother Talorcan. In 756 he allied with Northumbria against them, and the joint army took the British capital Alclwd, Dunbreatann, Dumbarton, the Fortress of the Britons. The British territory was divided, the Lennox going to the Picts. The decline of Northumbria allowed Cumbria later to recover some nominal independence for a time, but for most of the rest of that state's existence as a political unit it was under the Pictish or the Scottish Crown.

At Angus's death in 761 Pictavia had strengthened her dominance in the north, and in the south Mercia (which had assimilated East Anglia and Essex) had likewise been further strengthened by the great Offa (757-96) who extended his territories into Wales, and was the first to call himself *Rex Anglorum*.

---

[1] Not to be confused with Angus II, also MacFergus, in the next century.

Northumbria was falling into chaos. In the eighth century she saw five kings murdered or killed in civil war, five deposed, and four more who abdicated : by the end of the century Cumbria had broken away, and as was said above, recovered a brief and precarious independence. Dalaraidhe, after Angus's death, would seem also to have recovered for a while : but that generation is extremely cloudy. We know that in 789 Constantine MacFergus won the throne of Pictavia : and Donald, King of Scots, seems to be his son, presumably he ruled as his father's vassal, but even this point is not very certain.

Constantine's reign marks a turning-point, however, not only for Scotland but for Europe at large. The seventh and still more the eighth century had been a time of increasing consolidation. This island was well on the way to be drawn together into no more than three states. On the Continent the same process was going on on a much larger scale. In 732 Charles Martel at Tours had driven back the Moslem invaders, who in Western Europe were thenceforth confined to Spain, though they frequently, and for centuries thereafter, were to threaten Italy. The Frank power spread. Charles's son Pepin became King of the Franks, and Pepin's son Charles, Charles the Great or Charlemagne, by the end of the century had come to rule over all Western Europe save Spain and Scandinavia—from the Oder, the Carpathians and the Danube, to the Pyrenees, and from the Baltic to Central Italy. He was one of the great soldiers of history, a superb administrator, deeply religious, a fervent patron of scholarship and the arts. His character no less than his achievement made it seem time to make actual again a conception whose memory had never been lost, and in 800 he was crowned Emperor at Rome. The *res Romana* had revived again as the Holy Roman Empire. The four centuries of chaos and invasion seemed to have come to an end.

But they had not. Two years before Constantine won the Pictish throne, and over four hundred miles from his frontier, there occurred a small and violent incident, the first mutter of a long and bitter storm whose clouds did not clear until half a millennium later —that growled, indeed, for two hundred years later yet. In 787 three shiploads of strangers came ashore at Wareham on the English coast : the King's reeve came down to investigate the matter, and they promptly killed him. The ' Danes ' had begun to move, and all through the ninth century and the tenth, the people of all the coastwise parts of Europe had very good reason for frequent and fervent prayers for deliverance from ' the fury of the Northmen.'

The Gothic races of Scandinavia had so far played no part in the invasions that had washed across fifth, sixth, and seventh century Europe. For three centuries now they played a most active one. Scandinavia had already had trading contact with the South : the early remains show imports from the Black Sea, and the Imperial city of Constantinople was the sort of legend the Aztecs were to the Conquistadores. In the seventh and eighth centuries, however, the Scandinavians were prosperous at home. Then came the nemesis of prosperity: they increased, and there was over-population. They began to seek for ' a place in the sun ' overseas. The process recurs throughout all history, and always with painful results for somebody. The Northmen went out as armed emigrants, sailing their shallow-draught but seaworthy ships, full of men well equipped, well mailed, and hearty fighters, by three main routes. The Swedes crossed into Russia. The Danes (though the word is very loosely used) came past Frisia and the embouchure of the Rhine to Neustria (Northern France) and the English coast; and the Norsemen came west about and through the Isles to plunder rich and undefended Ireland, full of jewelled churches and cities without walls, and took the coasts of Scotland on their way. Within but little more than a century they had colonies in Scotland, England, Ireland, Russia, France, the Faroes, Iceland, Greenland, America, though not all of these were directly colonised from Scandinavia itself. Later, in the eleventh century, with their French colony Normandy as base, they founded a kingdom in Sicily and Southern Italy. England they captured altogether, twice, and the second time permanently. Later their descendants founded a chain of states in the Levant, took and held for a generation the Eastern Empire, and infiltrated, peacefully, the ruling class of every nation in Europe, ours among them.

In 793 (five years, that is, after the affair at Wareham)

the *Gall*, the Strangers, the Gentiles, sacked Lindisfarne. The next year they came to Jarrow, and also
laid waste the Isles. Next year again they sacked
Skye and the holy places of Iona, and the year after
that they were in Ireland. At Charlemagne's court
the great English scholar Alcuin heard of these things
as his modern equivalent might hear of the bombing
of Oxford and Westminster Abbey, and recalled how
Gildas, three hundred years before, had described the
invasions of the heathen Saxons. He wondered if
history would repeat itself; and repeat itself it did,
with a grim precision. The Danes treated the Saxons
as these had done the Britons, and achieved their
results in a shorter space of time. It was Scotland
and Ireland that bore the first brunt, however, for
they were nearer, and their rich monasteries were
attractive. Iona was burnt in 802 and again in 806,
when the monks were massacred. In 824 the invaders
sacked Bangor, in 825 Moville, and Iona again, where
St Blaithmac was martyred for refusing to give up
St Columba's relics. By 834 they held the whole
North of Ireland. In 839 they killed Eoganan King of
Scots, and their chief's wife was speaking prophecies
seated on the high altar at Clonmacnoise.

Meanwhile the Danes were likewise raiding England,
and Charlemagne's coast. England by now had been
showing the general tendency to unification and consolidation, for Ecgberht of Wessex had broken the
power of Mercia in 825, and by 830 had established
some kind of rather vague hegemony over all the

English states from the Forth to the Channel, drawing in West Wales and the little southern kingdoms of Sussex and Kent. No Anglo-Saxon king had been so powerful. Yet the Danes did not spare him. There had been a lull, but by the middle of the century their raids recommenced, and on a larger scale. In 838 they were back in the South of England ; in 841 they had formed a settlement on the lower Seine, coming not as mere pirates but as armed colonists : and in 850 they did the same in England, wintering there. From then on, for the rest of the century, only the great ability and courage of Ecgberht, his son, and his four grandsons, saved their dynasty. England was more than they could save, and their heroic efforts, culminating in the fine resistance of Alfred, could achieve no more than a compromise that in 878 gave half England to the Danes.

The small Celtic states northward were in no less danger. They were still separate when the first blow fell, and still at war with each other and with Ireland. (There was an Irish invasion in 819.) By the mid ninth century the Norsemen were masters of the Hebrides and colonising the coasts of the West and North. Ireland suffered most of all, being practically annexed by the invaders. She absorbed them in the long run : but they almost ruined the great Irish culture, though it was strong enough to revive again and endure until the coming of the English.

None the less, it was in the eight-forties, at the very high tide of this first great Viking onslaught, when the

North and the Isles were being rent from Pictavia, that we see the first of the successive unions that were to produce a United Kingdom of Scotland. Eoganan, King of Picts and Scots alike, had been killed, as we have seen, in 839, and his death had left the two kingdoms again divided. In Pictavia he was succeeded by Wrad and Bred, who reigned for no more than some three years between them. In Dalaraidhe his successor was his son Alpin : and Alpin's mother apparently had been a Pictish princess, the sister of Constantine and Angus II. Alpin died in 841, in a raid on Galloway : the Scottish throne passed to his son Kenneth, and on Bred's death Kenneth, by right of his grandmother, laid claim to the Pictish throne also. It seems that he had to fight to make good his claim : but he did so, and from about the year 843 [1] the two races of Picts and Scots make up one kingdom, commonly called Alba, or later, and increasingly, Scotia or Scotland. The name of Pict had gone out of use in a couple of generations, and the King was Righ nan Albannach, King of Scots. Kenneth MacAlpin was heir of the line of Fergus, already royal for more than three hundred years : and nearly eleven hundred after his time, his fifty-sixth successor, still his descendant, was crowned King of Scots and King of England also, and Emperor of a quarter of the world, on the sacred stone that by very ancient tradition Fergus had brought with him when he came from Ireland.

[1] This is the commonly accepted date : it is that given in the *Chronicle of Melrose*. But dates from 841 to 856 appear elsewhere.

II

THREE HUNDRED AND TEN YEARS
843–1153

Ituri in aciem majores vestros et posteros cogitate.

Tacitus, *Agricola*.

CHAPTER VII

THE UNITED STATES OF SCOTLAND

A HUNDRED AND NINETY-ONE YEARS: 843–1034

' O tu qui servas armis ista moenia,
Noli dormire, moneo, sed vigila.
Dum Hector vigil exstitit in Troia
Non eam cepit fraudulenta Graecia.'
Italian soldiers' song of the tenth century.

FOR two centuries after the Picts were joined with the Scots, this process of consolidation was continued, so that by the middle of the eleventh century there had come to be a sizeable kingdom of Scotland to confront the beginning of the Middle Ages and the great renaissance of the twelfth and thirteenth. The Celtic states came together by dynastic inheritance, though not without a certain amount of fighting. Northern England also was acquired, by conquest, and eventually, though not till the Middle Ages were well advanced, the lands lost to the Northmen were recovered. The process of welding together Picts and Scots, of drawing in the Cymry of Strathclyde, of conquering the northern part of Northumbria, went on to an accompaniment of constant wars with the Norse on the north and west, of constant defence against their coastwise invasions, and of intermittent wars with the English to southward, and later with their conquerors the Danes. Yet, thanks largely to the characters of the kings, the story of the next four hundred years, which is the substance of the rest of this book, is one of increasing strength, prosperity, and union.

Kenneth I, Kenneth MacAlpin,[1] Kenneth the Hardy, held the throne till he died about 858, and strengthened himself by alliance with his neighbours : a daughter was married to Aedh, King of Ireland, another to Rùn, King of Strathclyde. But his reign was stormy. The Britons burnt Dunblane, and the Northmen ravaged inland as far as Dunkeld, which in 849 he had made the ecclesiastical capital of Alba, transferring there the relics of St Columba. He himself harried the Northumbrians, invading England six times, and burning Dunbar, then, of course, an English town. He was briefly succeeded by his brother Donald I, then in 863 by his son Constantine I, whose reign of fourteen years was marked by new and fiercer incursions of the Northmen.

The attempts of Gorm, Eirik, and Harald Harfagr to consolidate the little Scandinavian states into the kingdoms of Denmark, Sweden, and Norway had driven their recalcitrants overseas in a fresh and

---

[1] From Kenneth's patronymic the line of the dynasty to 1290 is commonly known as the MacAlpin House. The usage is convenient, but loose, supplying a label rather than expressing a fact. The kings did not call themselves MacAlpin : and the male line from Alpin died out in 1034, the succession after that being carried on by descendants of Bethoc, daughter of Malcolm II, while the rival line which for long contested their claims were descended from Gruoch, granddaughter of Kenneth III.

formidable wave of conquest. France and all the British Isles suffered severely, including the Northmen already settled in Ireland, where Olaf the White became king in the North, sharing the power with the Danish Ingvar, whose descendants were the famous Hy Ivar. In France by the mid-century there was a strong colony on the Seine near Rouen, and in the middle of the 'seventies (towards the end of Constantine's reign, that is) Hrolf, Raoul, Rollo, son of Rognvald Jarl of Mori, landed there and seized Amiens, Soissons, and Laon. In England all through the 'sixties and 'seventies the English were being steadily driven back, precisely as they themselves had once driven the Britons: it was not until Alfred's victory of Ethandune in 878 that the heroic stand of Ecgberht's grandsons could halt the invaders, and even then it was only at the price of permitting them to colonise half England—Deira, East Anglia, and Mercia to the north of Watling Street. Alba was less easy, for geographical reasons, to get a grip on, but Strathclyde was attacked, and in 870 Olaf and Ingvar, invading from Ireland, captured Dumbarton after a four months' siege. They pressed heavily too on their predecessors in the Isles, who were already amalgamating with the native population to form the Gall-Gael. These resisted under Ketil Flatnose, whose daughter Aud the Deepminded is one of the great figures of the Sagas and a pioneer in the colonisation of Iceland. Further north, Harald Harfagr himself was raiding the Orkneys and Shetlands, which his expelled enemies

F

had been using as a base for raiding him. He conquered them, appointing as Jarl Rognvald of Mori (father of Hrolf), who however resigned the office to Sigurd his brother : and in time Sigurd allied with Thorstein, son of Aud and Olaf the White, and conquered the northmost provinces of Alba, Caithness and Sutherland, as far as the Oikil. Sigurd died in the business, slain by a dead man, for he slung at his saddle the head of Constantine's commander Maelbrighde : a tooth of it grazed his knee, and the wound poisoned. Thorstein drove south, and defeated Constantine himself at Dollar : the King was forced to make formal surrender of the North. Thorstein was killed very shortly afterwards, and the pressure eased somewhat : but within two years, in 877, Constantine also was killed in withstanding a raid upon the coast of Fife : some say he was taken and tortured to death in a cave.

He was succeeded by his brother Aedh, Hugh, younger son of Kenneth MacAlpin. (From this point the reader who wishes to understand the complex oscillations of the succession is referred to the genealogy opposite.) A bare year later, however, Cyric,[1] a chief of the Garioch, made war on Aedh, killed him, and seized the government. But though he contrived to hold it for eighteen years, it shows the firm status of the dynasty (even with the actual monarchy semi-elective) that he had to associate with himself as nominal king first Eocha, grandson of Kenneth and

[1] Also known as Cyr, Grig or Gregory.

THE DESCENDANTS OF ALPIN: 843–1034

(The prefixed numbers give the order of the succession)

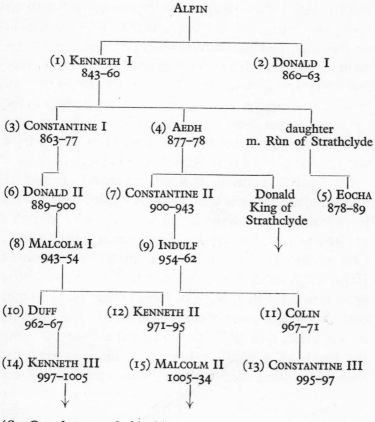

(*See Genealogy at end of book.*)

son of the King of Strathclyde, and then Donald II,
another grandson of Kenneth, and son of Constantine.
Again the story is chiefly one of Norse raids, for the
comparative stabilisation of affairs in England caused
the Northmen to concentrate on the coasts of Alba
and Ireland.[1] Fortviot, the old capital of the Southern
Picts, was burnt. Cyric defeated the raiders at Collin
on the Tay, and transferred the main seat of government to Scone, where the Kings of Scots, with very
few exceptions, were crowned thereafter till 1651. In
his time too begins the importance of St Andrews, for
by some rather vague enactment of his it received
certain privileges, also rather vague, on which it later
was to found a claim to ecclesiastical superiority.

On Cyric's death in 896 his colleague Donald II
reigned alone for four years, but was killed near Forres
in some kind of civil war, and succeeded, not by Malcolm
his young son, but by his first cousin and Eocha's,
Constantine II, son of King Aedh and grandson of
Kenneth MacAlpin.[2] Constantine II was a hardy
fighter, and his long reign of forty-three years brought
early, in 904, a great victory over the Norse invaders
in Fortrenn. In 908 Strathclyde came directly into
the hands of a younger branch of his own dynasty.
Donald its king died without heirs, and Constantine

---

[1] France was also suffering very heavily : a great siege of Paris
comes in 885.

[2] All through the later ninth century and the tenth, the throne
went alternately to the descendants of Constantine I and Aedh,
sons of Kenneth MacAlpin. Aedh's line ended with the death of
Constantine III in 997.

procured the election of his own younger brother, another Donald, whose line ruled there till it ended in 1018.

Soon there were fresh and violent attacks from the Northmen. Alfred had unified what was left of England, and his noble personality and great wisdom and courage had given the country a new spirit : his fighting children, Eadward the Elder and Æthelflæd, Lady of (South) Mercia, carried on his work and were pushing back the Danes. Elsewhere, however, the Northmen extended their power. In 911 Charles the Simple, King of France, made with Hrolf the Treaty of St Clair sur Epte, that, on condition of Hrolf's baptism, surrendered to him all the land between the Epte and the March of Brittany, which became the duchy of the Northmen, Normannia, Normandie, and a formidable factor in the history of Europe, including that of Scotland. The new duchy was a fresh threat to England and Alba, as it virtually completed their encirclement. Æthelflæd in 915 attempted to form a league against the menace, and made alliance with Constantine and the Britons : and in 918 the expected attack came in force. Rognvald Hy Ivar (not the Jarl of Orkney but the King of North Ireland) landed in Northumbria and seized York. Northumbria begged Constantine for help : he came, and close to Corbridge on the Tyne fought the invaders. Eadred, the Earl of (Danish) Northumberland, was killed ; the Northmen were still able to hold their conquests, but they were prevented from pushing north of Tyne. Rognvald

died soon after, and was succeeded by his brother
Sigtrygg. Constantine, possibly, re-confirmed with
Eadward the league already made with Eadward's
sister. Two MSS. of the *Anglo-Saxon Chronicle* (one
of which is clearly a very late version of the other) say
that in 924 he ' took Eadward to father and lord.'
Later English chroniclers, down to the present day,
make a good deal of the point, Freeman in special
building upon it an enormous structure, and declaring
that ' from that time to the fourteenth century the
vassalage of Scotland to England is part of the public
law of Great Britain.' Leaving out the general testimony
of subsequent events, we observe that the numerous
other MSS. of the *Chronicle* have no reference to such
an important matter, while Æthelward, who in the
next generation wrote a eulogy of the English royal
house for his kinswoman, Eadward's great-niece, the
Empress Matilda, has a great deal to say of Eadward's
wars, but nothing at all of this notable achievement.
And the actual story, where it does occur, does not
correspond with known circumstances of the time.
It seems probable that the chronicler who first wrote
it was confusing Eadward with Æthelstan his brother,
who succeeded him shortly after the time given, and
the King of Scots with another northern potentate,
Sigtrygg, Rognvald's brother and successor, who did
make some kind of alliance with Æthelstan. In any
case the point is of no great importance, as even if this
commendation of Scotland were as authentic as that of
England to the Pope, any legal effect would pass in 1097.

To come back to assurance, Eadward undoubtedly died in 925, and was succeeded by his son Æthelstan, the greatest save Alfred of his brilliant house, and the most powerful of its succession of Kings. Æthelstan had to begin, however, by recognising Sigtrygg's possession, and giving him his sister. Sigtrygg died in 926 : Æthelstan invaded his territory and recovered it, driving out Sigtrygg's son, who escaped to Ireland, while Godfred, Sigtrygg's brother, endeavoured to get Constantine to help them. Freeman has much to say of a *second* commendation of Scotland at this time : the sole authority is one MS. of the *Winchester Chronicle*, which, by the way, does not mention the other one, which he also accepts. This time Constantine, Eadred of English Northumbria, and two Welsh princes are said to have ' confirmed peace ' with Æthelstan and agreed to put down *deofol-geld*, devil-tribute, while Constantine's son was to be baptised. We happen to know that Constantine was not only a Christian but from the beginning of his already long reign had shown a keen interest in the affairs of the Church. Certainly Constantine showed friendliness to Olaf, Sigtrygg's exiled son, to whom he gave his daughter in marriage. He did not break the peace with Æthelstan, but the marriage may have roused the latter's suspicions : he may have thought that Constantine looked to establishing the same kind of dynastic connection with Northumbria that he had done already with Strathclyde, and paving the way to a later peaceful union. In 934 he invaded Alba and raided the whole east coast by sea and land, though Irish records (which at least are neutral) remark that the raids had very small result. They stirred Constantine to retaliate, however. In 937 he declared war, and with his son-in-law Olaf Sigtryggson, the latter's cousin Olaf Godfredson, King of Ireland, and his own nephew Eogan King of Strathclyde, landed in Humber-mouth. Æthelstan marched to meet him with an English army reinforced by Viking mercenaries. He did so at a place called Brunanburh, and was victorious in a hard-fought battle. Further war followed. Eirik Blood-axe, the son and successor of Harald Harfagr, was driven out of his kingdom of Norway by his own subjects : he descended upon Northumbria, and Æthelstan, still weak from a costly victory, bought him off by giving him the province, on condition that he should hold it against the Hy Ivar—the two Olafs. Eirik could not do so : they attacked him, and by 940 had won not only Northumbria but the Danelagh, the Danish half of England. Æthelstan died before he could counter them, and the expelled Eirik sailed to the Isles, where he made himself king, to be expelled a third time soon thereafter : as a popular sovereign he failed markedly. In 943 Constantine, now at least seventy and mourning a son killed at Brunanburh, resigned his throne and became a monk at St Andrews. He was succeeded not by his son Indulf but by Malcolm I, the son of his cousin and immediate predecessor Donald II : this Malcolm held the throne until 954.

Æthelstan had been succeeded by his young but

very able brother Eadmund the Elder, whose short reign saw hard fighting and much success. By 944 he had recovered Northumbria from the invaders, and about the same time he established some kind of control over Southern Cumbria, or Cumberland. In 945 he made an alliance with Malcolm, making over to him the province (perhaps only for life) *on þæt gerade*, on the understanding, that Malcolm became his *midwyrhta*, ' with-worker,' or precisely and literally, *collaborator*. (The later English chroniclers, who had the same difficulty with Anglo-Saxon as Lord Hailes was to have with the Norman-French of the *Scala-cronica*, mistranslate this as *fidelis*, and still later historians re-translate as *vassal* : but there is no sign of homage in the earliest records.) Eadmund died the next year, succeeded by his equally able and active brother Eadred : and Malcolm continued to hold Cumberland.

In 949 Olaf Sigtryggson demanded Malcolm's help in a fresh attack on Northumbria. Malcolm's conduct was more politic than honest. He squared his conscience by remaining neutral, but allowed old King Constantine, Olaf's father-in-law and now Abbot of St Andrews, to emerge from his cloister and lead a force that ravaged the luckless province as far as the Tees. Constantine then returned to his retirement, where he died in 952, and Malcolm in that year made an active alliance with Eadred and the Britons against the Vikings, which enabled Eadred to win back Northumbria once more. Olaf gave up his attempts

upon it and went back to Ireland, where he confirmed
the Norse domination there that lasted till Tara in 980
and Clontarf in 1014 restored the sovereignty to the
native kings. Malcolm himself was killed in 954, near
Forres, apparently in some kind of civil strife. He
left two sons, both to be kings in time, but in accordance
with the now usual arrangement, was succeeded by
Indulf, son of his own predecessor Constantine II.

Indulf's name is an anglicisation of Indulphus,
which appears in Gaelic as Illuilb, Ailuilb, and Illulfe :
it is probably a form of the Danish Hildulf, so Constantine's queen was possibly a Dane. His eight years'
reign is decidedly obscure : yet it seems to have held
a very important matter, nothing less than the acquisition of the present capital of Scotland, which at Indulf's
accession was still an English town. The cause, and
course, of his war with England are alike unknown :
he certainly made war on the English march, and
annexed the fertile country north of the Pentlands.
Oppidum Eden was abandoned to him. This may be
Caer-eideann, Carriden or Blackness, an important
coast fortress : but the phrase would also translate
Dun-eideann, Dun-edin, Edinburgh.[1] Certainly that
very important stronghold came into Scottish hands
about this time, and its loss laid open the northern
march of Northumbria. Indulf also repulsed a big
Viking raid in Buchan, and in 962 was killed in
withstanding another at Invercullen.

[1] Professor Watson has shown that *Edwinesburh* is not the original
form, but a ' rationalised ' corruption of the pre-Anglian name.

The next five years were filled largely by the struggle of his son Colin against Malcolm I's son Duff, who by now long-standing practice should have inherited. In 967 Colin contrived to kill—apparently murder—Duff near Forres, that town so strangely fatal to their race : but four years later he was killed himself in a burning house in Strathclyde, and the throne went to Duff's brother Kenneth II.

Kenneth's reign lasted from 971 to 995, but it is a cloudy time, for the surviving Scots records of the tenth century are very scanty. One picturesque event is frequently attached by historians to the second year of his reign—the famous story of King Eadgar of England, in token of supremacy, stroking an eight of vassal kings on the Dee, of whom Kenneth was one. One regrets to spoil so colourful a picture, but to trace its growth is an exercise not unamusing in the analysis of historical legend. The earliest reference to anything out of which it may have arisen is in a sermon of Ælfric's somewhat later, where describing the marvellous miracles of St Swithin, who was Eadgar's contemporary, he remarks that eight kings *gebugon to Eadgares wissunge* : this might conceivably mean ' bowed to Edgar's rule,' but it equally well can be rendered ' took his advice ' . . . and as Eadgar, himself advised by the great Dunstan, was a man of unusual intelligence, it is very likely that his various allies were accustomed to value his opinion highly. Had Eadgar's contemporary Æthelward, whose account of the glories of the House of Cerdic stops with the following year,

ever heard of the eight-oar, one would have expected
him to seize on the story : but though he has much to
say of Eadgar's greatness, he does not seem to know
anything about this. An eleventh-century MS. of the
Anglo-Saxon Chronicle describes Eadgar as reviewing
his fleet at *Leicester* (probably Chester—there is a
record of his doing so there) :

7 þær him comon ongean vi cyningas, 7 ealle wiþ hine getrewsodon
þæt hi wolden efenwyrhtan beon on sæ 7 on londe.[1]

A twelfth-century MS. repeats this, without any
embroidery : and also in the twelfth century, Florence
of Worcester, a gentleman with the quality of creative
imagination so manifest in our own Hector Boece,
repeats it enlarged, calling the kings *subreguli*, under-
kings, and making them eight : and he for the first
time tells the tale of the eight-oar. He also mentions
that Eadgar's fleet consisted of 3600 ships. He gives
a catalogue of the various rowers which shows him to
be badly out in his knowledge as to who was then
reigning, and where. We may take it, perhaps, as at
least reasonably probable that various potentates, of
whom Kenneth may very likely have been one, really
did pay a visit to Eadgar at Chester in order to concert
measures against the common enemy, and that they
fell in with Eadgar's policy. A review of the fleet,
intended to impress them, may have included some
kind of yachting party, which came down embellished

---

[1] And there came to meet him six kings, who promised to be his
even-workers (i.e. allies) on sea and on land.

in popular tradition. But even so much is rather conjectural.

Another story, also somewhat carelessly accepted, derives from the *St Albans Chronicle*, which makes Kenneth claim Lothian as an hereditary fief of the Kings of Scots, and so receive it from Eadgar. Lothian had been Anglian territory for generations before the union of the Scots and Picts had brought the Scots march anywhere near its border. Indulf, some ten years before the date assigned to this transaction, had certainly annexed its northern part : but there is no trace of any more in Scots hands until, three reigns later, Kenneth's son annexed the remainder of the province and pushed the Scottish frontier to the Tweed.

As for Kenneth's less mythical *faictes et gestes*, we have only rather general evidence. He had, of course, the running war with the Vikings that for nearly, now, a couple of centuries had been a commonplace of current events. Towards the end of the previous century, Einar, half-brother of Hrolf of Normandy, had driven out the Orkney Vikings and made himself Jarl of those islands. He was succeeded by his brother Thorfinn Skullcleaver, who died about the beginning of Kenneth's reign, leaving five sons. Their domestic affairs were complicated by the lovely and unscrupulous Ragnhild, daughter of Eirik Blood-axe and wife in succession of three out of the five. She brought two to their deaths : at last Liotr, her third husband, won the earldom after a war with his brother Skuli, and tried to push his dominion further south. There was considerable turmoil in the Far North, and a victory for the Norsemen, accompanied, however, by Liotr's death. His nephew Lodvar defeated an army of Kenneth's but had to withdraw : and in 995, the last year of Kenneth's reign, the Orkneys were forcibly pacified, and christianised, by St Olaf.

King Kenneth had considerable trouble in and with Angus, that brought him to his end : but its course and causes are impossible to trace. Fordun has a long and complicated story of how he brought about a civil war by attempting to change the principle of succession to primogeniture and secure the throne to his son, later Malcolm II, whose rights, on the usual principle, were subordinate to those of Colin's son Constantine, and of Kenneth's own nephew, Duff's son Kenneth. Constantine plotted against the King, with the aid of Finella (daughter of the Mormaor of Angus) whose son Kenneth had put to death : and Finella murdered the King by means of a piece of fantastic machinery that belongs to late-mediaeval romance. Local legend makes the lady a witch who could walk on the tree-tops : but there is some foundation for Fordun's story. The *Chronicle of the Kings* says that Kenneth was killed by his own men in Fettercairn, through the treachery of Finuele, daughter of Cunthar or Connachar, Earl of Angus, whose son he had put to death. Whether an attempt to change the Succession Law had anything to do with it is not clear : but certainly from that time onward there were a long series of succession quarrels, at times acute and very dangerous :

and uncertainty as to the principle of succession endured till as late as two centuries later on, when it helped to bring about the Three Hundred Years' War.[1]

Constantine now succeeded, but only at the cost of civil conflict. He was killed within eighteen months, in Glenalmond, by his rival Kenneth, son of Duff, who then came to the throne as Kenneth III, to be killed in turn, eight years later, in 1005, by the third claimant, Kenneth II's son Malcolm. The position with regard to the succession was now rather contestable, and decidedly paradoxical as well. The throne had gone turn about to the descendants of Constantine I and of Aedh. Aedh's line had ended with Constantine III : but a swing between alternate lines was still possible among the descendants of Malcolm I— between the lines of Duff and of Kenneth II. On that principle Malcolm was heir to the last king, Kenneth III. But if he did stand for the principle of primogeniture (and he tried to apply it to his own successor) then the lawful heir was not himself but Kenneth III's son Boedhe. It was a situation that promised storm : and in fact it gave rise to a long trail of conflict.

The first years of the reign of Malcolm II were marked by unsuccessful foreign war. Findlaec of Moray, brother and successor of the Mormaor Maelbrighde who had been defeated by Liotr of Orkney, now challenged Liotr's nephew and successor, Sigurd Lodvarson, to a formal battle. Sigurd accepted, and

[1] See *Robert Bruce King of Scots*, p. 44.

fighting under a magical raven banner, made by his
mother, defeated his challenger. Malcolm made peace
with Sigurd, and gave him the youngest of his three
daughters. From the marriage was born Thorfinn
Sigurdson, the Thorfinn of the Heimskringla Saga,
who succeeded his father in the mainland territories
of Orkney on the latter's death at Clontarf in 1014,
and thus gave his grandfather the King of Scots a
certain hold on the lost northern provinces.

Malcolm's main wars, however, were with England,
and though they were to include one of the three most
important victories in our history, they began with
disaster. Indulf, as we have seen, had won part of
Northumbria, the rich grain-growing country north
of the Pentlands. Malcolm coveted that which lay
south and east of them, the no less fertile district of
the Merse. Now opportunity presented itself. Under
Æthelred II, the younger son of Eadgar, known by a
bitter pun as Æthelred Unred,[1] Mercia, which Eadgar
had controlled, had made an attempt to recover
independence. The resulting disunion offered a clear
invitation to the Danes, who descended in force.
They were bought off by a tribute called the Danegeld :
but the tribute naturally provided an even warmer
invitation, and in the 'nineties they had invaded again,
under Olaf of Norway and Svend Forkbeard of
Denmark. Again Æthelred bought them off : then
in 1002 he tried a general massacre instead, the English

---

[1] Æthelred means 'Royal Counsel,' Un-red, un-counsel or evil-counsel.

falling by treachery on the Danish settlers. The
expedient was even less successful. Those murdered
included Gunnhild, sister of Svend, and for the next
four years—those covering Malcolm's accession—her
brother took bloody vengeance on the whole south of
England. Malcolm decided to fish in troubled waters,
and in 1006 he invaded Northumbria, and was beaten
before Durham by Uchtred, son of Earl Waltheof of
that province, who proceeded to decorate the town
with a frieze of Scots heads, neatly washed and combed
and set on palisades. (The four women who attended
to their toilet were given a cow apiece for the gory
business.) The Danish attacks continued, and in 1013
Æthelred fled overseas to the court of his brother-in-
law Richard of Normandy, the great-grandson of
Hrolf. Svend was proclaimed King of England, but
died almost at once. Æthelred returned, and un-
deterred by his previous experience, arranged another
massacre of Danes. He himself died then, just in
time to avoid the vengeance of Svend's son Cnut, who
landed in 1015, and forced Æthelred's son, Eadmund
Ironside, to share the kingship with him.

Eadmund died then : his young son was sent overseas for shelter, and found it at the court of Hungary,
with results that were not unimportant for Scottish
history. Cnut married Æthelred's widow Emma of
Normandy, and was formally accepted as King of
England, Æthelred's younger sons, Alfred and Eadward, taking refuge at the Norman court of their uncle
. . . also with results that were to be of crucial import-

G

ance to English history, and considerably to influence
our own.

Cnut rose to be the most powerful sovereign in
Europe save Henry II, who was then Emperor. He
joined Sweden and Norway with Denmark and then
with England, which he united once more, this time
for good : and he claimed some kind of suzerainty
over Ireland and Wales, although, in practice, it was
not effective : Ireland, indeed, defeated him heavily.
In spite of the series of political murders by which he
consolidated his position, he proved himself a just and
capable ruler, who restored a good deal of internal
peace to England.

In 1018 Malcolm challenged the new power. He
invaded England once more, and at Carham on the
Tweed defeated Eadulf Cudel, brother of Uchtred,
so heavily that *a flumine Tesa usque Tweedam populus
. . . pene totus cum natu majoribus suis interiit,* almost
the whole people from Tees to Tweed, with their
gentry, perished, and Northern England was thrown
into such confusion that when the Bishop of Durham
died of the shock, it was three years before a successor
could be appointed. The battle is one of the most
important in Scottish history. Northern Northumbria,
from Indulf's frontier of the Pentlands to the Tweed,
became and remained a part of the Scottish kingdom,
nor was Cnut able to recover it.

Apparently it was not until thirteen years later, in
1031, that he even attempted to do so. He invaded
Malcolm's dominions in that year, but we know very

little of what happened. Peace was made between the kings: so much seems certain. Later English historians declare that Cnut became overlord of Scotland : but they do not offer any explanation as to why the great province of Lothian, far the richest part of all North-umbria, should in that case have remained in Scottish hands : and we do know it did so. The Frank Rodul-phus Glaber, a contemporary and a neutral, describes Cnut as making a vigorous attempt to add Scotland to the rest of his great dominions, and failing : to be sure he attributes the failure to the earnest Christianity of Malcolm, but though he is probably wrong about the cause he may possibly have been right about the fact. The Irish chroniclers describe Malcolm on his death, three years after this invasion, as ' Lord and Father of the West'; and the *Chronicles of the Kings of Scots*, in a text completed during the next generation, call him 'most victorious King,' which even an obituary notice would hardly do if he had been so recently reduced to vassalage. The *Chronicle of Melrose* does not mention any submission, nor does Florence of Worcester, who would certainly have greatly liked to do so. The point, of course, is in any case no great matter. The certain fact, and the one that does matter to future generations, is that Tweed-dale, Teviotdale, Ettrick, and the Merse, with the as yet unannexed part of Lothian, were added to Scotland during Malcolm's reign. The South-east Lowlands were under the Scots Crown, if they hardly yet could be counted part of Scotland.

Malcolm also drew in, in effect, the South-west Lowlands. Eogan, his ally of Carham, was killed in 1018, soon after the battle. With him ended the line of Donald, son of Aedh and grandson of Kenneth MacAlpin. Malcolm, apparently peacefully, induced the Britons to accept as king another prince of the line of Kenneth MacAlpin—his own grandson Duncan, son of his eldest daughter Bethoc, by Crinan, Abbot of Dunkeld.[1] Duncan became King of Strathclyde: and Malcolm, who had no son of his own, determined that he should unite the kingdoms by becoming also successor to himself. The matter was not too easy to accomplish. By custom the throne would go at Malcolm's death to the line of his cousin and predecessor Kenneth III. Kenneth's son Boedhe, as it happened, was no longer living: but he had left a son whose name is not known, and a daughter Gruoch. Malcolm had the son murdered: but there was still a male descendant of Kenneth, for Gruoch had married Gillecomgan, Mormaor of Moray, and had a son Lulach. Lulach, however, was only a small child, and his father was killed in some kind of family feud, so that he and his mother had no one to make his claim

---

[1] The marriage of the clergy was not uncommon anywhere at this time: the Church had constantly raised objections to it, from St Paul's time onward, and it was frequently forbidden: it was not until the twelfth century, however, that a priest's marriage was *ipso facto* illegal. For a ' regular ' to be married seems odd none the less: but Crinan may have been a lay ' commendator ' of abbey lands. And in the decadence of the Culdees, or Columbite order, it was not an uncommon abuse for the members of the community to marry and bequeath the communal property to their children.

effectual.   Malcolm's desire accordingly bore fruit. On his death in 1034 his grandson Duncan, already King of Strathclyde, became King of Scots—of a kingdom that only thirty years before had for southern march the Forth and the Pentland Hills, and now had instead the Solway and the Tweed.   Our modern Scotland was coming into being, though its shape was not yet that familiar to ourselves, for Strathclyde still came a little way south of the Sark, and the Norsemen held the Far North and much of the West—Caithness and Sutherland and all the Isles, with the greater part of Argyle, the first Scottish Scotia.   None the less, there is now, from Duncan's generation, a kingdom we can identify with our Scotland : and if Kenneth MacAlpin first joined two out of its five component states and Indulf added its present capital, Malcolm II added the lands besouth the Forth.   But still two centuries and a third, or nearly, were to pass before the lost North and West were recovered.

CHAPTER VIII

NORTH AND WEST OR EAST AND SOUTH?

FIFTY-NINE YEARS: 1034–1093

'Sic fortis Etruria crevit.'

Vergil, *Georgics*, ii.

IN the next half-century there are two main matters. The first was dynastic conflict thrice in the next three reigns, that settled the principle of succession by primogeniture in the line of Malcolm II, though not without contest for generations after. The other was the posing of a question that was to affect the whole future history of Scotland—whether the country's cultural and political connections, through a time of powerful mental and spiritual activity, were to be, as before, with Ireland and Scandinavia, or with France and the Continent of Europe. The two points, in fact, are very closely connected, for had the dynastic question been otherwise answered, so in all probability would have been the other.

Malcolm II was the last king of the direct male line of Kenneth MacAlpin. Of the descendants of Malcolm I, Duff's (the elder) line had ended in his great-granddaughter Gruoch. Kenneth II's had ended in his three granddaughters, the daughters of Malcolm II.

Now, each of these four ladies had a son. Gruoch,
as was said above, had married Gillecomgan, Mormaor of Moray, and their son was Lulach. Bethoc,
the eldest of Malcolm II's daughters, had married
Crinan, Abbot of Dunkeld, and their son was Duncan,
King of Strathclyde, who now was King of Scots as
Duncan I. Donada, her next sister, had married
Findlaec, Mormaor of Moray, the uncle of Gruoch's
husband Gillecomgan : and their son was Maelbeatha,
the gentleman whom Shakespeare has ensured we shall
know as Macbeth.[1] Even allowing for the fact that
Thorfinn Sigurdson, Jarl of Orkney, the son of Malcolm's third daughter, was out of the running, there
were the makings of a fierce family quarrel, for Gruoch
had a blood-feud with King Malcolm over the murder
of her brother, and at Malcolm's death with the murder
still unavenged, the feud devolved on his heir, King
Duncan I. The feud apart, there was also cause for
trouble, for by Malcolm's own principle of primogeniture, and also by the regular practice of alternate
succession between two branches of the family, the
strongest claim to the throne lay with Gruoch's son
Lulach.

Lulach, however, was still, it would seem, a child,

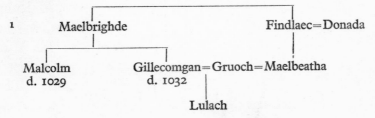

[1] Maelbrighde   Findlaec=Donada

Malcolm Gillecomgan=Gruoch=Maelbeatha
d. 1029   d. 1032

Lulach

and not a very intelligent one, as his later sobriquet was Lulach the Fool. Duncan, therefore, succeeded uncontested. But the widowed Gruoch now married her first husband's cousin Maelbeatha, who was also first cousin of Duncan through their mothers, and in fact stood next after him in the succession. Maelbeatha, by contemporary etiquette, was now in charge of the feud of his wife and stepson : and he was a man of energy and courage. Duncan's reign therefore opened ominously, and he deprived himself of a possible source of support by falling foul of his remaining cousin, Thorfinn of Orkney, and making an unsuccessful war against him. He was also tempted to make war in England. Cnut died in 1035, and his miserable sons were at war with each other, and with Æthelred's eldest son Alfred. Duncan and Alfred both were unsuccessful. In 1040, the sixth year of Duncan's reign, Maelbeatha carried his wife's feud into action, and avenged her brother on his slayer's heir. Duncan was killed, not, apparently, by murder at Glamis or Inverness, but in battle at Bothgowanan : and Maelbeatha took the throne by right of his young stepson, and was accepted, for the only other grown man with any claim was Thorfinn of Orkney.

Duncan, however, had left two young sons, Malcolm and Donald, and their mother, it would seem, was an English lady, of the great house of the Earls of Northumbria—the granddaughter of Cnut's sister Astrid and niece of Svend King of Denmark. The boys, accordingly, may have been taken to their

mother's country, then ruled by Cnut's younger son
Harthacnut : they disappear from sight for a long
time. Harthacnut drank himself to death in 1042.
The English had had enough of the dynasty : the son
of Eadmund Ironside—that is, the lawful heir of the
House of Cerdic—was out of reach at the Hungarian
Court, but his uncle Eadward was conveniently to
hand at the Norman one. Eadward was half Norman
by blood, wholly Norman by training and inclination,
and by temperament much nearer a priest than a
layman—that is to say, much more clerical than most
priests : but he was sober, just, and cleanly living, and
England called him joyfully to the throne. It is
probable enough that he gave shelter to the two young
princes, for he had been himself a prince in exile : and
if they were in fact bred at his court they came there
into contact with the Norman culture, which by now
was far less Scandinavian than it was French.

Maelbeatha, of course, had their return feud to look
for : but they were young. Their grandfather Crinan
tried to overthrow him and failed, and he was able
to hold the Scottish throne for seventeen years. The
records of his reign are very scanty, but he seems to
have made a good king. Apparently he went to Rome
a pilgrim : we learn that he there made great gifts to
the poor. He seems to have been friendly to Normandy : when in 1054 an anti-Norman *coup d'état*
drove Eadward's Norman favourites from his court,
Maelbeatha gave them shelter, with the result that
Siward, brother-in-law of the late King Duncan,

invaded his kingdom and defeated him. Birnam Wood, however, did not come to Dunsinane, for Maelbeatha reigned for another three years thereafter. In 1057, however, Duncan's son Malcolm, with what support is difficult to make out, attacked him and killed him at Lumphanan on Deeside. Lulach claimed the throne, and held a shadowy royalty for a winter : then he too was killed at Essie in Strathbogie, leaving a young son Maelsnechtain, and a daughter who was to bear some troublesome progeny.

Malcolm succeeded without further contest, and his thirty-six years' reign is one of the most important in our history, for it witnessed the beginning of the process that during the reigns of the four of his sons who followed made Scotland into a European nation.

This process of reorientation is often misdescribed because mis-seen. It is formulated as if it were no more than a conflict of native ideas and native culture with English. To see it thus is to see it in false perspective, and involves an odd ignoring of *English* history. It is true that many of the new ideas arrived via England, as one might expect, for that country, in the early Middle Ages, was our natural bridge to the Continent at large. But the culture of England in the high Middle Ages was emphatically not an English culture. Politically and culturally alike, England then was French. The class which gave her both her laws and her manners spoke French, thought French, took their scholarship, their letters, their arts, their whole social and political framework and point of view, from

France, and in French terms. There was, of course, an English England surviving, but without political or artistic voice. She retained her language, and (largely because of that fact) a considerable measure of national consciousness : in time, when the intimate bond with France had been broken, she was to assimilate her conquerors. But the time was a long one : for nearly a century after the end of this book the language of English schools was French or Latin. Such relics of English culture as survived did so only out of England, in Scotland itself, in the provinces Malcolm III's great-grandfather had won from England and made our South-east Lowlands.[1] The influence of these provinces was to be powerful, but not for a long time yet. English does appear as an ' official ' language in Scotland before it is so used in its own country : but while Scots state-papers of the thirteenth century, even those addressed to Norway, are sometimes in French, the oldest we have in English is of 1318, and then it merely translates a Latin one. At the coronation of 1249, the King's oath was trans-lated from Latin into French. French seems to have been the common speech of the Court, partly, no doubt, because it was almost as international as Latin,[2] partly also, perhaps, because from 1100 to 1363 every Queen

---

[1] So late as the end of the eleventh century these were still regarded as a sort of *Inghilterra irredenta* : the *A.S. Chronicle* remarks that Malcolm in 1091 *for mid his fyrde ut of Scotlande into Loðene on Englaland*—went with his army out of Scotland into Lothian in England : i.e. that he crossed the Forth.

[2] In the thirteenth century the Italian Brunetto Latini was writing in French because it was *commune à toutes gens*.

of Scots spoke French as her mother-tongue—Sibyl,
Maude, Ermengarde, Joan, Marie, Margaret, Yolette,
Elizabeth, and Joan again—while the next three, all
ladies of Scots houses, either probably or certainly
spoke it also, side by side with the Gaelic of their
native districts.[1]

To understand the time we are to consider one must
watch in Scotland the impact of tendencies general to
Europe—consolidation, centralisation, the building up
of a firm social framework, and within its walls a new
flowering of the intellect and the spirit. We have seen
that by the end of the eighth century there had already
been the promise of that. But the onslaught of the
Northmen brought it to ruin, and in Southern Europe
there were the Saracens also, driven back from the very
Loire in 732, and holding firm in Spain as a constant
menace that within a few years of the death of Charlemagne was threatening Rome and Constantinople both.
The Slavs were over-running Germany, the Magyars
a danger there and to Italy. The structure that
Charlemagne built fell into wreck ; and Ireland, the
Lamp of the West, was by 900 no more than a
plundered ruin.

---

[1] Evidence as to the precise use of language in mediaeval Scotland
is rather scanty. One observes, however, that a French romance,
by a Picard, is dedicated to Alan of Galloway, the head of a Celtic
house, who died in 1234 ; that the only extant correspondence of
Black James Douglas (who was not precisely anti-national) is in
French, though he no doubt spoke Gaelic also ; and that so late as
1394 Queen Annabel, a Scotswoman from a Gaelic-speaking
district, was writing in French to the English-speaking King of
England.

Yet there were men who fought in that despair, as
Syagrius or Boniface or Arthur had done four centuries earlier : certain kings of the House of Alpin
had been among them. Men who fight long odds may
be beaten, are often beaten : but they kindle a spark
in others who come after. By the tenth century, a
general resistance had begun to organise through all
Western Christendom. (The Eastern Empire, nar-
rowed but never disorganised, was quiet enough, and
the most civilised part of Europe.) The feudal system
began to shape itself, a system of social and military
organisation (the two were necessarily synonymous)
based on the only unit which had survived, the family.
It is worth noting that in tenth-century Latin *patria*
means nothing so large as a country or even district :
it means a man's family or kindred. The family held
its land : smaller families about a powerful one
demanded the protection of its *motte*, the castle that
was a refuge from the invader, and they paid for
protection by acting as garrison, while the lord of the
castle assured himself of a permanent garrison by
giving its members a holding on his land. The social
unit on the Continent was not, as with us, the clan of
common descent, but the castle and its people, the
lord's family and the followers settled on his land, a
unit which none the less inherited the Roman tradition
of the *paterfamilias*, whose *familia* included *clientes* as
well as kin. These separate little *patriae* grew by
accretion : as the lord became powerful more and
more people entered into the relation of ' manship,'

of *hommage*, with him. The area of his influence increased, till one castle was not enough. His ' men ' built others : but they were still on his ground, and owed him the service their garrisons of their own ' men ' did to themselves. So the system grew, up and down, till the process of sub-infeodation ran from the great fief, a province of the Empire, to the little peel-tower with a village below it. The network spread, and was regularised by custom and then by law, till all men on the land were included somewhere, and ' a masterless man ' was synonymous with an outlaw. A held X by service, vassalage, to its next lord, B, who held X, Y, and Z by service to *his* lord, C, and so forth : and the lord owed his men protection in return. The obligation was mutual : one must remember that, for it is too often forgotten by the historian, though the vassals [1] themselves remembered the fact very well, and when they considered their rights had been transgressed were by no means slow in transferring their allegiance, and were held to have a good moral right to do so.

One point must be remarked : the whole nexus of mutual obligation that in theory bound all laymen, from the Emperor down, was based on the tenure and defence of *land*. The clan grew up among invading settlers : it was essentially a bond of *race*. The fief grew from garrisons against invaders. And after its

---

[1] *Vassal* is supposedly derived from the Breton *gwaz*, one who serves. *Feu*, *fief*, and *feudal* are of unknown derivation, but have nothing to do (etymologically at any rate) with *feud* in the sense of hostility.

primary purpose had been served the fief with its solid concrete definition appealed to the intensely logical outlook that dominated the mediaeval mind, while its close association of the social unit with the tenure of a clearly marked piece of land must have done much to prepare men's imaginations for the concept of what we mean by nationality.[1]

Now, this military organisation worked. It held off the Northmen and the Saracens . . . or, in the chief Continental colony of the former, assimilated them within itself, though the Normans stamped it with their own character. Their genius for adaptation took it over as Normandy acquired the culture of France, but they took it over as a going concern. Therefore, while in France and the German states feudalism grew up from below, in Normandy, as later in the Norman colonisation of England, it was imposed from above, and took the whole state into one grasp from the start.

By the middle of the eleventh century this system had stabilised the social structure over great part of the Continent of Europe : and though the stabilisation was rather comparative than absolute, it gave the

[1] The towns, in many cases, grew up round the castle and were part of the fief. But quite often the towns were so to speak communal castles : indeed, so late as the twelfth century the great city of Rouen is called a *château*. The growth of a specialised craftsman and merchant class, which naturally concentrated in towns—and perhaps too the Roman tradition, perpetuated in the organisation of the Continental Church, of the city as the natural social unit—helped to lift the towns as it were outside the system, or to make the corporation a sort of collective lord. The corporative tendency so strong in an age of guilds, monasteries, and similar communities, would naturally go to strengthen this.

Church opportunity for revival. She had been in
bad case : in the chaos of the invasions her spiritual
offices had been secularised, had been given to those
men who could best defend, not to those who could
best use, her temporal possessions, until these had only
too often come to be looked on as so much heritable
property. Yet so early as 910 the tide was turning :
in that year William, Duke of Aquitaine, founded the
Abbey of Cluny in French Burgundy. There the
Rule of St Benedict was revived in its strictness, and
with a new and important characteristic. Before, the
monastic house had been a single isolated unit, dependent, if at all, on the local bishop. Now the Cluniac
foundations, that soon were many, came into being
each linked to the parent house, and formed a strong
and spreading transnational organisation, subordinate
only to the Pope himself, and strong enough effectually
to withstand any attempt at secular control. Cluny
and its great nexus of daughter-houses drew to them
the finest spirits of the age. These fought the secularisation, the slackness and degradation of the Church,
and brought back the conception of the *Civitas Dei*, a
community in the world but not of the world, whose
head was no secular prince, but Peter's successor.
Princes, however, gave them eager help, for with the
Cluniacs came spiritual revival, and the intellectual
that was its corollary. The Emperor Henry III (1039-
1056) proved himself an ardent supporter of the
movement, and in 1049 his cousin Bruno became
the first Cluniac Pope, as Leo IX. Leo's papacy was

brief, but of great importance : he held (and had a manifest case for holding) that lay control of the spiritual power was at the root of some of the time's worst evils. He fought the prevalent poison of simony, of the buying and selling of church offices ; and by forbidding the marriage of the clergy, which, often forbidden before, had grown common again, put an end to the inheritance of these, and also, by freeing the priest from family ties, gave him that independence which St Paul had praised.

The reforms in the Church led to a great revival in scholarship. Philosophy, law, theology, quickened again. Gerbert, who in 999 became the first French pope as Sylvester II, had studied in Spain the Saracen learning in science, in mathematics and astronomy : the Arab culture had inherited the tradition of the Greeks, and especially of Aristotle, whose works had been brought to Syria and Persia by certain heresiarchs banished from Constantinople. By the middle of the eleventh century the Lombard Lanfranc, the Burgundian Anselm, had brought the new learning to Bec in Normandy, founded in 1040 : and the light of Bec kindled Caen, Rouen, Jumièges, Fécamp, Avranches, and St Michel, and made the Duchy the very lamp of the North. With scholarship came a great quickening of the arts, centred upon a widespread revival in building. In central France, soon after the year 1000, comes the beginning of what we call Norman and the French Romanesque, the style of the great round vault, the round arch supported upon massive

H

pillars, as in the nave of the Abbey Kirk of Dunfermline. It derives fundamentally from Byzance and Rome, but our name of Norman is not without justification, for the Normans not only practised it superbly but added a convention of decoration whose feeling is very strongly Scandinavian—the interlaced fret that is closely akin to Celtic, the grotesque beak-heads, and the zigzag moulding that recalls the track of a light breeze over calm sea. Other crafts revived also, such as embroidery and work in metal : and even before 1000 there are the beginnings of the splendid French achievement in coloured glass.

The broad revival in the mind and spirit, the increasing dignity and responsibility of men with a defined place in an organised society, had their effect on general secular life. It was essentially a fighting age yet. The typical free layman was a soldier, less by profession than by birth itself. The Church needed the soldier for her own survival, and she humanised and christianised his calling by linking it to her structure and her service. She made him her champion, made him defender of those whom the Church de-fended. The conception of chivalry began to take shape, and a word which at first had merely meant a horseman took on a spiritual connotation : *caballarius* changed into *chevalier*, with a function, in the ideal, of God's police. Not only, now, must a man be brave in the danger from which life was seldom free for long at once, or be loyal to his lord and to his fellows. He must now be loyal to those whose lack of strength gave them need for his. There are noble manners in the Scandinavian sagas, in the Celtic epics, with a respect for honourable women, and in Christian literature, for Holy Church. From the beginning, courtesy and the self-discipline that is its basis had held a high place among the Christian virtues. Now they acquired a new colour. The knight was a man born to a special calling, to which, however, he must be ordained in form, and that only after a hard novitiate. He was ceremonially set apart, as a priest or a crowned king is set apart, with certain rights that implied a number of rigorous obligations which involved essential shame if they were neglected. The code that governed these rights and obligations became in time a thing too often of fantastic externals : yet even now the influence of its spirit remains in what is best of our civilisation. In its great days it was a very great thing. We may grant its ideals were seldom wholly fulfilled : but their constant presence in the assumptions and symbolisms of life gave decent men a reminder of something to which they were responsible, of a status from which they must not derogate.

Conspicuous among the ideals of chivalry was a new conception of the relation of men and women, and especially between a man and one woman, a woman and one man—of a *courteous love* [1] that exalted gentleness, self-control, and fidelity, and made a knight's

[1] *L'amour courtois* is conventionally rendered *courtly* love. But *courteous*, in the deep sense of courtesy, is much nearer to its fundamental spirit, though *courtly* may cover a number of later perversions.

lady inspirer of his deeds and seal of his honour. It
is true that in a class whose marriages were often made
in childhood as ratification of a transfer of land, this
ideal thinned to an artificial convention which could
be a mere decoration of lechery : but its essence was
a real and noble thing, and something new in human
evolution. It inspired a new art. By about 1100, in
Southern France, there was growing up a school of
lyric verse which expressed its ideals, and carried
them through Europe. Its intricate complexity of
forms, its elaborate analysis of feeling, were the work
not of professional men of letters, but of hard-fighting
soldier-politicians, and its influence can be traced for
centuries. Burns's favourite stanza, as a matter of fact,
was devised by one of the earliest of these Provençaux.

Throughout society, as its structure stabilised and
civilisation could grow up again, the reaction from
chaos brought a passion for order, definition, formula-
tion. We are apt to think of the Middle Ages as a
time of vague and muddled picturesqueness, emotional
rather than rational. It is true there was colour : men
loved grace and beauty and significant action : but no
age has ever shown such a hunger for system. It
is not for nothing that early Gothic building is as
' functional ' as the Forth Bridge. Hence the tendency
to organise everything, including society. A man
had his defined place in a group, which had its defined
place in the social order. Monasteries, the trade guilds,
the chartered burghs, the universities, the knightly
order itself, are all of them examples of such groups.

Now, the two major systems, which subsumed all the rest, were the structure of the Church and the feudal politico-military organisation. One claimed to include the whole spiritual life of man, the other at least to frame the material. But, as Scots history has incessantly shown, it is very difficult to divide, in practice, the things which are God's from those others which immediately are Caesar's : and a clash between these two primary organisations was bound to come as soon as they were defined. It came, and reverberated through all Europe, as the dominant issue of the later eleventh century, and still a major one in the two that followed. The *sacerdotium*, the spiritual power, claimed headship of the *regnum*, the temporal. Cluny bred Hildebrand, to whom the Emperor, like James VI to Melville, was ' God's sillie vassal ' : his theory, indeed, of the relation of spiritual and temporal powers was precisely that which Melville, Henderson, Cant, Richard Cameron, and Renwick were successively to put forward in our country : and Melville's words to James in 1596 would define it precisely :

There are two kings and two kingdoms in Scotland ; there is Christ Jesus and his kingdom the Kirk, whose subject King James the Sixt is, and of whose kingdom not a king, nor a lord, but a member. And they whom Christ has called and commanded to watche over his Kirk and govern his spirituall kingdom have sufficient power of him and authoritie to do so . . . the which no Christian king nor prince should controll.

We have seen already that the Emperor Henry III had supported Cluny : he was one of the greatest of the Emperors, bringing Poland, Bohemia, and Hungary

under him, and he had worked also reform in the
Papacy, inspiring it, under the influence of his French
wife, with the new and powerful Cluniac ideal.   He
died in 1056, just before Malcolm III had won back
his father's kingdom, and left his cousin Leo IX as
Pope.   Leo was Cluniac, and he brought from Cluny
a monk called Hildebrand, a carpenter's son.   In 1073
this Hildebrand became Pope as Gregory VII : and
in three years' time, with the Cluniac Order behind
him, he had challenged, victoriously, the Imperial
power, and forced the Emperor himself in person to
kneel to him in the snow outside Canossa.

The issue had been the right of *investiture*.   The
temporalities attached to the offices of the Church had
become fiefs, often very powerful fiefs.   The superiors
of these fiefs were often laymen, and wanted the
normal control over their vassal—the power to grant
the fief to their own candidate, who would back
them in any contest with their neighbours.   The result
had been a horrible prevalence of simony : the
Church's great offices, with their endowments, went
not to the best man but to the highest bidder.   Now
Gregory, following Leo, saw the Church in the light
of the Imperial tradition, a single transnational body
governing the spiritual aspect of all Christendom.
This had been really true under the Roman Empire :
but nationalities were coming into being, as the feudal
system united the group and the land : and these were
by this time tending to develop not as groups within a
larger temporal unit, but as autonomous units in

themselves. Under Christian Rome, even under Charlemagne, the Church had been the spiritual aspect of the State. Now a number of states were separate and often conflicting parts of the Church which formed their only bond of unity and the only force which could arbitrate between them. The Church, seen as a whole, had a good theoretical case to control the broken fragments of the Empire.

But there was also a case for the other side. The Church was the largest landowner in Christendom. If the kingdoms were only so many parts of the Church, the Church's fiefs were parts in turn of these kingdoms, and often powerful and important parts. To have heads of great fiefs appointed by a power outside the state upset the whole feudal nexus, blocked the circulation, so to speak, of authority. And in 1075 Pope Gregory forbade all holders of any spiritual office to accept investiture at a layman's hands. Henry IV defied him, and as we have seen, was beaten : but the controversy was not even partially settled until the Concordat of Worms in 1122, when the Emperor abandoned the claim to appoint bishops and to invest them with the ring and crozier, and the Pope conceded that they should not enter on their temporalities till the lords of these had agreed that they would accept them. Though the actual Investitures Quarrel was thus settled, the strife between the Papacy and the Empire went on till the death of Frederick II in 1250 ended in practice the lingering idea of a transnational *regnum*.

All these factors—feudalism, chivalry, the Cluniac
Reformation, the Investitures Contest, the growing
sense of nationality and of national organisation, the
intellectual and spiritual renaissance—were coming to
daylight and growing more clearly defined and formulated in the last third of the eleventh century, the time
covered by the reign of Malcolm III : and all of them,
as they developed, impinged upon Scotland in one
way or another. Their impact should be watched
through the following chapters.

Malcolm came to the throne a young and active
man, apparently in the late twenties. We know but
little of him personally, save that he was a good fighter
and a true lover, was concerned for the prosperity of
his kingdom, and had a natural gift for leadership,
that shows in the story his youngest son told Ailred—
how he learnt that one of his nobles had plotted his
murder, and keeping silence, invited him to a hunt
where having led him out of sight of the rest, he confronted him with ' So you desire my death ? A knight
will hardly choose the knife or poison. We are alone
now. Come and fight it out.' The man fell at his feet,
promised loyalty, and kept it. Malcolm said no more,
until in his later years he told his son.

Of the opening of the reign, we know nothing whatever. We may take it that by fighting or personal
influence, or both, the young King consolidated his
position. The first events of which we have definite
knowledge were repercussions of events in England,

with whose stormy affairs he was all through his life
to be closely involved. Indeed, the complex situation
there had so much to do with foreign policy and even
domestic affairs through the next generation that it is
worth while to explain it in some detail. The course
of events was at this time beginning that made England
for three centuries a French kingdom, or, to borrow
a phrase from modern India, a kingdom living under
a French *raj*, whose natives were very much less
articulate and had a much smaller share in the government than the natives of India in our present time.
Its root was in the growth of Normandy. By Malcolm's
accession that duchy had become a virtually independent state, small indeed, but powerful, and set
between a France divided in warring fiefs, with a King
almost helpless to control them, and an England in
process of painful recovery from the Danish conquest.
Normandy now was French-speaking, and the intellectual centre of the North, for the mixed Franco-
Norse race had shown an extraordinary power not only
of material acquisition but of the assimilation of ideas,
political and cultural alike, and no less of the adaptation
of goods and ideas to their own purposes, and of themselves to circumstance and place. As their fathers had
gone out from Scandinavia, so they spread in turn
from Normandy, seeking their fortunes. By the early
eleventh century Norman adventurers were founding
cities as far off as Italy. In the 'thirties, one of the
twelve sons of a poor knight of Coutances had set out,
with thirteen men, and founded a state which already

had become the Duchy of Capua and Apulia, and by
1127 was to be the Kingdom of the Two Sicilies. The
Norman soldier of fortune was already as familiar a
figure in Europe as the Scots in the late Middle Ages
or the centuries of the Religious Wars. When Norman
subjects were thus active, it was unlikely that the
Norman Duke, whose father had forced Brittany to
submission and extended his duchy almost to Paris
itself, would be less ambitious. In fact he was not :
and already he was the most powerful man in France.

Now, Duke William's relations with England were
very close. His great-aunt Emma had been the wife
of two English kings, the Saxon Æthelred and his
conqueror Cnut. Cnut's sister Astrid was his father's
wife, which may have helped to take her rival's son
on to the Saxon side in the English struggle. Eadward,
Emma's son by Æthelred, had now been King of
England since 1042—king by election, not by inheritance, for the son of his elder brother was still
alive, a married man at the court of Hungary, with three
small children, one of them a boy. And Eadward had
not only been brought up in Normandy : half his blood
and all his preference were Norman. He was a scholar
and lover of the arts, much more at home in the great
Norman abbeys, alive with the new life of Cluny, than
in an England whose culture had gone to pieces : he
was also of frail physique and a fervent piety that made
him, though nominally a married man, take upon himself a vow of virginity.

This meant a thorny problem at his death. His

natural heir was a nephew on the other side of Europe, who had never set foot in England since he was a baby. Close at hand, united by culture and by kindness, was his young Norman cousin. And closer still was the very powerful Godwin, Earl of Wessex, whose daughter was Eadward's queen. Godwin headed that faction at the English court which looked with suspicion on Norman influence and Norman ways. In 1051 he had risen in unsuccessful armed revolt, and the upshot had been a vague promise of heirship to William. In 1053 Godwin died, and the leadership of his party went to his sons Harald and Tostig: the latter was a close friend of the young exiled Scots prince Malcolm, whose sympathies were thus on the English side. The influence of Godwin's sons increased. On Siward's death in 1055 Tostig was made the Earl of Northumberland, and in 1057, the year in which Malcolm won back his father's kingdom, Eadward was induced to call home his exiled nephew from Hungary. The prince came, but only to die almost at once, leaving his three small children at Eadward's court as the last survivors of the House of Cerdic. And Harald, shipwrecked on the Norman coast, was captured by William and forced to take an oath to support the latter's claim to the English succession. It was growing evident by the late 'fifties that there would be storm in England when Eadward died.

The precise relations between Scotland and England in Malcolm's early reign are not very clear. He began in friendliness, undoubtedly: but in 1061 he was

raiding Northumberland, whether through a quarrel
with his old friend Tostig, or because he thought that
since he was Siward's nephew it should have been
given to him, is not very clear. His army went home
with the plunder of the province, and that is all we
know, save that any quarrel with Tostig must have
been mended, for the latter appears four years later as
Malcolm's ally.

About this time his father's cousin, the great Earl
Thorfinn, died, whom the Heimskringla Saga calls
' The noblest earl of the Islands. . . . He possessed
Shetland, Orkney, the Hebrides, and great dominions
in Scotland and in Ireland,' the Scots ones including
most of the Far North. He left two young sons who
inherited his lands, and a widow, Ingebjorg, of high
Norse blood.[1] Malcolm married this lady, who bore
him one son at least, and probably three,[2] but died in
a few years' time, before 1067.

In 1065 the English explosion came. Northumbria
was in revolt against Tostig, who fled to his father-in-
law the Count of Flanders, and was replaced by a
descendant of his father's rival Leofric of Mercia.
Tostig invaded, but was beaten off, and fled to Scotland, where Malcolm gave him shelter. Then in
March of 1066 King Eadward died. The lawful heir

---

[1] She was a daughter of the Jarl Finn Arnison, and a descendant
of Harald Harfagr. Her mother was a niece of St Olaf and of Harald
Hardradi, then King of Norway, whose wife Thora was Ingebjorg's
cousin on the other (her father's) side of the house.

[2] Of two of these sons there are only the barest traces, but nothing
suggests that either was illegitimate. All three reached manhood.

was Eadgar, his young great-nephew : but Harald Godwinsson seized upon the throne, and drove out all Normans from the English court. At once he found himself with war on both sides : his brother Tostig hated him, and he had broken his oath to the Norman Duke. Tostig tried to get Malcolm and also Svend of Denmark to join him in an invasion, but neither would come. Queen Ingebjorg's great-uncle, the wild Harald of Norway, made alliance with him, and so did her young son, Earl Paul of Orkney. They landed in England, defeated Morkere, Earl of Northumberland, and were defeated by Harald at Stamford Bridge, Tostig and Harald Hardradi being killed there. Almost before Harald Godwinsson could turn, William of Normandy attacked his south coast. Harald swung back to meet him, and in October was defeated and killed in turn near Hastings in Sussex. For more than four centuries after that defeat—for seventeen reigns —England was ruled by a series of French princes, who were still French-speaking three-quarters through that time.

William did not win England easily, however. The country had a long tradition of racial and cultural homogeneity, hammered hard by the Danish invasions, and kept in being by a dynasty brilliant almost to its end, the House of Cerdic, whose heir was the young Prince Eadgar. Morkere of Northumberland, his brother Eadwine of Mercia, and Stigand, Archbishop of Canterbury, carried through the form of electing Eadgar as King. Had the young man been either of

his sisters, the Norman Conquest might have been
undone.   But he inherited from Æthelred Unred
rather than Ecgberht, Æthelstan, or Alfred : he surrendered almost at once, and did homage to William,
who rapidly consolidated his power, though he never
really held the far north of England.

When William went back to Normandy the next
year, Eadgar, Eadwine, and Morkere alike went with
him.   By spring, however, Eadgar had broken away,
and—perhaps after some abortive rising—set sail with
his mother, Agatha 'the Hungarian' and his two
sisters Margaret and Christina, intending to return to
Hungary.   Foul winds drove them up the North Sea.
They ran for the Firth of Forth, and landed at St
Margaret's Hope, near Dunfermline, the town that
was Malcolm's virtual capital : and there the King
received them and gave them shelter.   Margaret was
now a woman grown, of uncommon beauty, charm,
and intelligence.   She had been bred first of all at the
court of St Stephen, in touch with the traditions of
Byzantium, then at that of St Eadward, in closer
contact still with the new intellectual brilliance of
Cluniac Normandy, and had grown up wise, scholarly,
and a saint.   Queen Ingebjorg was dead and Malcolm
free, and he loved at once this banished princess-
errant.   At first she refused him : she and her sister
were destined for the cloister.   In time she changed,
but not for a year or two.

The events of that time are violent and obscure.   In
1069 William set about making sure of the North of

England, where it seems that legitimist feeling had endured. He sent Robert de Comines (whose descendants came to Scotland as the Comyns) to hold Northumberland and garrison York : and of Comines and 700 men, only one escaped with his life. Eadgar joined the rising, but it collapsed, and York was sacked by the Normans as punishment. Eadgar tried again, with a Danish fleet in support, and stormed York : but William bought off the Danish admiral and proceeded to ravage the whole North of England. Malcolm seems to have been acting in Eadgar's support : he invaded England, found the English legitimists already crushed, and reached Wearmouth only to discover that Eadgar was already on board ship, with his family and the chief of his followers. Eadgar, according to Symeon of Durham, did him homage for England in return for shelter . . . and Malcolm had news that William had given the earldom of Northumberland, which as Siward's nephew he desired for himself, to his cousin Cospatric, the son of Duncan I's younger brother Maldred by a daughter of Uchtred Earl of Northumberland. And Cospatric, who had been a supporter of Eadgar, and whom Malcolm had lately sheltered from King William, was raiding Cumberland, which Malcolm also claimed. Malcolm turned on Cospatric, sacked his chef-lieu of Bamborough, and took home so many English prisoners that according at least to an English chronicler there were English slaves in every house in Scotland. It was an odd wooing for an English princess : yet in that year, 1070, Margaret married Malcolm, and though she may have done so unwillingly, the marriage was to prove singularly happy.

In the next year, 1071, William marched north to take vengeance : but the *Anglo-Saxon Chronicle* remarks 'he found nothing there for which he was the better'—or England either, for between Saxons, Danes, Normans, and Scots, the unhappy Northumbria was a ruinous desert. Eadgar did not attempt to resist him, but fled to Flanders. William marched on into Fife : but Malcolm apparently did not see further reason for launching his country into further war in support of a brother-in-law who had flagrantly refused to be supported. He met William at Abernethy and arranged terms of peace. William agreed to pay Malcolm a yearly subsidy and to give him twelve English manors, to be held, of course, as fiefs of the English Crown : and Malcolm, on his part, sent his son Duncan as surety for his performance of the arrangement. The treaty has been represented as a conquest of Scotland : but for one sovereign to hold land in another kingdom and to do the needful homage to its king, was a commonplace of feudal politics. William himself and all the English kings for centuries were vassals of the French Crown for lands in France, but this did not give France suzerainty over England. Had Malcolm been forced to be William's vassal for Scotland, he would certainly, in the latter's various wars, have been called on for the usual feudal service. Being William's vassal was no sinecure : but no Scottish army ever fought for him.

The peace gave both kings a chance to settle their kingdoms. Eadgar came back to Scotland the next year, with the information that the King of France had offered him Montreuil on the Norman march. Malcolm advised him to take it and settle down, equipped him and his suite very handsomely with gold and silver plate and mantles of purple royally furred with ermine, and sent them off . . . and in no long time had them back on his hands again, ship-wrecked and homeless. Malcolm knew Eadgar by now : he had also met William, and had formed a personal friendship with William's son Robert. He declined to break the peace for the feckless Eadgar, and advised submission. Eadgar took his advice, did homage to William, and was given a Norman castle as residence.

There were wars at home then. Maelsnechtain, son of Lulach, had grown up, and apparently laid claim either to the throne or to the Mormaorship of Moray, which had been held by his grandfather Gillecomgan. At all events, Malcolm in 1077 had to fight him. The King was successful, though Maelsnechtain lived till 1085. In 1079 the Anglo-Scots peace was in danger for a while. William went to war, in Normandy, with his eldest son Robert, who was Malcolm's friend, and Malcolm invaded England as a counter. Apparently Northumbria welcomed him : at all events, in the next year William sent up the Bishop of Bayeux to ravage that province, and Robert, to whom he now was reconciled, to do as much for Scotland. Robert,

I

it seems, disliked the attack on his friend. He did march to Falkirk, but turned and went back again, and compromised between friendship and filial duty by building a New Castle on the Tyne as a frontier guard, in lieu of the lost Edinburgh. There was peace with England then for fourteen years, until at William's death war broke out again, and brought Malcolm to his death, and his Queen likewise.

Within this framework of intermittent war, many other matters progressed. The new ideas, and ideals, were touching Scotland, and Malcolm and Margaret spread their influence. Their marriage was a very happy one : the grave hagiography that tells of it is full of small revealing human touches—Malcolm, in the early days, torn by jealousy at his wife's constant retreat to a cave in the woods, following her there, to find her in a passion of prayer for himself, and falling penitently at her feet ; Margaret, having spent all her own money on her poor, pillaging his pockets and being caught and chaffed for her burglary ; Malcolm in turn stealing her beloved books, and bringing them back to her bound in gold and gems. These stories do not suggest the presently fashionable picture of a grimly pious schoolmarm dragooning the luckless Malcolm to foreign habits : in fact, from what we know of the King in general, the attempt would have gone ill for the wife who tried it, and we do know that their union was complete. The Queen could not keep him out of English war—nor perhaps, being of her

time, did she wish to do so, for the English kings
against whom he carried it had stolen the rights that
should have been her brother's—but she could, with
his enthusiastic support, be his companion and
colleague in other matters. Both, in their youth, had
come in contact with the new standards of the rising
civilisation of France, that St Eadward had brought
from Rouen to Westminster. They accepted them.
The Scots court took on a new splendour and beauty
of externals, yet a new sense of moral discipline. Its
centre was a pure, dignified, and devoted family life,
based on the constant practice of religion, and alongside its pomp went a wide and thoughtful charity to
the poor. The combination is characteristic of the
time : King, Queen, and court went brave in rich
foreign stuffs, and the merchants brought new fashions
from overseas : yet both fasted rigorously and were
constant in prayer, and no poor man ever asked in
vain for help. It was not for nothing that her husband's
kingdom was to canonise Queen Margaret before the
Pope did.

In passing, one may make an observation on the
common remark that Margaret's children were all
given English names. In the first place, it is not true
of three of the eight. In the second, it seems to be
overlooked that since at Margaret's marriage she had
three stepsons, two of whom outlived her, none of her
sons was the probable heir to Scotland, while as the
nephews of her childless brother, they were the
legitimate heirs to the *English* throne. For a princess

of a dispossessed house, with a proud record, it was
not unnatural to mark their claim by giving them the
names of her own near kinsmen, the more as those of
her husband and his near kin, his father and brother,
were already appropriated by her stepsons.   So her
eldest son bore the name of her own father and of the
venerated great-uncle to whom both she and her
husband alike owed much :   her eldest daughter
Eadgyth that of the Confessor's queen, and of a
canonised princess of Margaret's house.   The second
son bore the name of Æthelred, last king of that house
before its previous dispossession ;   the third, of her
fighting grandfather Eadmund Ironside ;   the fourth
of her brother, *de iure* king of her country, to whose
throne, at their birth, she may still have hoped that
one of her sons would succeed.[1]   The names of the
three youngest children witness the new ideas of the
time, in both literature and devotion.   The boys bear
those of two of the Nine Worthies, the hero-kings of
Greece and Israel (were these Malcolm's choice ?)
and the girl that of Our Lady, an increased devotion
to Whom was both cause and effect of the new chivalric
attitude to women.   These last names were novelties,
like Margaret's own :   but Margaret, Mary, Alexander,

[1] The English crown did in fact go to her great-grandson, but
through her daughter. And English historians down to this present
day make a good deal of the fact : we are even gravely told that
Eadgyth-Maude brought the rights of the House of Cerdic to
her descendants, though such a very unusual circumstance as
that a sister whose brothers have left male heirs should precede
these latter in inheritance would seem to call for at least an
explanation.

and David have ever since been favourite names in
Scotland.

Margaret, undoubtedly, was an innovator, and with
Malcolm at her back, a powerful one. But apart from
her natural dynastic hopes, her outlook was European
rather than English. In special, the Cluniac movement
stirred her strongly. Its leader in England was the
Italian Lanfranc of Canterbury. He had been Abbot
of Bec in Normandy, and was set at Canterbury by the
man who had usurped her brother's throne : but she
valued his character and his scholarship, and made a
friend and counsellor of him. Her Cluniac sympathies,
and her own disposition, made her deeply aware of
the evil condition of the Scots Church, which had
grown corrupt, decayed, and secularised. She became
from the start its generous patroness. Malcolm had
already founded the abbey-bishopric of Mortlach.
Now between them they repaired the wrecked Iona,
gave great gifts to the cathedral of St Andrews, and
founded the abbey of the Holy Trinity at Dunfermline
where they had been married : it was richly adorned,
with altar plate of pure gold (Turgot, her biographer,
says he had charge of it) and the famous Black Rood
with a relic of the Cross. To other churches they
gave constant gifts : Margaret's ' bower ' was a work-
shop of fine embroideries, and her maidens were
trained to delicate skill with the needle.

Yet she did not serve only the externals of the
Church. The slackness of its discipline troubled her,
and with the transnational Cluniac point of view she

no doubt found it isolated and provincial, cut off from the main stream of religious life : the rich spiritual vitality that had quickened its missionary work in England four hundred years before was almost dead, strangled by the long turmoil of invasion.   With Malcolm's support, she set herself to reform it.

These reforms have often been misunderstood. Margaret, it is clear, had no prejudice against the Scottish Church as such.   She herself is recorded, by her own chaplain, as having affirmed that it was in no way heretical in belief, and she showed continual reverence to those who had preserved its noble old traditions.   There were still many anchorites who retained the true spirit of Columban monasticism, and to these she paid great respect, visiting them, and asking their counsel in charitable works, while both she and Malcolm and their elder sons gave grants to the Celtic monks of certain houses.   She does not seem to have brought in those of any Continental rule, even that of Cluny itself : and the specific reforms she is described as pressing are almost all returns to neglected Columban practice.

Malcolm, at her desire, called his high clergy together.   The Queen was a scholar and a theologian : he was neither, so he left the lead to her, and contented himself with acting as interpreter, for he spoke English well and she had never been able to learn Gaelic. They discussed various abuses.   The Sabbath was profaned with secular work.   The marriage law was flagrantly violated : men married the widows of their

fathers or brothers.   Lent had been shortened, by
counting its Sundays (which are not fasts) among its
forty days.   And there was a general neglect of the
Easter Communion incumbent on the faithful.   Apparently this last point was defended : the Scots bishops
claimed that in this case the omission was due to
humility and not to neglect, but Margaret argued that
the penitent sinner had both a need and a right to
approach his God, and that the Sacraments were open
to all who came to them in reverent contrition.   Turgot
says they discussed also certain strange rites in the
celebration of Mass : what these were we do not know.
It has been suggested that Mass was said in Gaelic
instead of Latin : but a difference in language is hardly
a ' rite,' and vernacular masses were not unknown
elsewhere.   We know that there were some unusual
customs—that the celebrant after consecration thrice
took three steps backward, prostrating himself each
time before the Host, and that the broken pieces of
the Host were laid in elaborate symbolic patterns :
it may have been points such as these that she disliked.
One would have expected her, with her Cluniac background, to protest against the sale of benefices and the
marriage of the clergy, which Gregory VII had forbidden a few years after she came to Scotland : but
she is not recorded as having done so.

For most of the last third of Malcolm's long reign—
for the twelve years after 1079 at least — the Scots
kingdom was free from foreign or civil war.   Malcolm

had established firm government at home, and he kept the peace he had made with William of England. William, however, was growing an old man, and it was possible that England at his death might pass not to his eldest son Robert, Malcolm's friend, but to William, the next, a violent and ill-conditioned creature, who would make a stormy neighbour. It may have been with an eye to future contingencies that Malcolm began to negotiate a marriage for his elder daughter with Alan of Brittany, for to have Brittany and Normandy (which would go to his friend Robert) as his allies would be useful in the event of an English war.

In 1087 William the Conqueror died an ugly death, and left his three sons involved in a bitter quarrel, that at once flared into war. William did in fact make himself the King of England, but in 1091 they made a sort of peace, and in its readjustments dislodged the luckless Eadgar, who had lived quietly in Normandy for years. He came, as usual, to his brother-in-law. Malcolm himself had a grievance against William II, who had, it seems, revoked his father's grant of the English manors. He raised an army, and made to invade England. Robert and William counter-invaded with another, suffering badly from the weather. He moved to meet them : but Robert and Eadgar opened negotiations, and contrived to induce the two Kings to make peace and renew the Treaty of Abernethy. *Later* English chroniclers affirm that Malcolm, ' stricken by terror,' did homage to William for his kingdom. Contemporary ones merely remark that Malcolm

Williames man wearþ to eall swilce gehyrsumnisse swa he ær his fæder dyde—became William's man to such obedience as he had previously given his father : i.e. his manors having been restored, he did homage for them. Eadgar's grievances also were promised redress, and he went amicably south as William's guest . . . and in a few weeks William had broken so many promises that Eadgar and Robert both left his court in disgust.

The arrangement with Malcolm also does not seem to have been implemented. At least there was tension once more between the courts, and William rebuilt and fortified Carlisle, which had for long been a ' devastated area,' and imported, willy-nilly, a fresh population : for over half a millennium thereafter that town and Robert's Newcastle were the principal strongholds of the English Marches. In the spring of 1093, however, William grew seriously ill, and came near enough hell-fire to be somewhat alarmed. He decided that it might be better for his probable future to keep his promises, and invited Malcolm to visit him at Gloucester, giving hostages for his safety and sending Eadgar with a royal escort to meet him. Malcolm came, but at leisure, for he was by now turned sixty : he paused on his way to lay the foundation-stone of Durham Cathedral. He did not reach Gloucester till August, and by that time William had become convalescent. He refused discourteously to receive his guest, and as for the disputes that they were to have settled, Malcolm must ' do him right ' in an English court, where his case should be arbitrated by English barons. To do so would have been to admit them his peers—to admit, by implication, that he was William's vassal for all his possessions. Malcolm was of course in grave danger, for he was far from his own frontier, and William's safe-conducts were of doubtful value. He declared firmly that in an international dispute the Kings of Scots ' did right ' on their march and with the judgment of the peers of both kingdoms—i.e. that he had no intention of considering himself William's vassal, but had still no objection to peaceful settlement —and left.

William, with a certain lack of humour, proceeded to charge him with a breach of faith, and refused the arrangement. War was inevitable, and Malcolm decided to strike the first blow. Sorely against the wishes of the Queen, who foresaw disaster, he raised an army, and in November took it over the March. Margaret lay ill in Edinburgh Castle. On the 13th of the month she was convinced that something evil had happened to her husband. Nor was she mistaken. Malcolm had been ambushed on the banks of the Alne, and struck down by his personal friend, Morel of Bamborough. Edward, the eldest son of his second marriage, was borne back wounded, to die at Edward's Isle, near Jedburgh. Eadgar, his brother, brought word of the disaster to the Queen. When she heard of her husband's death she prayed for her own, and on the 16th November her prayer was granted. Her body and his were buried side by side in that Dunfermline where they had been married. In death as in life she was honoured as a saint, and in 1250 formally canonised : by a charming touch of something like gallantry, the Lesson and Gospel for the Mass of her day are the account of the Virtuous Woman in *Proverbs* (which indeed describes her character very well) and the Parable of the Pearl (*margarita*) of Price.

CHAPTER IX

THE SONS OF MALCOLM III

SIXTY YEARS: 1093–1153

'Of the familiar Scotland of Bruce and the Stewarts, David was unquestionably the creator.'

E. W. Robertson, *Scotland under the Early Kings.*

MALCOLM'S death plunged the country into chaos. She was at war, she had lost in one breath a strong and capable King, and the Queen his wise counsellor. Moreover, a succession war was threatened. Malcolm, like most kings of his time, not only in Scotland, had named his heir in his lifetime. He had chosen Prince Edward, and Edward now was dead, while there were still living six sons of the King, of whom three were grown men, besides his brother and certain other descendants of Kenneth MacAlpin. The passing over of Prince Duncan is explicable. He had been released at the death of William the Conqueror, when Robert of Normandy had knighted him, but instead of returning to Scotland had preferred to remain at the English court, where apparently he was popular. Of his full brothers (if, as is probable, they were his full brothers) Donald had died in 1085, and Malcolm was also passed over. This last does not seem to have been a man of much vigour, or we should probably have more trace of him than a single mention as witness to a charter of 1094. It has been suggested that these sons of Malcolm were illegitimate : indeed, there is a statement to that effect in the *Chronicle of Melrose*. But there seems to be reason for thinking this an error, based on the fact that their legitimacy *might* have been contested, as Queen Ingebjorg had been the wife of Malcolm's cousin once removed : Melrose, in Scottish England, would naturally side with the sons of Queen Margaret.

With Edward dead and no successor named, the heirship lay between Duncan and Edmund, the second of Margaret's sons. Duncan claimed it, and was opposed by Edmund in alliance with their uncle Donald Bàn, who in fact was aiming at the throne for himself. A little oddly when one looks at the facts, it is customary to describe Donald as a Celtic prince opposing the half-English sons of St Margaret. In fact Donald was allied with one of them, and he was himself the son of an English mother, and bred in England, while his opponent Duncan was not St Margaret's son, and though bred in England likewise, was half Norse, a fact which might help him in the North and West, but was hardly likely to do so anywhere else. The opposing princes, however, found a political division by which they profited. There had been a good many English *émigrés* at the Court, to whom Margaret and her husband had shown favour. Donald, in spite of his alliance with Margaret's son, posed as the champion of those who had been jealous of this favour, and won their support. Duncan played into his hands : his Norman upbringing had apparently given him the Norman international outlook. To secure help, he offered fealty to William in exchange for an army, which was given him. The move probably secured Donald's election as King, but though elected, he could not withstand his nephew. Duncan defeated him, and assumed the throne.

The reign of Duncan II, however, was brief. Perhaps in an attempt to secure the support of Scottish England, the great conquered and as yet but half-incorporated province of the South-east, he married Æthelthryth, daughter of his father's cousin Cospatric, whom Malcolm had pardoned and given the rule of Lothian.[1] It did not avail him : Donald had roused the North-east, and allied with Maelpeter MacLoen, Mormaor of the Mearns. Duncan went north to deal with them, and within six months of his accession was murdered on the Bervie.

Duncan left a son William, but William was a baby, if indeed he was even born when his father died. Donald succeeded without active opposition : his nephew Edmund was still in alliance with him. Ethelred, the next brother, Earl of Fife and Abbot of Dunkeld, died about this time, Edgar the next was only a young lad, and the two remaining brothers were

[1] Cospatric, son of Maldred (brother of Duncan I) by Ealdgyth daughter of Uchtred Earl of Northumberland and of a daughter of King Æthelred Unred, was the ancestor of the Earls of March or Dunbar.

small boys, whose guardians sent them, with their sisters, to England. Donald held his power for three years, and shared it with Edmund. So much we know. The latter may perhaps have been Prince of South Scotland, which was still considered as an appanage or colony rather than an integral part of the Scottish kingdom : or possibly he governed Scottish England, where the son of an English princess would be welcome. Such an arrangement, at all events, obtained when the kingdom was shortly thereafter divided once more.

There is nothing else that we know of Donald's reign : but that time saw certain reverberant matters in Europe that complete the transition to the true Middle Ages—the great international movement of the First Crusade. So long as the Roman Empire, whether integral or reduced to its Eastern part, had held the Holy Places of Palestine, the access of pilgrims to these had been unimpeded. Even the Moslem conquest had not changed this : the Arabs regarded Issa ben Yusuf, Jesus the Son of Joseph, as a great prophet. In the four centuries and more since the fall of Jerusalem, the number of Christian pilgrims had if anything increased : so late as 1064, in the reign of Malcolm III, a single pilgrimage had included 7000 people. But the Turks were by that time pressing on the Arabs : in 1076 they had taken Jerusalem, had closed it to Christians, and were threatening Constantinople, the bulwark of Europe. In less than a generation they had captured and desolated Asia

Minor, and founded a state there, Roum, whose capital, Nicaea, was not a hundred miles from the Bosphorus.

The Emperor Alexius turned west for help. The strongest force within reach was Pope Gregory's Church. Alexius did not belong to it, but he could appeal, as the desecration of the Holy Places was the concern of Catholic and Orthodox alike. Gregory died before he could respond, but his vigorous French successor, Urban II, took up the cause. In 1095, when Donald III was barely consolidating his position, he preached a Holy War at the Council of Clermont. The response was instant, and great. The popular and emotional appeal was for the recovery of the Holy Places, but below that was the sense that Europe, Christendom, was threatened once more, as was indeed the case, with recurrence of that ghastly age of invasion that had filled the ninth and tenth centuries with destruction. Thousands took the Cross, the badge of her defence. It was a movement of the people—of all peoples, but especially of the French. The Kings played no part. The Emperor and the King of France were excommunicate, and in any case weaker than their own great vassals. The Kings of Spain had their own permanent local crusade on their hands. The Kings of Scandinavia and of England had no care for such matters, and the King of Scots was defending a precarious throne. King Philip's brother came, though, and Robert of Normandy, with the Marquis of Provence and Godfrey of Boulogne, Duke of Lower Lorraine. Europe marched east.

It was a strange business, for there was no unity but that of the common aim of the common soldiers. It was not until 1097 that the Crusaders were in Moslem country, and not until July of 1099 that after a desperate war, Jerusalem fell. Godfrey became its King, though he would not use that title, or wear a crown where Our Lord had been crowned with thorns. Besides his kingdom, the Levant was divided into small Christian states, facing permanent siege. They formed a barrier against the Moslem, and though after some forty years they began to shrink, the attempt to defend them is one of the constant threads of purpose in politics all through the next century and three-quarters. While they acted as a wall against the Moslem, their establishment had other results as well. They served as a bridge to the culture of the East, to its science and its letters and its crafts, and the various endeavours to keep them in being gave Christendom a sense of common purpose, strengthening the transnational, transracial bond, at the very time when the stabilisation of races was producing a sense of national consciousness. The constant traffic back and forth across Europe of great numbers of men (and before long of their women) caused a general stirring and mixing together of cultures—which in practice meant largely a general contact with French—and bred a sense of travel, and distant travel, as something part of ordinary life.

While the Crusaders were marching to the East, and Donald III seemed to be settling on his throne,

K

Scotland was roused once more to a war half dynastic, half international. As was said above, the younger children of Malcolm III had been sent to England. The girls went to their mother's sister Christina, now Abbess of Romsey, and she brought them up—not without danger, being even reduced to dressing the beautiful Eadgyth in the habit of a nun for her protection. The young princes, Eadgar, Alexander, and David, were received at William's court. Eadgar was now a little over twenty, a gentle, pious, and apparently rather lethargic young man, yet not without ambition of a sort. He seems to have been on friendly terms with Duncan II, as his name appears as a witness on one of the latter's charters. Evidently he did not approve of the rule of his uncle and his elder brother, or William contrived to play upon his ambition. At least the latter induced him to follow Duncan's example, and promise vassalage in return for support. In October of 1097 he was sent north, with his uncle Eadgar and an English army. There seems to have been a lively little war, ending in the defeat of Donald and Edmund.

Eadgar was crowned, but his uncle and elder brother still carried on the struggle, and there was a new invasion in the West. The Isles by now were peopled by a mixed race called the Gall-Gael, or as we should say, Norse-Celts. One need not go in detail into their turbulent history since Eirik Blood-axe had been driven out about the middle of the previous century. They broke up or were reunited according to the power of various leaders, and they plundered constantly all that came within reach. Jarl Thorfinn of Orkney, Malcolm II's grandson and the first husband of Queen Ingebjorg, had welded them together for a time, achieving a rule that ran from the North Isles to Dublin. After he died (about 1056) there was a great Gaelic recovery in Ireland, and in 1061 the South Isles came under Dermot King of Leinster, to be won back in the 'seventies, after his death, by Godfred Crovan, son of Harald the Black of Iceland. In 1095 Godfred died, and just about the time of Eadgar's invasion, Magnus Olafson, called Barefoot, King of Norway, decided to win back the Isles under the Norwegian crown.

In 1098, while Eadgar's war with his uncle was still in progress, Magnus seized the Jarls of the Orkneys, Duncan II's half-brothers, and raided all the Isles with a powerful fleet, capturing Man and Anglesey. Eadgar is said to have ceded him the Hebrides : as a matter of fact they were not his to cede, but he may have made some treaty of definition. Magnus was killed in 1103, and for another century and a half the Isles and a good deal of the North-western seaboard, including the original Scotia, swung back and forth between a vague independence and a vague allegiance to the Norwegian crown, with a constant turbulence and a constant hostility to their Scottish neighbours.

While Magnus was thus driving through the Isles, Eadgar carried on his own war. We know little about it, but in 1099 Donald III was captured at last, and suffered the common fate of deposed princes in the Dark Ages, being blinded and imprisoned, at Rescobie in Angus. Prince Edmund also was captured, or surrendered, and apparently resigning any claim to the crown, became a Cluniac monk at Montague in the farthest south of England, where in time he died in the odour of sanctity, and was buried, by his own desire, in chains : and since Donald left only a daughter, Bethoc, and Duncan's son William was a small boy in England, Edgar's position was reasonably secure.

In the same year also the death of William Rufus removed a difficult neighbour. He was succeeded by his brother Henry, later remembered as Beauclerc, the Scholar, the most able, and stable, of the Conqueror's sons. Now Henry was friendly to the young Scots princes : also he loved their beautiful sister Eadgyth. In 1100 he married her, she taking the name of Malde (Mahault, Maude, Matilda) in compliment to his mother. The match was popular : Good Queen Maude was her mother's daughter in beauty, saintliness, and scholarship, and though it certainly did *not* join the rights of the House of Cerdic with the *de facto* crown of the House of Normandy, the fact that her mother was the Confessor's great-niece did a good deal to please Henry's Saxon subjects, though their Norman overlords, for that very reason, were apparently somewhat inclined to sneer at it. The marriage was not, for the Queen, a happy one : the House of Normandy rarely made good husbands.

But it made for friendliness between Scotland and England. Henry does not seem to have claimed any feudal superiority over Eadgar, though such a claim would of course have been justified. He certainly received no submission from Eadgar's brothers and successors, but he was wise enough not to demand it, and during all his life was at peace with Scotland.

Eadgar reigned for some seven years after his uncle's capture, but we know hardly anything of that time. He was a benefactor of the Church, giving lands to St Andrews and to his parents' foundation of Dunfermline, and founding a house of Benedictines at Coldinghame, in Scottish England. He made gifts also to Durham, for which both Malcolm III and his sons seem always to have felt a good deal of affection. Turgot, St Margaret's chaplain and biographer, was then the Prior. There are rather vague traces of foreign alliances : in 1102 his younger sister Mary was married to Eustace Count of Boulogne, the crusading brother of Godfrey King of Jerusalem, and three years later (did he get it from Eustace ?) Eadgar sent a camel to Murchetagh King of Munster, which suggests some sort of Irish alliance, perhaps to counter the troublesome Norse of the Isles.

For the rest, his nine years' reign is merely a blank. He died in Edinburgh Castle, still unmarried, in the first days of 1107. Dying, he named his heirs, and not too wisely, for according to a bad Continental precedent, he divided his kingdom between his surviving brothers. Scotland proper—that is, Scot-

land benorth Forth, Alba—went to Alexander, the
elder, with attached to it Lothian north of the Lammer-
muirs and the Border strengths of Edinburgh and
Stirling.   The great appanages or colonies besouth
the Forth, Strathclyde in the west (the old kingdom
of Cumbria, with a vague frontier in the Eden valley)
and Lothian or Scottish England in the east, with a
march no less vague, that might be anywhere from
Tweed to Tyne, were granted to his younger brother
David, whose wise counsel, it seems, had already
been of value.

Eadgar's death marks the end of the period of
transition.   With Alexander we come to the full
Middle Ages . . . and enter them with Scotland less
united than she had been for nearly a century past.
Had Alexander's marriage produced a son, the country
might have stayed permanently divided, and been
eroded piecemeal by England and Norway.   In fact,
though no thanks to Eadgar, the issue was otherwise.
David in time achieved a united kingdom, and he and
his brother Alexander between them laid the foundations, in the next half century, on which Malcolm IV
and the later Alexanders were in time to build the
Scotland of Bruce and the Jameses.

Alexander is called ' a lettered and godly man,' and
in fact the most important points in the history of his
seventeen years' reign are ecclesiastical.   He was also,
however, called Alexander the Fierce, and some of the
qualities which gave rise to the name were shown in

his dealings with ecclesiastical matters, perhaps
because points which were not ecclesiastical, but
concerning Scots independence, became involved.
He himself was a man of high character, deeply
religious, swift and strong in justice on the evil-doer,
courteous and openhanded to all others. He loved
splendour : we hear of his Arab horse, his Turkish
armour, which show the new Eastern luxuries touching
Scotland, and he was reputed in England to have the
finest collection of pearls of any man living. But he
was no mere dilettante : he could lead and rule, and
unlike his elder brother he took a firm stand on the
question of Scots independence. It speaks to his
statesmanship and that of his brother-in-law that in
spite of it he was able to keep on most friendly terms
with England : in 1111 he even assisted Henry in a war
with the (still independent) Welsh. The relation of
the two Kings was drawn closer by the fact that
Henry was not only his brother-in-law but his father-
in-law also : he had married Henry's natural daughter
Sibyl. The match was hardly a suitable one for a
king, but as Alexander was about thirty at accession
it presumably took place at a time when that still
seemed unlikely : it was not a happy marriage, for
though the lady was very beautiful, she had little
beyond her beauty to commend her.

The reign began with a threat of civil war. The
North-east, old Northern Pictavia, had never greatly
loved the descendants of Alpin. Now Moray and the
Mearns rose against the King, and he was attacked in

his favourite residence of Invergowrie. He was warned in time, however, and with a vigorous counter-attack drove his assailants over the border of Ross. They turned in the corner of the Moray Firth, and made a stand at the crossing called the Stockford. King Alexander with his mailed knights behind him swam it on horseback at the full of the tide, and fell upon his foes to such effect that the insurrection was shattered. (His standard-bearer won the name Scrimzeour—Skirmisher, or quite literally Scrim-mager—and was granted the hereditary right to bear the Royal Banner : at the coronation of King George the Sixth it was duly borne by his descendant, Mr Scrimgeour-Wedderburn.) It would seem that the King's personality won over his surviving opponents : when in 1114 he founded the Abbey of Scone, Heth, Earl of Moray, and the other Gaelic nobles of the North—the Earls of Strathearn, of Athol, Mar, and Buchan—set their seals to the charter as his witnesses, side by side with those of Constantine of Fife and Cospatric of Dunbar.

This rising gave Alexander his only war. For seventeen years he ruled Scotland firmly and well, and kept peace with his neighbours. We know little else directly of his reign, but we may take it that the new influences general to Europe touched Scotland as elsewhere, and that in Scotland as elsewhere the more conservative objected to them. Like his mother he sought to reform the Church, which was probably none the better for the general disorders after his

father's death. He gave great gifts to his parents'
foundation at Dunfermline and his brother's at
Coldinghame. It would seem by now that the Celtic
custom of appointing monastic bishops, attached to a
community, not a diocese, was dying out. At least
there was now but one bishopric in Scotland, whose
jurisdiction covered the whole kingdom. It was an
impossible post for any one man to fill satisfactorily.
Alexander therefore founded two more bishoprics, one
with jurisdiction from the Tay to the Spey, with its
seat at Dunkeld, the other the diocese of Moray,
beyond the Tay, whose cathedral later came to be at
Elgin. Both date from the first months of the reign.

He was also in sympathy with the new reforms that
were revivifying the monastic life of the Continent,
and with one in special. Under Gregory VII, St
Peter Damian had appealed to the example of St
Augustine's ' clerks of the Bishop's household ' as a
pattern for cathedral clergy. This revived rule of
St Augustine was intended to bridge the gap between
the ' regular ' or monk, cut off from the world, and
the ' secular ' or parish priest, who lived isolated. It
established communities of clergy living under a
common rule and attached to a cathedral or a church,
but carrying on the duties of secular priests. As
might be expected, they were a great missionary order
from the beginning. Alexander saw their possibilities,
and brought in these Canons Regular, as they were
called, for his new house of Scone. They came from
the newly founded Pontefract in England, and the

name of the Prior suggests he was a Norman. Later,
in 1123, he founded another house for them on
Inchcolm, in gratitude for delivery from a shipwreck.
One gathers that like his mother he had no hostility
for the Gaelic Church so long as it was true to its own
ideals, for the dedication of this house of a new order
is, significantly enough, to St Columba.

The most conspicuous ecclesiastical matter, however,
was his ' ganging feud ' with Canterbury over St
Andrews. It began as a by-product of the general
' investiture ' quarrel, which was still in full violence
on the Continent : the Concordat of Worms, which
settled its central and original point, was not arrived
at till 1122, only two years before Alexander's death.
Small local versions of it had broken out over Europe ;
before Alexander had come to his own crown he had
seen a very conspicuous one in England, between King
Henry and Anselm of Canterbury, which was settled
in the year of his accession.

In the Scots dispute the question of lay versus
secular investiture of a prelate was soon involved in,
and swamped by, other matters. Alexander, at his
accession, found the see of St Andrews vacant. He
wished to place there his mother's old chaplain (who
had already written her biography) Turgot, the Prior
of Durham, a Saxon Englishman of noble birth and
high character. The chapter agreed, and Turgot was
elected. Then there were difficulties. Turgot was
not, of course, in episcopal orders, and the natural
person to confer them on him was the metropolitan

of his own province, that is to say, the Archbishop of
York : [1] and the Archbishop was only newly elected,
and not yet consecrated to his own see. He undertook,
however, to consecrate Turgot as soon as he was
qualified to do so . . . and declared that as Archbishop
of York he had jurisdiction over the Scottish bishops.
Ranulph, Bishop of Durham, intervened, and offered
to consecrate Turgot himself, *associatis sibi episcopis
Scotiae et Orcadarum Insularum*, with the assistance
of the Bishops of Scotland and the Orkneys. (The
proposal shows the international character of the
Church, for the Orkneys, of course, were under the
Archbishopric of Drontheim.) Anselm of Canterbury
then intervened, affirming that such consecration would
be invalid : it must be done by the Archbishop of
York after his own consecration. The Scots clergy
protested against York's claims, and a compromise
was arrived at. Thomas of York, being consecrated
himself, did consecrate Turgot, in 1109, but with an
express reservation of the rights of both churches.

The episcopate thus begun did not go well. Turgot
and Alexander soon found themselves in active dis-
agreement. The reasons are not known, but possibly
Turgot was too much inclined to give in to the claims
of York. We know that, though clearly a good and
likeable man, his attitude to ' foreigners ' was charac-

---

[1] A ' province ' of the Church is a group of dioceses, normally
under an archbishop : there were two such in England, Canterbury
and York. Canterbury was held the senior in rank, but without
any jurisdiction over York. Scotland until 1492 was a single
province.

teristically English. He came to the point of resigning his see at last, but died in 1115 before he could do so.

The dispute, however, continued. Alexander wished to bring in a new man, more in touch with the new ideas than any of his own higher clergy. He wrote to Ranulph of Canterbury, and asked his advice. Apparently he had learnt his Scots history in England, for he tells Ranulph—quite incorrectly, of course—that *Canterbury* had once had the right to consecrate Scots bishops, but had made it over to York. Ranulph did not, apparently, enlighten him, but he did nothing else. In 1120 the see was still vacant, and Alexander wrote to Ranulph again, asking this time for a specific man, one Eadmer, a monk of Canterbury, a good man and a pupil of the great Anselm, who like his teacher had taken the Papal side in the Investitures Dispute : and he demanded that Eadmer should be sent free of all English ties. Ranulph and Henry agreed that this should be done. Eadmer (who tells himself of these proceedings) was duly elected, and went to St Andrews. Alexander did not ask him to receive lay (i.e. royal) investiture in the temporalities of the see : but King and Bishop-elect at once found themselves at odds on the other matter. Eadmer claimed that Canterbury had jurisdiction over the whole island, and wished to be consecrated by its Archbishop. Alexander had evidently been studying history, for he would not hear of it, and in fact lost his temper and flung out of the room, declaring that

Eadmer should not have the see. They were reconciled in time : but now the King insisted on investing
Eadmer himself with the temporalities, by giving him
the ring. But still he was not consecrated, and still
he wished it should be done at Canterbury, and still
Alexander held firm, while King Henry backed him.
Eadmer at last wrote to a friend in England, Nicholas,
probably the Prior of Worcester. Nicholas knew his
history, and pointed out that though York had received
more than one bishop *from* Scotland, she had never
given one *to* Scotland, excepting Turgot—that England,
in fact, had no jurisdiction over the Scottish Church.
Let Eadmer avoid all grounds of dispute between
York and Canterbury, Scotland and England, by
applying for consecration to the Pope, to whom
neither party could raise any objection. It was sound
advice, but Eadmer would not take it. He returned
to the King his ring and crozier, and went back to
England . . . whence in a while, having studied some
history himself, he wrote to Alexander, owning that
he had been wrong, and offering to come back.
Alexander refused. The dispute had dragged on to
1122. It served to make clear the relation of the two
Churches, but the English claims, in spite of papal
pronouncements, were renewed again and again,
until so late as the sixteenth century.

In 1122 Queen Sibyl died, childless, and was buried
on an island in Loch Tay. Her husband was still
only in the forties, but he seems to have made no
effort to marry again. In any case, he did not survive

her long, for he died at Stirling on the 23rd of April 1124, and was buried beside his parents at Dunfermline.

Alexander had been a popular king. There could have been a contest for the heirship, as Duncan II's son William was still alive, and there were also a couple of grandsons of Lulach. The Crown, however, went peaceably and without opposition to the dead king's brother David, ninth son of Malcolm III, whose long reign is one of the most important in our history. David found a kingdom in process of integration. He united to it the great appanages of the South, that for seventeen years had thriven and prospered under his wise rule. To Scotland proper, he was his brother's heir: to Scottish England, the heir of the House of Cerdic: to Cumbria the grandson of her last independent king and the restorer of her desolation: to all, a man known and reputed for good government. He was then in his early forties, of high personal character, just, scholarly, devout, and capable, in touch with the new life stirring strongly in Europe. He had, and deeply, the mediaeval passion for order, system, articulated structure, and it was in him no merely abstract idea, for he had a genius for practical organisation, and a broad vision of its concrete ends, whose eventual purpose was 'life more abundantly' for all his subjects. While his character commanded men's respect, his tact and charm won also their warm affection and enabled him to establish and make welcome a number of important new institutions and to reform a number that had decayed. Kings who innovate are seldom popular, but David's kingdom came, and before very long, to venerate him as a father : when he died, though never formally canonised, he was to go down to tradition as St David.

To amateurs of the romantic and picturesque, his reign has never made any great appeal. In private he showed the sober domestic virtues : he married for policy, apparently, but became a most loyal and devoted husband, and no less was devoted to his brilliant son : the one headstrong and unconsidered act of his reign was his war with Stephen to avenge a slight on Prince Henry. In his dealings with his own kingdom his record is one of steady, constant, and far-seeing labour, with a broad grasp of all details of administration. His foreign policy has been described as vacillating and greedy : but it must be remembered that he was coping with a situation of great complexity, in which certain elements are too often forgotten. His record in foreign affairs is in fact successful, but again it lacks the picturesque and romantic : he fulfilled his obligations to his niece by supporting her so long as any part of her own kingdom seemed willing to receive her, but was not quixotic enough to waste Scots lives in forcing her claim on an unwilling England. He lost his one full-dress battle, by faulty generalship, for though brave enough he was not an instinctive soldier : yet he won the campaign of which it was a part, for he gained, and retained, what he desired to win, and having received the provinces he wished so handled them as to make them well content to find themselves brought under his control.

Foreign policy, through his reign, meant for practical purposes, English policy : the Norse attacks had ceased for the time being, and outwith his dealings with England foreign relations consisted in general encouragement of trade and of the new and stimulating cultural influences, with regard to which he looked, as did all enlightened men, to France and especially to the work of the Normans. In English relations two sets of complex factors were present and interacted one on the other. As background to both was his desire to unify and organise his kingdom. Part of his plan was a final definition of its still rather fluid and uncertain marches. We think of the present line of the Border as something natural, to be taken for granted. David lived at a time when the expansionist policy of Indulf and Malcolm II had comparatively lately pushed the march from the Forth and Clyde to *part-way* through the old kingdoms of Cumbria and Bernicia. The north parts of these states had now been loosely attached to the Scots Crown for over a century, in part by inheritance, in part by the same right as that by which most of England had been, for a much shorter space of time, under the rule of the House of Normandy—that is, by conquest. To a mediaeval king, or indeed to many modern potentates, the obvious course would be to advance his frontier to the old southern marches of these two states, the Tees on the east, the head-waters of the Eden on the west. For this course he had legal justification. As the direct heir of the House of Cerdic, he had a clear claim by descent not only to Bernicia and to English Cumbria, but to England itself, whose king at his accession was the son of a usurper and himself had usurped his elder brother's place. David was fully aware of his own heirship : in English territory he flew the Dragon of Wessex. On more than one occasion, during his reign, a united Scotland and wildly distracted and all but ruined England would have made it feasible to press his claim, and between his position as heir of her old kings and the contrast between his own wise rule of Scotland and Stephen's appalling misgovernment of itself, Saxon England at least would in all probability have risen for him.

On the other hand, he was bound by ties of gratitude, of personal friendship and close family kinship to the House of Normandy. Henry of England was not only his sister's husband, but had acted as a father to himself when he was a young and all but a fugitive prince. Henry had trusted his daughter's rights to him, and David was ready to fulfil the trust, by defending his niece's claim against her rival. Yet since he was above all things a realist, he would not force her on England against its will : and her claim soon proved to be against that will. In the circumstances he recognised her rival as head of a *de facto* government, but refrained from embarrassing Maude's claim, or her son's, by putting forward his own over her head. With regard to that, he was willing to compromise. He wished, as was said above, to round his march by including under

L

his rule the rest of old Bernicia and Cumbria : to that he held firmly, and in that he succeeded. But he never attempted to go any further, and he was even willing to leave those parts of these two provinces that lay outside his own previous dominions under the suzerainty of the English Crown, to hold them as Henry or Maude held Normandy, in fief and not in absolute sovereignty.

His first attempt to win the march provinces was made early, and peaceably, when he was still Prince of South Scotland, and may have desired (not looking then to succeed to his brother's crown) to create a sort of Middle State, which would have lain between the two British kingdoms as later Burgundy lay between France and the Empire, and being nominally dependent upon both, would in practice have held the balance of power between them. About 1114 he married the heiress of the greater part of old Southern Bernicia— that is, of Northumberland. This was Maude, daughter of Waltheof the son of Siward by Judith, niece of William the Conqueror. The lady was thus his own second cousin and cousin once removed of Henry of England : she was countess in her own right of Huntingdon, and Countess of Northampton by her first marriage. The marriage was probably made for politic reasons, for Maude was a good deal older than her husband : it turned out in fact to be singularly happy, and no doubt added to that serenity which was a part of David's gifts as a leader : but successful as it was on the personal side, it was a failure on the political.

David became guardian to his young stepson and was invested with the great estates which were actually held by his wife, the earldom of Huntingdon and lands in six English counties : most of these fiefs remained for some time in the Scottish royal house, and added considerably to its revenues. But he did not receive Northumberland, merely a strengthening of his moral claim, which it is unlikely that he would forget.

He kept peace, however, with his brother-in-law. Then, some half a dozen years after the marriage, while David was still only Prince of Strathclyde and Lothian, an English succession problem began to threaten. King Henry's son was drowned in the White Ship. His only other child was a daughter, Alice or Maude, who was married to the Emperor Henry V. The only male descendants of William the Conqueror save Henry himself were his elder brother Robert, Robert's son, and the son of Adela, sister of Robert and Henry : this last was Stephen, Count of the great French fief of Blois. Robert had been in prison since 1106.

The situation remained thus for a time : but in 1125 the young Empress was widowed, childless. Free to marry and with no ties in the Empire, she became at once an important factor in England. Henry decided to name her his heir, and made his barons swear fealty to her as his successor, David her uncle swearing with them as Earl of Huntingdon. In 1127 she strengthened her position by marrying Geoffrey Plantagenet, the powerful Count of Anjou, to whom in 1133 she bore a son. Her rivals with a senior claim by descent, Robert and Robert's son, were removed from the scene, the latter dying in 1128 and Robert himself in 1134, which left a straight fight between Maude as the elder heir and Stephen as the senior male. And David was closely connected with them both, for Stephen's wife was another niece of his, the daughter of his younger sister Mary.

The English succession war took some time to develop, and before it David had his only civil ones. About 1130, Lulach's son-in-law Heth Earl of Moray, who had lived peaceably since his defeat by Alexander, died, leaving two sons, Angus and Malcolm. These rose in revolt. David was absent in England, but the two were met at Stracathro by Edward the Constable, and Angus was killed. Malcolm carried on what threatened to be a rather serious war, and David returned, bringing with him as allies a number of Norman knights from Northumberland. The rising broke: Malcolm's supporters gave him up, and David imprisoned him in Roxburgh, and declared Moray forfeit to the Crown.[1] The turbulent province, which had caused so much trouble to David's dynasty for generations, was divided in fiefs among his own personal followers, Scots and Norman.

[1] This is the usually accepted version. There is some evidence for making Malcolm an illegitimate son of Alexander I: contemporaries, however, call him MacHeth. Mr Anderson suggests that Heth may have been his *mother's* name. This seems rather far-fetched, as no one doubts that his partner in the insurrection was a son of Heth Earl of Moray. Malcolm may have been a son of Heth's wife: but that Alexander should have an intrigue with Lulach's daughter seems rather unlikely.

There was another rising, in 1134. A little later a
monk who had become Bishop of the Southern Isles,
the jovial, large, and unmonastic Wimund, took to
arms, proclaimed himself son to the Earl of Moray, and
with a force of Manxmen set about pillaging the South-
west. He submitted, however, to David, who gave him
Furness in Cumberland : but he made himself so unpopular with the people that they captured him, put
his eyes out, and imprisoned him for the rest of his life
at Biland.

Wimund's affair was the last of civil war in this reign.
The foreign complications were already active, however.
In 1135 King Henry died at Rouen : the Empress was
out of the country, and before she could cross, Stephen
had landed, won over the Treasurer and the powerful
Bishop of Salisbury, and had himself crowned at once.
The great English barons had all taken oaths to Maude.
They all broke them now, and took fresh oaths to
Stephen. David, however, raised an army and led it
over the Border. Carlisle and Norham, Wark and
Newcastle, received him and did homage to his niece.
Further south, however, no one rose for her : instead,
they supported Stephen, who marched to meet David.
To fight most of England to instate a Queen for whom
the country clearly did not wish was obvious folly. A
conference was arranged, and the Kings made peace.
Stephen offered back Huntingdon, with Carlisle
and Doncaster, and made some half-promise of
Northumberland. David would not take the necessary
oaths as Earl of Huntingdon, but compromised by

England by now was beginning a civil war, for Robert of Gloucester, the Empress's half-brother, seeing Stephen thus occupied in the North, lifted his sister's banner in the South. The North, however, disgusted by the methods of the Galwegians, turned out for Stephen, and the Archbishop of York preached a holy war.

David moved with a considerable army to join Gloucester. On the 22nd August 1138 he came face to face with Stephen's force at Northallerton. The Norman barons who held fiefs in both countries (there were several of these) were in a quandary. They decided for Stephen, but David's personal friend, old Robert de Brus, the lord of Annandale and of Skelton in Yorkshire, came to him now with Bernard de Baliol, and attempted, even with tears, to make a peace. David might have agreed, but his nephew William (says Ailred who had known him) was a fire-eater, and succeeded in talking the King out of it. The Normans denounced their fealty and rode off, and David made ready for battle. He was personally brave enough, but a better commander in peace than in the field, and now he made a serious error of judgment. He had meant to meet Stephen's mailed cavalry with his own, *secundum artem*, but Clitheroe had gone to the Galloway heads. Their owners now claimed the van, and threatened mutiny if it were not granted : and David permitted them to have their way.

The English force was drawn up under the sacred standard that gives the battle its name—a ship's mast

with banners of saints and the Host above it. The
Galloway men charged the mounted Norman knights,
and the wild force of their charge drove these back :
but the knights were fully mailed, and their assailants
wore no kind of armour. The knights had archers
behind them : these played on the unprotected line of
the Scots van, and broke it up. Prince Henry counter-
charged with the Scots knights : he broke the English
wing opposed to him, but drove them back too far, and
was delayed, and meanwhile an Englishman raised a
hacked-off head, and shouted that the King of Scots
was killed. The trick worked : the Galloway men,
already severely punished by the archers, fell back in
disorder, breaking up those behind them : the Lothian
Angles panicked and broke. David in person tried to
rally them, but was forced off by his own guard. There
was considerable slaughter, but David succeeded in
pulling his defeated force together, and fell back in
good order on Carlisle, being joined there by Prince
Henry and the knights.

David proceeded to re-form his army. The Pope's
Legate came to Carlisle, and tried to make peace, but
David's blood apparently was up, and the Legate had
to go down upon his knees to win him to consent to even
an armistice. The Legate then tried to get Stephen to
offer peace. The English nobles refused, but Stephen
assented, and put the negotiations in his Queen's hands.
Queen Maude had charm, ability, and courage. She
met her cousin Prince Henry at Durham, and they
made terms. By the Treaty of Nottingham in the next

year, Northumberland was granted to Prince Henry, saving Newcastle and Bamborough, in lieu of which he was to receive two towns of equal value in the South : and he on his part agreed to keep their laws as he found them, and respect the local rights of the Archbishop of York and the Bishop of Durham.

There followed a brief interval of peace. In spite of the recent desolations, Henry made himself popular in his new dominions. He was the pattern of knighthood, ' pride of youths, glory of knights, joy of old men,' courteous, kind, brave, devout, and honourable. The Englishman Ailred of Rievaulx, his close friend, praises his bearing that combined humility with a natural gift for command, and incidentally tells a revealing story. In the ride to Carlisle after the Battle of the Standard, the knights flung away their armour to make more speed. Most of them dropped it where they happened to be, but Prince Henry kept his until he found a poor man to whom he could give it, as something that could usefully be sold.

During the peace the Prince married, in 1139, a Norman lady, Ada or Adela, daughter of the great Count de Warrenne by a granddaughter of Henri I of France : her brothers were Counts of Warrenne and of Melun and Earl of Leicester, and the family were partisans of Stephen.

England by now was in a dreadful condition, reflected vividly in the *Peterborough Chronicle*. The good type of Norman baron was a just and excellent administrator : but Stephen's weak rule gave scope to

those who had no more desire than to exploit a conquered colony. They built great castles, and from them
racked the country to famine point, stripping the very
churches, and capturing men who had any sort of
possessions to torture them into yielding their last
penny : men said at last that *Crist slep and his halechen*,
Christ slept and His saints. In 1140 civil war broke
out again, between Stephen and the Earl of Chester :
the chronicler says pithily *noht forpi ꝺæt he ne iaf him
al þat he cuthe axen, alse he did all othere, oc æfre þe mare
he iaf heom, þe wærse hi wæron him*—not because he
[Stephen] did not give him all he could ask, as he did to
all others, but ever the more he gave them, the worse
they were to him. On the confusion, the Empress
landed and tried to take London, but was repulsed.
Soon after, however, the war turned in her favour :
Stephen was captured, and David, who had brought
down an army to help his niece, rode with her into
London. It was their first meeting since her childhood,
and they did not agree. The Empress was a vain ill-
tempered woman, and would not listen to her uncle's
counsel. He went with her to Winchester, however,
and there Stephen's Queen attacked them, and they
were defeated. David was almost captured, but made
an adventurous escape. Stephen, released, defeated
the Empress and all but took her in turn. She fled
oversea, and carried on the war in Normandy. David
had not forgiven the quarrel : he was on excellent terms
with his other niece, Queen Maude. He gave up the
Empress's cause, and though he showed kindness to her

son, he made peace himself with Stephen. He had gained by the war what he desired for himself, for while Southern England in the 'forties was anarchic misery from side to side, the North, under David's good government, was peaceful and thriving, and his invasions were already forgotten. His frontier, for practical purposes, was the Tees and the Eden, but his sphere of influence extended further south, for when in 1151 a dispute arose as to the ownership of Skipton, well south in Yorkshire, it was to David that the case was appealed.

Against this background of intermittent war, Scotland throve steadily. David's passion all his life was his kingdom's progress and the unity of her heterogeneous elements. Like James VI later, and more effectually, he desired to be 'a universall king.' He inherited his ideals from his brother, enriched them by his own knowledge of men and affairs, and left them to flower in the hands of the last Alexanders and revive in those of the greatest of the Stewarts : indeed, the two, Alexander I and David, the heirs of the House of Fergus, the House of Cerdic, the old British line with its heritage of resistance to invasion, the immemorial descent of the Kings of Picts, forged and established an ideal of kingship that but for the strange exception of Bruce's son and the futile puppet-play of John Empty Jacket, was held wisely or foolishly, capably or weakly, by every King of Scots till the Union of Crowns : indeed, one can trace a certain inheritance of it, mishandled, so late as the reign of James VII and II. There were brilliantly good kings : there were unsatisfactory kings : but except for John Baliol and David II, there were no kings who merely owned the country as property. Their relation to it was always personal, as a husband's or father's relation is personal. They did not own a land, but headed a people : they were not Kings of Scotland but Kings of Scots.

David had seen the Norman political and administrative structure at close quarters : he did not copy Norman methods mechanically, but he appreciated their spirit, and freely adopted their means when they served his purpose. His first aim was to build a framework of law and order, with the Sovereign, the chief of the people, as its apex, that should grasp and unite the kingdom as a whole. To do this, he must have men whom he could trust, and like other organising kings—like James I later, or Louis XIV in France—he chose them from men whose place and power depended on himself, whom he could hold responsible to himself. Later kings, attempting the same system, could choose from the small gentry or the middle class, earlier from the Church. David used churchmen largely, as we shall see : but churchmen alone could hardly police his kingdom—a kingdom of fluid marches, of mixed races, of possible foreign invasions from all four airts. There was no middle class worth speaking of; its power begins with this reign, as a matter of fact : and the small gentry were for the most part out of touch with the court and the

new ideas. David took his men where he could find
them, and many of them came from that floating body
of Norman adventurers, cadets of good houses for the
most part, who in Europe of the early Middle Ages
were as omnipresent as the Scots in the later or (I have
elsewhere drawn the parallel) as the Jew in the modern
commercial aristocracy. These men were bred in the
new chivalric culture : they were fighters, and their
race inherited, more than any other, the Roman genius
for organisation and administration. As a boy at his
sister's court he had been bred among them, made
friends among them. When as a young man he became
Prince of Strathclyde and Lothian they helped him to
secure his principality (for Alexander at first had been
somewhat unwilling to yield him his legacy) and when
he was King he found them useful servants. Strathclyde was devastated by the wars : Moray was forfeited.
He gave large grants of lands in both districts to these
friends. Among them was a cadet of a family from the
Cotentin, whose brief name has an astonishing number
of spellings, but at this time is commonly given as De
Brus : Robert de Brus was granted the Marcher lordship of Annandale, where Scots Cumbria pushed
against its English neighbour. The youngest son of
Alan, Sheriff of Shropshire, the son of a Breton knight
of the Conqueror's, was given Renfrew and Kyle, and
David also made him head of his Household, High
Steward, an office from which his descendants took a
surname. Both founded houses that later were to be
heard of. Another, De Moreville, was made Constable

—that is, Commander-in-Chief : as the Covenanters realised half a millennium later, an ' outside appointment ' for the headship of a mixed Scots fighting force precluded a good deal of jealousy : he had Cunningham. And there were many others, Somerville, Umfraville, Lindsay, Baliol, Comyn, Gordon, Sinclair, while the first Fraser, though not Norman but Fleming (as the first Stewarts were Breton) may be classed with them.[1] Many of these received fiefs from David himself. Others married them. The Norman knights were inveterate marriers of heiresses, and it so happened that during the course of the next century several noble Gaelic lines ran out in a daughter : several earldoms of the early Three Hundred Years' War were in the hands of descendants of these matches. The system had the seeds of trouble in it, for several of these men acquired or inherited other fiefs in France or England, and were thus vassals of more than one sovereign, a very awkward matter in a war, as David himself found out at Northallerton. In the main, however, the device worked. These new vassals and their other new companions—for Angles from Lothian and Gaelic Scots were also settled on vacant or forfeited

---

[1] It has been noted before, but is often forgotten, that a territorial name with the French particle is no proof that its owner was a Norman. Surnames began when French was in common use among the landed class, and the identification of laird and estate has lasted almost or quite down to our own day, though we express it differently in English. The Douglases are apparently of autochthonous stock, but their mediaeval representatives called themselves *De Dufglas*. William FitzDuncan's French surname and Norse-Saxon-Gaelic descent were remarked on above.

lands—became the nucleus of a feudal system that organised the nobles in a direct and legal relation to the Crown on one side and the lesser lairds on the other : and since the King was in a position to pick his men, he could see that the new fiefs went to those who could carry out in practice the public duties, military and civil, that were in theory implied in their status. He strengthened the bond to the Crown by an insistence upon written charters, a novelty in the tenure of secular lands, though in this it is possible that he was carrying out a practice begun already by his brother : for ecclesiastical fiefs it had been in use as early as the brief reign of Duncan II.

While he thus provided a new organisation of the secular side of his kingdom, David also gave a parallel one to the ecclesiastical. His brother had already done much to restore discipline to the Church, and had introduced the new Continental reforms by bringing in the Canons Regular. These reforms now were going on vigorously abroad. At the end of the eleventh century, in David's boyhood, St Bruno at the Grande Chartreuse had founded a new rule whose stern discipline was so well planned that the order, though never widely popular, was to escape the corruption that at one time or other fell on all the rest. There were several attempts to revive the full observation of the Benedictine Rule, with its insistence on *laborare et orare*. One notable example was Tiron in Burgundy, but wider ranging were the Cistercians, or White Monks, founded in 1098 at Cîteaux, also in Burgundy :

before very long this order had produced St Bernard, one of the greatest forces of his day, who in 1115 founded the famous house of Clairvaux. The Cistercians were severe in discipline, practised a stark simplicity in all their buildings and their way of life, and laid much emphasis on the spiritual value of hard work : unlike the Tironensians, who turned mainly to the handicrafts, the labour in which they specialised was agriculture. The desert places where they established their houses were soon made fertile, and as their order, like the Cluniac, was internationally organised, ideas spread quickly from one house to the other. All Benedictine orders laid emphasis as well on mental labour, and the revival of St Benedict's Rule brought with it a great revival of scholarship. The schools of the Church were filled with flocks of students, who used, of course, the international Latin, so that they were able to gather from all countries about the rostrum of a famous teacher. Laon was a great centre of theology ; Chartres of letters ; Paris another, of the new and exciting scholastic philosophy, and one of its noted teachers at this time was a Scotsman, Richard, at the Abbey of St Victor. It was during David's reign that Abelard (who died in 1142) carried on his intellectual war with St Bernard. These great schools gave rise to the universities, were in fact universities, still unregulated and unorganised, but thirsty for learning, and very much alive.

David was fully awake to these new movements. He was anxious to bring new blood into the Church,

M

and when he reorganised his parents' foundation of Dunfermline he brought up some Benedictines from Canterbury, whose schools under the learned Burgundian Anselm of Bec had a high reputation. (In 1140 the Constable, De Moreville, brought monks thence to found Kilwinning.) He had, however, been watching the work of the newer orders, and most of his many foundations belong to these, and to those among them most likely to influence the life of lay-folk, not only spiritually but intellectually and in material well-being. So early as 1113 he had brought the craftsmen-monks of Tiron from their mother-house to Selkirk, removing them to Kelso fifteen years later, where they would be near the important town of Roxburgh. The Cistercians also interested him. Monks from Clairvaux founded a house at Rievaulx in Yorkshire: in 1136 David invited a number of them to come north, and gave them Melrose, which had long lain in ruin.[1] Melrose colonised Newbattle in 1140 and Kinloss in Elgin ten years later, and it was from Melrose that Prince Henry brought monks to found a house at Holmcultram in Cumberland. David also established a house at Berwick for nuns of the order, and Cistercian work was appreciated by others, for in 1142 Fergus, Prince of Galloway, brought monks from Rievaulx and set them at Dundrennan, to civilise his wild principality, which was by no means out of the need of it.

David did not forget those orders already in Scotland.

---

[1] In 1148 David's younger stepson, the gentle and attractive St Waltheof, became its abbot.

His brother had found the Augustinians useful, and David himself had established them at Jedburgh in 1118 : in 1128 he brought them from Alexander's St Andrews house to Edinburgh, and built them an Abbey of the Holy Rood outside the walls, at the foot of Arthur's Seat. In 1147 he founded Cambuskenneth for them outside Stirling, though this time he brought his canons from Arras in Picardy. The Augustinians also had a junior, reformed, branch, founded in 1120 by St Norbert at Prémontré near Laon : these spread quickly, founding, among other houses, one at Alnwick, in Prince Henry's great English fief, whence David took men, in 1150, to establish them on the Tweed at Dryburgh. The order seems specially to have appealed to Fergus of Galloway, no doubt from its missionary activity, for he brought men from Prémontré itself to Soulseat, whence they founded Tungland, Dercongal, and a new Whithorn. The new crusading military orders, soldier-monks, were founded in David's time, the Templars in 1128 and the Hospitallers, who were nurses as well as monks and most vigorous fighters, two years later, both of them in Crusading Jerusalem. One would have expected them to be popular in Scotland, but they never were. Each soon had a house there, however, in David's lifetime, the Templars at Temple in Midlothian, the Knights of St John of the Hospital at Torphichen, whose mediaeval church has still an odd look of being less a kirk than a castle.[1]

---

[1] Crusading Palestine suffered a serious blow in 1144, when a fresh wave of Turks attacked it, and re-took the County of Edessa.

These details of foundations are not otiose : they
reveal the international mind of the age, and show how
new forces impinged upon Scots culture.[1]

David also reorganised the secular clergy. Already, in
his principality of the South, he had so early as about
1115 revived the derelict see of Glasgow, which had
suffered heavily from war and invasion, and for long
had had no bishop. He placed there his own tutor,
one John, a Briton : John, however, *nolebat episcopari* :
he tried to get out of it by going on pilgrimage
to Jerusalem, but was driven back to his see by the
Pope, who consecrated him with his own hands.
David investigated the old lands of the see, and restored
them.   York claimed jurisdiction over the diocese.
John refused to admit it, and in 1122 appealed to the
Pope, with what result is not known.

David's general principle after his accession was to
guard the autonomy of the national church, but to
bring it within the great international organisation of
the Church at large, while at the same time he amplified,
and strengthened, its general administrative machinery,
as he was doing that of secular life.   So early as 1126
there was a General Council of the Scots Church at
Roxburgh, headed by the Cardinal Legate of the Holy

St Bernard preached a fresh Crusade, and Louis VII of France and
the Emperor both took the Cross, setting out in 1147.   The Crusade
was to be unsuccessful : Edessa was never recovered, and the
decline of the Crusader states begins at this point.

[1] Miss I. F. Grant makes the interesting point that by this time
the Culdees, the oldest order in Scotland and the successors of the
Columbite monks, included Normans : the last Provost of the
Culdees of St Andrews was a Comyn.

See. We know that the Legate was empowered to deal with the question of the claims of York, but we do not know what happened, though David in that year was certainly attempting to settle the matter by inducing the Pope to give the pall—the insignia of an Archbishop—to St Andrews. York opposed, successfully,[1] and Innocent II bade the Scots bishops obey its Archbishop. They refused : he threatened them with excommunication. They still refused, and backed the anti-pope Anacletus, and the quarrel was not composed till 1138, when another Council, also under the Papal Legate, was held at Carlisle, immediately after the Battle of the Standard. The nationalist attitude of the pre-Reformation Scots Church was to be of immense importance later on.

The process of ecclesiastical organisation that paralleled the secular went on *pari passu* with the introduction of new men and new ideas and the definition of the Church's national status. Alexander I had broken up the unwieldy jurisdiction of St Andrews, but there were still only four dioceses, even counting David's Glasgow, which was outside the kingdom as held by Alexander. In 1125 Malcolm III's foundation of Mortlach was transferred to Aberdeen, and dioceses were created for Ross and Caithness, though the latter district was only very loosely attached to the Crown. It is probable that David was also the founder of the sees of Brechin (which had a Culdee chapter) and of

---

[1] The Archdeacon of York was much annoyed with the Pope for not believing that Scotland was part of England.

Dunblane. He certainly joined with Fergus of
Galloway in re-establishing that of Whithorn or
Candida Casa, whose second, English, succession
of bishops had died out : its chapter was formed of
Premonstratensians from Fergus's abbey of Soulseat.
David also strengthened the existing dioceses. Bishop
John built a cathedral at Glasgow in 1136. Robert,
Prior of Scone (who from his name was probably a
Norman) became Bishop of St Andrews in 1138. (He
was consecrated by the Archbishop of York, but
' saving the rights of both churches,' a formula which
avoided the ' ganging plea.') He proved a devoted
helper to the King, building a cathedral and staffing it
with a body of Canons Regular, who in 1147 were
recognised by the Pope as its chapter, with right of
election. It was ordained that this body should in-
corporate those of the Culdees of St Andrews who
would receive the Augustinian Rule, those who did not
retaining their possessions for life. These were to go
afterwards to the new chapter, but the provision was
never carried out, for the late Culdees tended to marry
and hand down the temporal goods of their office to
lay descendants, who were difficult to expropriate.

The general organisation went downward also from
the dioceses. There is at least the beginning of a
division of these into smaller units, parishes, containing
each at least one priest responsible for its welfare, and
one church to which he was attached. And—this
change would be very far from popular—a system of
teinds was established for their upkeep.

This infusion of new blood, the growing nexus of organisation and articulation that marked religious and secular life alike, brought changes in the working machinery of both. The legal system in special was overhauled. Not only were there vigorous new laws against violence and robbery, and an enforcing and completion of the feudal nexus by the provision that every man had ' to find him a lord,' but new officials were introduced, and a new mode of trial. The officials were the Sheriffs, whose duty (by a sort of lay analogy to the episcopate) was to safeguard the King's Law in a given district. The Sheriff was in fact the King's deputy, who held the royal castle at the *Caput Comitatus*, the county town. His duties included the organising and leading of local military services, including police-work, the keeping of the castles in repair, the holding of what, under the Justiciar's, was the most important court for both civil and criminal cases, and a good deal of fiscal work : he collected the taxes and sent in accounts to the Great Chamberlain.

The new mode of trial showed a fundamental revolution in the method of administering justice. The determination of the matter of fact, in cases of doubt, had previously been by *ordeal, compurgation,* or *wager of battle.* All three appealed to supernatural judgment. In compurgation, testimony was given by a number of friends of the accused, who swore that he was innocent: the oaths, in the sight of Heaven, were what mattered, and evidence, in our sense, was not led. In ordeal the innocent accused could, for example, pick up hot iron

or put his naked hand in boiling water, while the
guilty would be injured. Wager of battle was in
its essence a kind of two-sided ordeal : pursuer and
defender fought it out with arms under supervision,
on the assumption that the power of Heaven would
give the victory to the innocent. The possibilities
of abuse are obvious, though trial by ordeal was
in fact revived after the Reformation in cases of
witchcraft . . . but with a further complication
added, for in the usual test of ' swimming ' at
least, it was the innocent who would be harmed,
and the accused who did not drown who was guilty.
David, who lived in an age of formal logic, when
dispute as to the nature of a fact was a regular part
of academic method, preferred the *visnet, voisinage,* or
jugement del pays, where the issue was decided by a
group of the local free tenants, who having heard the
evidence for both sides, decided on the fact in the
absence of the presiding judge, who accepted their
verdict and gave sentence accordingly. The older
forms, however, long endured, as for certain litigants
they had an obvious convenience. The four Pleas of
the Crown—treason, murder, rape, and fire-raising—
were withdrawn from the jurisdiction of the lesser
courts, and special protection was given to the
poor, whose possessions were to be ' as the King's
possessions.'

The Sheriff was not the only new official. The great
officers of the Royal Household became not merely
household servants or ornamental figures holding an

honorary and ceremonial dignity, but Ministers of the Crown, with defined and onerous duties in the administration of a kingdom now sufficiently organised for them to reach it. Here again David continued work already begun by his brother. Alexander had appointed a Constable, Justiciar, and Chancellor, the two former as heads of the military and judicial systems, the last as keeper of the Great Seal and head of the Great Council of earls, barons, and prelates : he was later responsible for the elaborate registration by charter that controlled the tenancy of land, which was the basis of the whole social structure. David added to these the Chamberlain, the Marischal, and the Steward. The last was in charge of all the Royal Household, no light matter in those days of a peripatetic court : the Marischal led the cavalry in war, and was supreme judge in Courts of Honour : the Chamberlain was the Royal Treasurer, and as such had much to do with the fiscal affairs of the burghs, presiding in their assembly. Certain of these posts were hereditary, the Stewardship going down in the family of Walter FitzAlan of Renfrew, to whom it gave a surname, and the Constableship in that of De Moreville of Cunningham. The Chancellor and Chamberlain being generally churchmen, the hereditary principle could not be applied in their case. David naturally gave these offices to men close about him, and in sympathy with the work of organisation. This, as a rule, the Gaelic earls were not, and the only Gael among David's great officers was Constantine, Earl of Fife, the Justiciar,

whose earldom lay far south, and included the favourite
royal seat of Dunfermline.

One more point in David's organisation was notable.
This time it was in a sense a process of devolution : he
is the real founder of the burghs, which formed a
system of their own, theoretically within the feudal
one, actually and increasingly outside it, and gave
scope for the rise of a new and very powerful social
class. There had, of course, been towns for centuries,
but they were rather aggregations of people produced
by geographical or military necessity than corporate
communities.

Nothing, however, is more characteristic of the
Middle Ages than the intense feeling for organised
corporate life. All over the Continent the cities were
taking rise, and they made for the arts of peace, and
for peace itself. The great absentee manipulator of
finance may make wars for his profit, but he scarcely
existed. The craftsman has something else to do, fully
as interesting : he will defend it hotly, as mediaeval
princes were to find, but he does not go to war for his
amusement, or even for his profit. Moreover, these
corporations were actual producers of wealth : they
were desirable tenants, so to speak. David encouraged
—he would hardly have needed to initiate, for it was
the general tendency of the time—the formation in the
parts of the kingdom most accessible to overseas trade
of walled towns on the Continental model, corporate
castles, with the royal castle as core, peopled by an
organised body of artisans and traders, who had each a

responsible share in the communal life. Each burgess
had to possess a fixed minimum of property within the
burgh, and to swear obedience to its magistrates, whom,
on the other hand, he helped to elect.[1] The Provost
was head of the burgh's organisation, four bailies heads
of its four wards : burgesses were judged in their own
courts by their peers, and before their own magistrates,
out-taken only the Four Pleas of the Crown. They
had a monopoly of trade within fixed districts (except
at fair-times) and freedom from imposts on the transfer
of goods. The Constable of the royal castle had
certain privileges : he could borrow forty pence for
forty days from any burgess, and at Christmas, Easter,
and Pentecost could demand kain of pigs, geese, and
fowls : but his privileges were strictly defined, and
there was machinery for settling disputes. The castle
was not necessarily a royal one, for towns grew up
round the castles of great nobles, or the seats of bishops.
The burghs soon formed an inter-burghal organisation.
Already, before David came to the throne, there had
been *hanses*, groups of towns organised for (especially
overseas) trade. The four chief towns, Berwick,
Roxburgh, Edinburgh, and Stirling formed one, which
was to grow into the powerful Convention of Royal
Burghs, which still exists, and can even yet make at
least a certain impression upon a government outside
the kingdom.

The burghs gave an enhanced security to craftsmen

[1] Scotland appears to be the first country whose burghs had this
right.

and traders, which caused an increased circulation of goods. Supply and demand, as usual, increased each other : but since the Gael has never been much of a trader, or much given to the more mechanic crafts, they increased by the attraction of incomers, from Scottish England, from England itself (from which peaceful merchants were glad to escape to David's good government) and from the great commercial towns of Flanders : and the English and Flemish speech began in this way to penetrate above Forth, to the new trading settlements on the East Coast. Scots merchants, too, were active overseas. The chief export was wool : the great Border abbeys did much trade in that, Kelso owning 7000 sheep. Others were salmon and herring, including *aleci rubei* or kippers. There was also considerable import trade. The Crusades had given fresh impetus to the circulation of goods, and Scotland under David was importing not only iron, dyes, teasels, linen thread, knives, soap, onions, honey,[1] and wine, but such luxury foodstuffs as rice, figs, raisins, almonds, ginger, and pepper. No doubt, though we happen to know less of them, these would also be accompanied by such matters as fine Flanders cloth (the staple trade of that country) and silks from the East, while if King Alexander possessed an Arab horse and Turkish armour, his nobles were not likely to let him outshine them.

By the end of David's reign the country was pros-

---

[1] Sugar was a rare luxury, imported from the East and considered as a sweetmeat. The usual cooking sweetener was honey.

perous, and like to be more so. Thanks largely to the Cistercians, her basic occupation, agriculture, had been greatly improved, and under the new organisation, the new peace, trade flourished, taxes were paid, and payable, and a man could make himself a decent fortune without lifting it by the strong hand from someone else. The intellectual and artistic condition is difficult to assess, for the only relic of that side of the time's life is what is left of ecclesiastical building : and most of the great churches of the time were rebuilt later, while all were to be ruined. There are relics of Romanesque in one or two parish kirks, as at Lamington and Leuchars ; and David's two major monuments, the abbey kirks of Kelso and Jedburgh, show a very beautiful later type of it, where its mailed-fist temper has given way to a grace and lightness, at Jedburgh even a sort of gaiety, that is due as much to the delicate proportion as to the lovely warm colour of the stone. Jedburgh shows the beginning of further transition. In the first third of the century a new style, based upon the pointed arch, intensely ' functional ' and extremely beautiful, was rising in Northern France. This new French architecture, *opus francigenum*,[1] became a rage, and rapidly spread from Spain to Hungary, great churches not yet fifty years old being torn down to rebuild in it. Jedburgh shows its influence touching Scotland, and Dryburgh and the lovely Dundrennan wholly belong to it.

[1] Characteristically known in England as ' Early English.' The most accurate name for it would be First Pointed.

These great mediaeval churches were more than mere buildings. They were enriched with all the other crafts : Chartres is said to have 10,000 painted or sculptured figures in its fabric, though this presumably includes those in the windows. The sculpture of the Scots churches, and their paintings, have almost disappeared, except for a few broken relics of later times, and a trifle of wood-carving, also late. Of the glass that was one of the glories of the age—the twelfth and thirteenth centuries are the greatest time of that very lovely art—not a scrap is left. Scotland produces some of the most beautiful modern stained glass in the world, but of her pre-Reformation work not so much is left as would cover a fair-sized hearth-rug, and that is of the sixteenth century, a time whose work is much inferior. Yet so fine is the masonry, so beautiful the proportion shown in these churches, that we cannot doubt that their equipment must have corresponded. We know that David gave to several of them gifts of gold and silver plate, and many jewels. Secular building, in this as in other countries, was largely wooden, even the great castles on their *mottes* or earthworks : timber, of course, was plentiful, for the Caledonian forests were not yet depleted. These wooden buildings have naturally vanished, and cannot help us to reconstruct the life lived in them. But if beauty and richness were sought for in the churches, it is likely that they would also be in demand in the more secular apparatus of living.

What the less material arts were like is hard to say.

Music, at all events, appears to have flourished, for a generation later Giraldus Cambrensis remarks that the Scots derived their music from Ireland but had greatly advanced upon the work of their teachers : and Giraldus, half Welsh, with a Welshman's love of music, delighted in Irish music, though he loathed Ireland. He adds that Ireland used two instruments, the harp and the *tympanum*, which in classical Latin means a percussion instrument, but seems to be used here for the psaltery, whose strings were struck with hammers : Scotland used both, and added also the *choreus*, perhaps a *crowd* or rudimentary violin, since the context makes clear that it was an instrument. He declares that ' in the opinion of many today, Scotland has not only equalled her teacher but far surpassed her, so that *ibi quasi fontem artis iam requirunt*,' they seek there as it were a fountain-head of the art. Besides the native music, the new monastic orders would do a good deal to enrich that of the Church, for the Benedictine Orders were famous for the singing of the daily offices.

With literature we come up against a wall. The fact that none survives does not mean that there was none : a shoal of Scots writers of the *late* Middle Ages, and later, known by name to have existed as men of repute, are utterly lost : and we cannot infer that these men did not matter, as so much of the best of what has survived has done so in a single manuscript copy, made for casual pleasure by a private hand. By what we know of the times before and after, the Gaelic epics were being read, and perhaps written : Scots and Irish Gaelic were as yet hardly differentiated. There were too many monasteries of learned orders not to produce a certain amount of Latin, though most was probably chronicle, some of which remains. English was in a curious position : the gap here really does seem to imply that there was none, for in England, whose history has given a better chance of survival to mediaeval artefacts in general, there is no English literature for a hundred and fifty years except the tail-ends of two monastic Chronicles : the fact is the measure of Norman cultural domination. It was not until the thirteenth century that English began once more to be a literary speech.[1] French work, like Latin, was virtually international. French was the mother-tongue of all David's *novi homines,* and probably that which he most used himself, though judging from the circumstances of his up-bringing, he was probably tri-lingual from childhood, adding Latin later : a know-ledge of languages must have been as useful to him as later it was to be to James the Fourth. His reign largely coincides with the age, in Northern France, of the *chansons de geste,* the great heroic epics : *Roland* was

---

[1] There is one extremely curious fact, however. Pre-Conquest English verse was made upon a quite different system from post-Conquest. Now in Scots *late*-mediaeval verse we find not only traces of this early system incorporated in work whose general form belongs to the later, but actual examples of it, written as late as the end of the fifteenth century, in an accomplished and courtly literary tradition. The mediaeval man was not given to deliberate archaising, and the survival seems only explicable by some sort of vanished continuity.

made about the time when David himself was born. In South France, from the beginning of the century, there was springing, as we have seen, a new school of lyric poetry—lyric in the most literal sense, for it was meant to be sung—whose inspiration was *l'amour courtois* : and it soon spread over Europe. David's reign indeed covers the great age of the Troubadours, and Scotland, where interest in music was so keen, could hardly have missed so prevalent a fashion.

So the long reign went on, with increasing stabilisation, peace, and prosperity. King David was loved as the father of his people, and although he was growing old he had as heir a prince of high character and great charm, in the prime of life and with experience of successful rule, who had three sons in turn. But the last years were to be clouded. In 1149 there was the threat of war in England again. The Empress Maude had a son by her second marriage, now a lad, Prince Henry, who had been a good deal about the Scottish court. In 1149, he came to Carlisle to seek knighthood at David's hands. He was now sixteen, and old enough to press his mother's claim. He concerted, with the Earl of Chester, an invasion of England, and promised his great-uncle to confirm his ownership of Northern England. David made preparations to support him, but the Earl of Chester surrendered to King Stephen, and the boy gave up his plan and returned to France, peace between David and Stephen remaining unbroken.

Within three years, both King and kingdom suffered

N

a serious loss.   On the 12th June of 1152 the good
Prince Henry, hope of the country, died, leaving three
sons who were only small boys.   He had no brother
living :   Queen Maude had died in 1131, and David,
who mourned her deeply, had never re-married.   The
loss broke the old King, who was then seventy, a great
age for the time.   He would not show signs of grief,
and dined in state that day as was his custom, but from
that time he prepared for his own death, doubling his
alms, increasing his devotions, and making his will.   He
tried to secure his grandsons in the succession, sending
the Justiciar, the Earl of Fife, to take Malcolm,
the eldest, all through the Scots kingdom, to
receive recognition and allegiance, while he himself
took the second, William, to Newcastle, where the
Northumbrian lords of his father's fief came to do
him homage.

Within a year of his son, David died himself.   He
came to spend the next Easter at Carlisle, and died
there on the 24th May 1153, meeting his end very
patiently and devoutly.   He had found Scotland an
isolated cluster of small half-united states, barely
emergent from the Dark Ages :   he left her a kingdom,
prosperous, organised, in the full tide of mediaeval life,
and fully part of Europe, as she remained through the
rest of the Middle Ages and some time after.

III
A HUNDRED AND THIRTY-THREE YEARS
1153–1286

Out of the wrong and the right . . . something new had come. And everybody had played a part in it, even the traitors.

Stephen Vincent Benét, *The Devil and Daniel Webster.*

CHAPTER X

THE GRANDSONS OF DAVID I

SIXTY-ONE YEARS : 1153–1214

*' Progress is not merely the solving of problems : it is always also
the setting of problems.'*

G. K. Chesterton, *As I was Saying.*

DEVELOPMENT, however, was not continuous and
constant : and the second half of the twelfth century,
the period covered by the reigns of David's grandsons,
shows a slackening of the process, though it went on
none the less in spite of civil disturbances and one
serious set-back which almost ended the kingdom's
independent existence. The eldest son of Prince
Henry, Malcolm IV, succeeded to the throne of his
grandfather, and the chief drawback of the system of
primogeniture was at once revealed, in the first of the
recurrent minorities that were to be such a constant
curse to Scotland, for the new king was not yet twelve
years old.

The death of a strong king, his replacement by a
child, had grave and immediate consequences. Within
a few months, the King of Norway in person was leading an attack on the East Coast, that sacked Aberdeen.
It does not seem to have been more than a piratical
raid for loot, but before the year was out more serious
trouble had risen in the Highlands. Moray, never too

friendly to the descendants of Malcolm II, objected to
the rule of a child : and a grown man was to hand of
the royal house, for Lulach's grandson Malcolm
MacHeth, whom David had captured in 1135, had left
a son Donald, and Donald had a very powerful ally,
for his mother was the sister of Somerled, the lord of
Morven, Lochaber, and Argyle.   Somerled is rather
difficult to ' place,' since he is described as Pictish,
Gaelic, Norse, and a man of the Gall-Gael : he appears
as heading a kind of Gaelic revival in the Isles.   There
was a dangerous little war, that went on for some time.
In 1156, however, Somerled was distracted by ambition
that took him elsewhere.   The Norse King of the Isles,
Godred Olafson, was his nephew : and Godred made
himself so unpopular with his subjects that some of
them called in Somerled's son Dougal.   Somerled
took his son's part against Godred : his war was
partially successful, for Godred, though he kept
Man and the North Isles, had to cede the South
Isles to Dougal.   Meanwhile, Donald MacMalcolm
was deprived of his strongest supporter, and the
Moray rising, though not yet definitely put down,
hung fire.

While it was still a serious danger, however, there
was a threat of worse danger in the South.   In 1154
King Stephen died.   His son had predeceased him,
and he was succeeded, as had been arranged, by King
David's young great-nephew and Malcolm's second
cousin, Henry of Anjou, Henry Plantagenet.

The change was important to Scotland.   For one

thing, it gave her as neighbours, through the rest of the Middle Ages, a series of Plantagenet kings, with the Plantagenet temperament, and running, for the most part, true to type. They were often men of great intelligence and almost always of great personal charm, but with a quality that their contemporaries explained by giving them, as immediate ancestor, the Devil in person—a strain of wild and violent instability which, side by side with equally violent greed and frequently with marked ability, had much to do with the stimulating of a constitution in England, and made them most dangerous neighbours to other countries. Their foreign policy won England Wales and a rather loose hold on Ireland : but it also plunged her into the Hundred Years' War with France, the Three Hundred Years' War with Scotland : and these, though they sorely damaged her opponents, won as payment for centuries of spilt blood and treasure no more than the town of Berwick, the Isle of Man, and the retention of the Channel Isles, which had been part of the Duchy of Normandy.

Henry was now twenty-one, and in a very different position from the lad of seventeen who four years before had promised Northumberland to his great-uncle. In those four years he had won, without a war, not only England but a good half of France. His mother had made him over Normandy : his father had died and left him Anjou and Maine. In 1152 the Queen of France had procured the annulment of her marriage, and married Henry : and she was Duchess of nearly all Western France, from the Loire to the Pyrenees and inland to Auvergne. She was to describe herself, in time, as ' Eleanor by the wrath of God Queen of England,' but the marriage gave her husband enormous power. He was no prince-errant now, looking for help to a strong King of Scots, but a grown man, ruler of a great dominion that ran from the march of Scotland to that of Spain : and the King of Scots was a small boy of twelve, with a rival for his throne rousing civil war, and the threat of a Norse war on his hands as well.[1]

By 1156 Henry had put down all opposition in England, and was demanding the return of the English fiefs which David had held—so Henry claimed—from the Empress Maude. Malcolm was in no case to fight for them. The kings met at Chester. Malcolm restored to him Northumberland and Carlisle, but was granted his grandmother's earldom of Huntingdon, *salvis omnibus dignitatibus suis*, saving his (royal) dignity : in other words, he was Henry's vassal for the earldom as Henry was Louis's for his French fiefs.

Relations continued peaceful, if somewhat grudging. In 1158 Malcolm visited Henry at Carlisle. He was then eighteen, and apparently he wished Henry to knight him, as King David had in the same place knighted Henry. Henry refused. The reason may have been that the lad had seen no

---

[1] One rival was removed in 1157, when Malcolm MacHeth gave up his claim to the throne, and a part of old Moray was made into an earldom of Ross for him.

kind of active service. Malcolm, in spite of the matter of Northumberland, seems to have felt a boy's admiration for his brilliant kinsman, who was already a seasoned soldier, and next year, in spite of the opposition of his own lords, he insisted on going with Henry to the latter's war in the South of France, took part in the abortive siege of Toulouse, and having received his knighthood at Tours, returned to his kingdom in 1160.

He found himself at once in serious danger. His nobles had strongly objected to his conduct towards Henry, which they considered lacking in dignity, and half a dozen of them, headed by the Earl of Strathearn, attempted now to kidnap him at Perth, perhaps with the intention of crowning his brother. Malcolm, however, was by now a man. He put them down with a vigorous counter-attack, and then crushed a simultaneous rising in Galloway, so effectually that old Fergus (who may possibly have been in the band with Strathearn) gave up his son as a hostage, and himself became a monk at Holyrood, while his turbulent and half-independent province was brought into feudal subjection to the Crown.[1]

Malcolm was now nineteen, and for the brief remainder of his life, he ruled with vigour. He seems to have tried to follow his grandfather's footsteps,

---

[1] The history of Galloway is a virtual blank from the time of Kenneth I to that of David. Fergus is the first Lord of Galloway of whom we know anything : he was connected with England and the Isles, as his wife was a natural daughter of Henry I, and his daughter was married to Olaf King of Man.

especially in connection with the Church, for several important foundations belong to this reign, though not all are the King's. He brought Cistercians to Coupar Angus, and established a spital for travellers on the English road over Soutra, and a house of Cistercian nuns at Manuel. The most notable feature of the church history of the reign is the number of women's houses that were founded. His mother built the famous priory at Haddington, also for Cistercian nuns, and Cospatric Earl of March give them houses at Eccles and at Coldstream : another, at North Berwick, is possibly his as well, while Uchtred of Galloway, son and successor of Fergus, brought Benedictine nuns to Lincluden. The Cistercian influence penetrated beyond the borders of the kingdom, for Somerled's son gave that order a house at Saddell in Kintyre. The most notable religious foundation of the reign was not Cistercian, however, being Walter the Steward's great Cluniac abbey of Paisley.

It was possibly in pursuance of David's policy of encouraging trade that Malcolm made alliance with the Low Countries. In 1162 he married his sister Ada to Florence, Count of Holland, 'the type of all honour and probity,' who fetched her ' with great array and decoration and military force of ships.' His other sister, Margaret, had been married in 1160 to the Duke of Brittany : she had one daughter, the most unhappy Constance, who for her sins was to marry a son of Henry's.

The promise of Malcolm's early personal reign was

not to have a chance of being fulfilled. In 1163 he was dangerously ill while on a visit to King Henry of England. He recovered for the time, and was present at Woodstock when King Henry's vassals swore to accept his son as his successor. The next year brought renewal, and removal, of a past danger. Somerled landed in Renfrew, the Clyde shore opposite his own dominions, with the whole force of Argyle and the Isles, accompanied by various Irish allies. He sacked Glasgow. Walter the Steward successfully opposed him, and somehow he was slain, apparently by his own men, and his force dispersed. His dominions were broken up, the Isles being divided between his sons, while Man apparently returned to Godred.

It ended the Western menace for a time, but Malcolm did not live to profit by the victory. Before the next year was out, on the 9th of December 1165, he died at Jedburgh. He was then not quite twenty-four, and still unmarried.

The heir was his brother William, who was at once enthroned. William had reached manhood : he was then twenty-two, red-haired and powerfully made. But though he had considerable personal charm, and plenty of courage of the obvious sort, he was an un-stable creature, apt *de cunseilz noveler*, to change his mind, and rather a romantic knight-errant than a responsible king. A contemporary Anglo-Norman calls him *pruz, merveillus e hardi . . . chevalier bon e de grant vasselage*, courageous, arrogant, and bold, a good

knight and of great chivalry : the praise, as far as it
goes, appears deserved : but the King of Scots needed
other qualities. His impressionable and impetuous
mind made him easily swayed by women, and his
youth and middle life were marked by a series of
mistresses. Later, he sobered, and ruled

cum lenitate simul et mansuetudine cum religione magna . . .
eleemosynarum largitione, pius, providus, et pacificus, justitia
ubique cum aequitate servata,

with gentleness and mercy, great religion, and generous
almsgiving, pious, prudent, and peaceable, keeping
everywhere justice and equity. Giraldus Cambrensis,
Henry II's chaplain, who pays him that tribute on a
personal acquaintance, considers him *rector felix et
moderator*, a fortunate ruler and controller of Scotland :
but though increasing years—and he lived long—did
bring him an increased sense of responsibility, it seems
clear that the responsibility overweighted him, and
that he had not the stable strength to shoulder it with
the serenity of a good leader. His time stands between
those of David and of the later Alexanders like a spell
of grey east wind and dusty drift between two others
of sunshine and lively growth.

He inherited the Scotland of David I, though
possibly a little the worse for wear : but he did not
inherit David's great Northern English fiefs, and the
endeavour to recover them against the overwhelming
strength of the Angevin Empire was—aided by
William's own lack of stamina—to bring grave disaster.
He still retained the remaining English possessions,

as held by his brother : and when in 1165 he went to do the regular homage for them, he claimed the Northern fiefs also. Henry refused them, and with violence : one of his councillors spoke in favour of William, and (as an eyewitness reported in a confidential letter to the Archbishop of Canterbury) Henry flew into a most Plantagenet rage, tearing off his clothes and the silk cover from the couch he sat on, snatched handfuls of the straw that served as carpet, and sat gnawing them in the middle of the disorder.

William was probably less demonstrative : but he did not feel friendly. Henry was engaged in a violent feud with the Church, in the person of Becket, whom he had himself made Archbishop of Canterbury. There was also considerable tension between him and Louis VII, his overlord for all his vast French fiefs : and their personal relation—for Louis was Queen Eleanor's former husband—did not sweeten tempers. In 1168 William made a league with Louis, which was the beginning of that long alliance that in the fifteenth century was to save France, in the sixteenth Scotland, at moments of supreme danger, and leave a tradition of ancient friendliness that still has pleasant results for the travelling Scot. Henry and Louis returned to peaceful relations, however, and in 1170 William was at Windsor as Henry's guest at the coronation of the heir to England, ' the young King ' Henry, whom his father, for the sake of security, had crowned in his lifetime, his barons swearing fealty.

The year, in England, ended with Becket's murder,

that shocked all Christendom, and even, in time, shocked Henry. The next brought an English war of annexation in Ireland : that country had been somewhat recovering from the long Norse domination, but in 1156 Pope Adrian IV, the only Englishman who ever wore the Tiara, made a present of its temporal lordship to Henry : it did not happen to be his to give, but it gave England a case for claiming that law was on her side. Nothing had been done for some time, but 1169 and 1170 had seen Norman incursions, in nominal alliance with Irish kings, and these were so handled as to give a foothold. In 1171 Henry went in person, and made a surface conquest of the country, that set a running sore in the side of England, and for Ireland brought long centuries of suffering.

In 1173 William was drawn into an English civil war. Henry's sons were growing up, and a fierce hatred between son and father was a regular part of Plantagenet tradition, while Queen Eleanor's infatuation with her husband had now given place to a very hearty loathing. They joined now in revolt against Henry, supported by Louis of France, Philip Count of Flanders, and some of the strongest of the English nobles. The young Henry offered William Northumberland, with Cambridgeshire for his younger brother David. William accepted, and in the late summer of the year invaded, giving siege to Wark and Carlisle. The Justiciar and Constable of England brought up an army, and William fell back to head them off from the Marches. Before the two forces could come to grips, the English leaders had word that the Earl of Leicester had landed in the South to support the insurgents. They hastily made a truce with William, whose intelligence service appears to have been defective, and went back to confront the new threat. The war continued, but William, bound by the truce, could take no part. The truce ended in January, and he allowed Henry's commanders to buy another, till Easter. His brother, however, was leading the English forces of the young prince, who himself was in France : and in summer King William invaded England in support of him.

It was a bad moment for Henry : it even roused his conscience. He did public penance for the murder of Becket, going barefoot in procession to his shrine and being flogged before it. That day, as Becket's admirers did not fail to remark, his luck turned, and spectacularly. The beginning of William's advance had been successful, and he had taken several towns and castles. Now, in July, he sent most of the army forward under Duncan, Earl of Fife, to ravage Yorkshire, he himself remaining behind. On the 13th of the month, a party of English knights set out from Newcastle in a thick fog, and got thoroughly lost. When the fog lifted, they found themselves close to Alnwick, and in sight of a small party of knights and men-at-arms who, their helmets off, had dismounted for a meal.[1] Then

---

[1] The traditional story is that they were tilting in a meadow : but Jordan de Fantosme gives this more probable version, and he says that he was actually present.

they realised, from the banners and coat-armour, that these were William of Scots and his personal guard. William's men saw the English, but apparently took them for a detachment of Fife's force until they were almost on them. The English party was a good deal the larger, and common sense would have dictated escape. William, however, forgot that he was King and head of an army, remembered that he was a knight with *un biau faict darmes* in sight of him, flung to horse, and charged. An English sergeant stabbed his horse from beneath, and the King went down with the beast on top of him, and was dragged out a prisoner. His knights refused freedom when he had been taken, some who had got clear riding in and surrendering themselves to share his fortunes, and he was handed over in triumph to Henry.

It ended the rising. The Scots leaders quarrelled and went home, the English ones surrendered to King Henry : the fleet that had threatened invasion melted away, and in three weeks Henry was master of England again, and could cross the Channel to deal with his son and Louis, who were besieging Rouen. It took him a month, but by the end of summer he was victorious in Normandy also, and his sons had submitted.

William, a prisoner, had been carried overseas, and was held at Falaise. Henry confronted him now, demanding as ransom nothing less than the complete feudal subjection of the Scottish kingdom. William's courage was adequate to a charge of horse : it was not

adequate to imprisonment and a personal contest with
the terrific force of the Angevin. It may in fairness be
advanced as excuse that William's continued imprisonment meant virtual abdication, or probably death :
the heir to Scotland was his brother David, also in
Henry's hands, and neither of them, at this time, was
married. The only possible alternative heirs to the
Crown were the enemies of their house, Donald
MacMalcolm, the descendant of Lulach, and Donald
MacWilliam, the grandson of Duncan II : and the
accession of either of these two would probably mean a
first-class civil war, on which Henry would certainly
intervene, with the force of England and of his huge
French dominions. William surrendered, accepted
whatever terms Henry dictated, and at Falaise in
December signed a treaty that for the next fifteen
years made Scotland an English possession. William
was to become Henry's liegeman, in the same manner
as his own vassals were to himself : and a significant
clause is inserted here. A usual formula for allegiance
was ' against all men ' : here it is varied to *contrv
omnen hominem de Scotia et de omnibus aliis terris,*
against all men of Scotland and other countries. All
Scots prelates should do homage to Henry as did the
English ones, and the Scottish Church was to give the
English that obedience *qualem facere debet et solebat,*
as it ought and was wont to do. The barons of Scotland and the King's heirs must do homage to Henry.
Roxburgh, Berwick, and Jedburgh, Edinburgh and
Stirling, were to be handed over as sureties—the chief

o

strengths of the Border and those commanding the march between South and North. Prince David, four earls, and the Constable were to be hostages for their delivery, and on their release were to leave their heirs with Henry. And those who had taken the oath were to induce others to take it also.

William put his seal to these terms : and the fifteen years that follow provide an interesting commentary on claims to previous feudal subjection. On this occasion there was no doubt of it : and the natural consequences followed, as they had never done on any previous occasion for which claims have been made. William had to come when Henry wanted him, and to bring his barons. He could not make war on his own rebellious vassals without Henry's permission. He could not marry without Henry's permission. When Galloway was subdued after a rising, he had to bring its lords to swear fealty to Henry. No Papal Legate might enter his kingdom without an oath to do nothing detrimental to English claims, and without returning through England. These were the logical consequences of feudal subjection : and now, and for the first time, they were enforced. And Giraldus Cambrensis makes it very clear that the whole affair was held, at the English court, to be a quite new and unprecedented glory—that by bringing *totam insulam Britanniae, sicut oceano clauditur, in unam monarchiam*, the whole island of Britain, as the sea encloses it, under one monarchy, Henry had done something that had not been achieved since Claudius Caesar (who had not achieved it, by the way) and won *tantum . . . tam magnificum honorem . . . perpetuum et impretabile decus*, so great and so magnificent an honour, an everlasting and priceless distinction, above all his forebears since the time of the Picts and the Scots. The frank admission, now that those were not called for, that earlier claims were totally unbased, oddly parallels Edward I's abandonment, at Wallace's trial, of his previous claim to be legally lord of Scotland : at that time he had made himself its lord in fact, and legal fictions were no longer needed.

William's subjects did not take kindly to the surrender. Nationalism, in the modern sense, was hardly yet in being anywhere. But it was to be in Scotland that it began, and apparently the germs were already stirring. He found himself, on return to his sold kingdom, confronted with a general unpopularity, a general disorganisation, and a general slackening of government. In Galloway there was a serious civil war, though not on any nationalist grounds. It was only fourteen years since the province had been brought under the Scots Crown, and it saw its chance in the weakening of William's authority. It rose, and drove out the royal officers . . . and then plunged into a civil war of its own. Its joint lords were Gilbert and Uchtred, the two sons of Fergus : Gilbert now set his son Malcolm to capture Uchtred, who was blinded and mutilated, so roughly that he had the good fortune to die. Henry had shown himself willing to back Gilbert, at the price of submission : but the fratricide scan-

dalised him, and he drew off. On William's release, in
the February of 1175, Henry gave him permission to
deal with Galloway. Gilbert was forced to submit and
to pay a fine, but on returning to his lordship he
promised death to any of his subjects who should
swear fealty to the King of Scots.

The Church also was in revolt : and this time the
grounds were very definitely nationalist. The old
dispute with the Archbishop of York had been revived
again under Malcolm IV, in 1155, when the English
Pope, Adrian IV, had vainly attempted to force the
subjection of the Scottish bishops. Falaise had been
intended to settle the question : but the treaty had not
been made with the agreement of the Scots prelates,
and they declined to give assent to it now. In 1176
William brought them to Northampton, to swear
allegiance to Henry. With the Bishop of Glasgow and
Gilbert de Moray [1] as spokesmen, they resisted with
vigour. The Bishop, apparently fixing on the clause in
the Treaty, *qualem facere debet et solebat*, declared that
the submission which the Scots Church ' owed and was
used to give ' to the Archbishop of York was precisely
nothing. The Archbishop said it had been given in the
past, and was owing now, and Gilbert rose, *ignitus velut
ferrum excandens*, glowing like hot iron, and spoke
fiercely, reminding the English churchmen of the days
when *Ecclesia Scotica Catholica* had been the mother of

[1] Not St Gilbert, who could not have been old enough to speak
there, but apparently a member of his family, who a hundred and
twenty years later—and after that—were to prove themselves
notable defenders of Scotland.

their own. The speech was founded on good history,
and some of the English were convinced by it : others,
however, *naturaliter* (says Fordun) called him a vapour-
ing and headlong Scot, *fumosus Scoticus et impetuosus,*
and the Archbishop laughed, and playfully smacked
his head. The Scottish bishops, however, agreed with
him, and there was a deadlock. The situation was
saved by the Archbishop of Canterbury declaring that
he, not York, should receive the desired submission,
whereon he and his brother of York quarrelled so
violently that as Henry had no wish for another
Becket, the conference was adjourned with the question
pending, and the Scots had leisure to appeal to the
Pope. A letter of William's to His Holiness expressed
the King's willingness that they should swear : it is
held by some authorities to be forged, but in any case
did not achieve its purpose. In May of next year the
Pope—not the English Adrian but the Italian Alexander
III, the vigorous opponent of Barbarossa—sent the
Scots prelates a copy of the letter, and in July decided
on their case, and told them not to take the oath, con-
firming the decision next year by his Legate. It is
possible that the episode had something to do with
William's sole religious foundation, for he built, next
year, the Abbey of Arbroath . . . and its dedication was
to St Thomas à Becket.[1]

Before the abbey walls were well above ground,
William was quarrelling with the Pope himself. The
quarrel raised the old question of investitures ; and

----

[1] The monks were Benedictines from Kelso.

Alexander held the general principles of Gregory VII, which had already brought him into violent conflict with the Emperor, whom he had excommunicated and with whom he was only becoming reconciled. In 1178, when the last of the Emperor's series of anti-popes had just surrendered pretensions to the Tiara, the see of St Andrews fell vacant. The Chapter elected John the Scot.[1] The King wanted the see for his own confessor, Hugh, and ordered his bishops to consecrate him. The Chapter appealed to the Pope, who bade his Legate consecrate John for them. William let the consecration go forward, but swore his favourite oath, by the arm of St James, that Scotland was too small to hold John and himself: he made room by banishing John and his family, who included the Bishop of Aberdeen, John's uncle.

The gesture roused Pope Alexander. Until now he had been pro-Scottish, but he responded by appointing as Legate to the Scottish kingdom no other than the Archbishop of York, and threatened an interdict—that is, a general suspension of all religious services—and excommunication for the King. William then offered John the Chancellorship and a promise of the next see that should be vacant, but Alexander would have none but that to which John had been canonically elected; and William, Hugh, and all of Hugh's supporters, were excommunicated in due form. The

[1] Johannes Scotus. *Scotus*, so late as this, can hardly mean Irish: the probability is that he was a man of Scots (i.e. Gaelic) stock, born in Scottish England, where his race was scarce enough to give him a nickname.

quarrel, however, was very shortly settled. In 1181 both the Pope and his Legate died, and William made peace with the new Pope, Lucius III. Both the rival bishops were to resign the see and be reinstated by the Pope, who would leave Hugh at St Andrews and allow John to accept Dunkeld, now vacant. The Pope's authority and the King's desire, if not that of the Chapter, being satisfied, the excommunication was recalled, and Lucius even sent William the Golden Rose.

While this struggle was still going on, there was civil war. In 1181 certain nobles revolted, and attempted to dethrone the King. Malcolm MacHeth was dead and his son in prison, and the rebels turned to the other rival line, and put forward Donald, son of William FitzDuncan. By midsummer matters looked serious in the North, and William was further handicapped by the fact that he had to get Henry's permission before he could move. The Galloway men also raided Lothian, and William was powerless to crush either rising : he succeeded in checking them, but could do no more, and all through the early 'eighties war threatened on both sides.

In 1184 Henry apparently considered that his teeth were drawn, and began to treat him with more consideration, returning Huntingdon, which William subenfeoffed to his brother David. William was middle-aged by now, and growing more sober : he was turned forty, still unmarried, still without lawful offspring, although he had several of the other kind. He decided to marry. He could not do so without Henry's permission, and the lady on whom he fixed was Henry's niece, Matilda of Saxony.[1]   Henry disliked the match, as it gave William inconvenient Continental allies, but professed to forward it.   Nothing was done.

Next year, the civil war took a fresh turn.   Gilbert of Galloway went to his own place : his son was a hostage in England, and Roland, son of that Uchtred whom Gilbert had murdered, was about the Scots court, where he had married Helen de Moreville, daughter of the Constable.   He raised a Scots army, and fell upon the province, retaking it quickly.   The success annoyed Henry.   William's marriage negotiations were still hanging fire, as Henry had found a more suitable—i.e. less useful—bride, Ermengarde de Beaumont, a rather distant French cousin of his own, and was offering her, with Edinburgh for dowry.   He bade William force Roland to give an account of his doings, and Roland declined, blocking the Galloway passes by felling trees, which suggests a good many changes in that landscape.   Henry brought up the whole armed force of England : Roland had to submit, and abide by the decision of English courts over his cousin Duncan's claim to partition.[2]

This quieted the South.   William allowed his

[1] So the English chroniclers call her, after her mother.   Her real name seems to have been Richenza.
[2] William later settled the matter by creating Duncan Earl of Carrick, leaving Roland the undivided Galloway.   Duncan's granddaughter was the mother of Robert I.

marriage to be arranged (as was, of course, King Henry's legal right) and married Ermengarde at Woodstock, sending her up to Scotland alone thereafter. North of Forth the rebellion in favour of Donald MacWilliam was still in progress, and spreading. In 1187, the year after his marriage, William raised all the men he could and marched to Inverness. His own supporters would not let him lead them. They demanded that he should stay while they went on, while others refused to go unless he led them. A nasty situation was saved by Roland of Galloway, who, operating with a small detached force, met Donald at Mamgarve near Inverness, engaged him at once, and ended the rising by killing him on the spot.

Before that year was out, there was news from the East that thundered through Christendom, and was to have important results for Scotland. The early century had seen the power of Islam in the East restored to unity, and the first-fruits of the restoration had been the fall of the Crusader state of Edessa and the inglorious failure of the Second Crusade, which had ended in 1148. Now Saladin encircled the Latin states, and this year the King of Jerusalem challenged him. Saladin attacked, and in a great battle at the Horns of Hattin shattered the Christian power with appalling slaughter, and in October took Jerusalem.

The Pope died of grief. His successor preached a Holy War once more. The Italian Normans were the

first to respond, but the Emperor took the Cross, and
the King of France : and Henry, who was growing old
and remembering his sins, would have joined them.
He needed money, much money, to raise an army.
William's relations were friendlier with him now : the
kingdom was settling down from the civil wars, and
Edinburgh, as Queen Ermengarde's dowry, was in
Scots hands again. William now offered 4000 merks
for Roxburgh and Berwick. Henry refused, but offered
them in exchange for the tenths of the kingdom.
Neither clergy nor nobles would accept the bargain . . .
and then the elder of Henry's surviving sons went to
war with his father again, and the youngest, and dearest,
John, rose with his brother.

It killed the old man. In July 1189 he died, dread-
fully, at Chinon, in the triple château high above the
Vienne, where a peasant-girl later came to a King of
France. Henry, the eldest of his sons, the one whom
he had once had crowned, was dead, and Richard,
Count of Poitou, was King of England. Now Richard
desired to go on the Crusade, and he had a depleted
treasury. Moreover, he was on friendly terms with
William, and David of Huntingdon had supported him
in his war against his father. He set about raising
money by every means, including a sale of the earldom
of Northumberland to the Bishop of Durham.
William, and Scotland behind him, saw the chance.
The King offered 10,000 merks for rescission of the
Treaty of Falaise. Whether greed, crusading fervour,
or statesmanship moved him, Richard made the

wisest decision of his life : it annoyed his subjects
exceedingly at the time, but it gave them a century of
peace with Scotland, and growing friendship. He
accepted the offer. He was crowned, with Prince
David carrying the Sword of State; and six weeks later,
in November 1189, William was escorted with pomp
to Canterbury, and there on the 5th December they
made the treaty which completely annulled the bargain
of Falaise, and restored her independence again to
Scotland.

Roxburgh and Berwick were returned, by perpetual
hereditary right. The earldom of Huntingdon and all
other English lands of the Kings of Scots were to be
restored as they had been held by King Malcolm.
And William was declared free and quit from all pacts
which Henry *per novas Cartas et per captionem suam
extorsit*, had extorted by new charters and by William's
capture. The allegiance of William's vassals was
restored : all documents bearing on the surrender
were to be returned, and any overlooked and not
returned were formally declared to be invalid. The
arrangement opened a hundred years of peace, though
a precarious peace in its early stages. The Scots kings
in that time were to join in wars in England, but
always as allies of an English party—and the popular
party. The English ones were to intrigue against
Scotland, but not to implement the intrigues by war.
As for the nations themselves, there was before long a
real friendliness between them. Scots and English
freely entered each other's countries, to the great benefit

of trade in both.[1] The Scots kings were personally
liked in England—better liked, in fact, than three of the
four English ones of that period : and when, at the end
of a century of peace, proposals were made to federate
the kingdoms, the Scots received the suggestion
willingly.

The friendliness, of course, took some time to
develop, but the benefits of the treaty soon were felt,
the more as in the previous year, 1188, Pope Clement
had clearly defined the relations of the two national
Churches : that of Scotland was categorically declared
to be subject to the Holy See alone, with no inter-
mediary, and no excommunication could be pronounced upon the kingdom of Scotland save by the
Pope or a Legate *a latere,* while only a native of Scotland, or the Pope's own emissary from the papal court,
could be appointed legate to that country. The civil
wars too were over, and for some years Scotland
enjoyed a much-needed quiet.

The Third Crusade opened with promise. The
Emperor, the King of France, and Richard of England
led armies well equipped and reasonably disciplined.
But their jealousies, and the hostility of the Emperor
of the East handicapped them heavily. By spring of
1190 the German effort was broken and the Emperor
killed. Richard was delayed by private wars in Sicily
and Cyprus, and though the Crusaders at last captured
Acre, Richard and Philip Augustus quarrelled them-

[1] In 1242 a Scotsman was mayor of the great English port of
Dunwich, now under salt water.

selves to a standstill, and the former went home. In
the autumn of 1192 a truce was made that left Jerusalem
still in Moslem hands, though Christian pilgrims were
given access to it. There were to be other crusades at
intervals for nearly a century yet : but the failure of
the Third marks the turn of the tide.

Richard, returning, was captured by the Duke of
Austria, and handed over as prisoner to the Emperor.
John his brother and Philip of France intrigued with
the latter to prolong his imprisonment, for John, who
had inherited no more than a ghostly lordship of
Ireland, was aiming at his brother's heritage, and
Philip, thinking John a less formidable vassal than
Richard, supported him. They tried to win King
William to side with them, but he would not, sending a
free gift instead of 2000 merks towards Richard's
ransom, while David of Huntingdon and the Earl of
Chester (whose sister David had married in 1190)
took arms for the prisoner.

Early in 1194 Richard was released : he had been
forced to pay an enormous ransom, and to become the
Emperor's vassal for England, which was restored to
him as a fief of the Empire. In April he was back
again in his kingdom. William went to meet him, and
claimed the northern fiefs his father had held—
Northumberland, Cumberland, Westmorland, and the
Honour of Lancaster. Richard was non-committal :
he declared that he must consult his barons, and
having done so, refused on the grounds that if he gave
them up to William it would seem as if he feared

William's ally France.   He protested his affection for
William, however, and attempted to soften the refusal
by drawing up an elaborate protocol of the honours
and privileges to be enjoyed by Kings of Scots whenever they should visit the English court.[1]   William took
the refusal amicably enough—the two kings seem to
have been personally friendly, and in fact, though
Richard was a better soldier, they had a good deal of
temperamental likeness—and when Richard thought
wise to be crowned a second time, he came as the chief
guest . . . and made another effort for Northumberland.
The Bishop of Durham had resigned his purchase, and
William offered now to buy it himself for 15,000 merks.
(The sum is interesting : it was half as much again as
the ransom for Scotland, and as William would have
had to raise it himself, it throws some light on the
revenues of the Crown.   The disproportion is explained
by the fact that Northumberland was firmly in English
hands, while Scotland, even nominally subject, never
had been.)   The huge sum tempted Richard : he
offered the fiefs, but without the castles : that is,
William would have drawn the revenues, but gained no
political or military advantage.   They left the matter
open, and William went home.

Next year, he was seriously ill, and seemed likely to
die.   His queen had borne two daughters, but still no
son, and William proposed the succession should

---

[1] Among them was a daily ' livery ' or ration, which included
twenty-four royal loaves, twelve pints of wine, specified as royal
and expensive, and *two pounds* of pepper.

devolve, not on his brother or his brother's sons, but on a foreigner, Otto of Saxony (heir to that duchy, nephew of Richard of England, and brother of the Matilda William had courted) on condition that Otto should marry his elder daughter Margaret. The Scots nobles would have none of it, the Earl of Dunbar protesting that the Crown could not devolve by way of a female line so long as the King had a brother or a nephew. William saved the immediate situation by recovering, but he tried to go on with the project for the marriage, and he and Richard set going negotiations, William offering Lothian as the bride's dowry, while Richard offered to give his nephew Northumberland. The arrangement would almost certainly have meant war sooner or later, and very fortunately it came to nothing.

1196 brought fresh war in the North, the results of a long-drawn-out succession struggle in the Orkneys, between the rival lines of Paul and Erlend, the sons of Jarl Thorfinn and Queen Ingebjorg. The wild story of the feud need not be told here : the murder of St Magnus (Erlend's son) by his cousin Hakon Paulson was its beginning : and Kirkwall Cathedral was built in memory of that killing. Hakon held to the earldom, which went in time to his sons, Paul II and Harald, Harald taking the Mainland territory, which then came as far south as Dingwall. By the mid century the feud had somewhat died down, and the earldom was divided between Erlend's grandson Rognvald and a second Harald, nephew of Paul II and Harald I, and son of

Mordach Earl of Athol.[1]   But Harald II's cousin,
another Erlend, son of Harald I, appeared on the scene,
induced Malcolm IV to grant him Caithness, and
demanded the partition of the Orkneys.   The feud
reopened, and for a while it ran a triangular course.
Harald II lasted longest, and by 1158 was Earl of
Caithness and Orkney both.   He married a daughter of
the Earl of Fife; and Fife was a strong supporter of the
Crown.   In 1196, however, he put away this lady, and
the successor whom he chose for her was a daughter of
Malcolm MacHeth, Earl of Ross, whose house had
hereditary claims to Moray, and even to the kingdom.
Moray lay to the south of his own dominions, and he
seized upon it, and threatened to make himself master
of much of the Highlands, for mediaeval Moray
stretched as far west as the head of Loch Duich.

William marched against the rebels : near Inverness
he met and defeated Harald's son Thorfinn, and

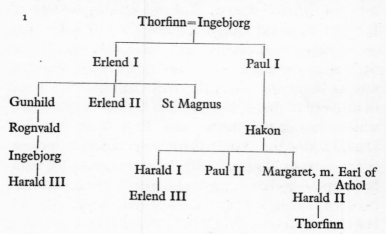

[1]

advancing, ravaged Caithness. Harald offered to make peace, to give Thorfinn as hostage, and to bring in the leaders of the rising. William accepted, but Harald arrived with his nephew instead of his son, and frankly announced that he had allowed his prisoners to escape. William therefore took Harald himself as hostage, until Thorfinn should arrive : and meanwhile the Orkneys were attacked by another Harald, Harald III, the representative of the other and senior branch of the house, who had procured a grant of half the earldom from both the King of Scots and the King of Norway. He was killed, however, in a battle at Wick, which ended the line of Erlend, and its claims. Harald II was now left undisputed head of the dynasty, and he tried to buy back the earldom from King William, who said he might have it if he put away his MacHeth wife and took back her predecessor, which Harald declining, William sold the fief to Rognvald King of Man, with the result that there was another war, which ended in Harald surrendering and repurchasing his fief for 2000 pounds of silver. The Crown had been intermittently involved for some eight years, and the whole episode probably did a good deal to stimulate the reorientation of foreign policy that is characteristic of the next century, when Norway and the Isles, rather than England, became as it were the current enemy.

Before this northern war was over, certain other things had happened. The position of the dynasty was improved by the birth of a prince, Alexander, on the 24th August 1198: and at Musselburgh in 1201 the

P

barons did homage to him as heir to the Crown. His birth was soon followed by fresh complications with England, that nearly brought the Hundred Years' Peace to a premature end. In 1199 King Richard was killed. The natural heir was his nephew Arthur, son of his dead brother Geoffrey and of William's niece, Constance Duchess of Brittany : but Arthur was a boy of twelve, and Richard named as his heir his brother John, the most evil though not the least able of his house.

England accepted John, and he was crowned in May 1199, a few weeks after Richard's death. William recognised him as King, but his kinship to Arthur made John suspicious of him, and when William again laid claim to Northumberland, John promised it, on condition that he would pledge himself to refrain from making war. John's promise was not kept. William renewed his claim, and was put off with smooth words and an invitation to meet John and talk it over. John in fact set out to the meeting, but by this time the barons of Anjou, Maine, and Touraine were up for Arthur, and William decided to back his great-nephew. He threatened John with war : John made truce and fresh promises, and went off to France, the promises unfulfilled.

William hung irresolute. He was elderly now, his health broken, his heir a child, and his own throne uncertain : he was not popular, and there was still a male descendant of Duncan II and apparently also one of Lulach, who could be set up in his place. A war in

England for a foreign prince whom England had not accepted, or for fiefs which concerned the King and not the nation, would have been dangerous whether he won or lost.   In his doubts he made a pilgrimage to Dunfermline, kept vigil by the tombs of his grandfather and great-grandmother, and sleeping, dreamt a dream which warned him from war.   He did not attack John, but was still irresolute, refusing to meet him in peace, and negotiating for an alliance with Philip and the marriage of his young heir to Philip's daughter.

In 1200, however, John and Philip made peace, and William agreed at last to the interview.   He came to Lincoln in November, and did the customary homage for Huntingdon, *salvo iure suo*, saving his own rights. There was a fresh argument over Northumberland, and John, no doubt using to effect the great personal charm which he seems to have possessed in spite of his vices, promised a definite answer in six months.

He had grasped by now, though, that William would not fight.   His next move was to build a new strong castle at Tweedmouth, where it menaced the harbour of Berwick, then the chief centre of Scots foreign trade.   Twice the Scots razed it.   John could do nothing, for in 1202 his French barons rose once more and proclaimed Arthur, and Philip supported them. Arthur, however, was captured, and disappeared. Philip, as John's overlord, demanded a reckoning, and declared John's French dominions forfeited : and in 1204 Normandy, Anjou, Maine, and Touraine were lost, and John's lands in France reduced to his inheritance from his mother, who had been Duchess of Aquitaine. He made no attempt to recover them. England was turning against him, and though in that year he met William at Norham and quarrelled with him over the Tweedmouth razing, he could not afford a war. By the next year, John had quarrelled with the Pope over the Archbishopric of Canterbury : and Innocent III was no man to accept defiance. The struggle went on for some years (William expressing sympathy with the Pope) and in 1208 England went under a six years' interdict, while next year John was excommunicated.

A strained peace between Scotland and England still endured. In 1209 it was very nearly broken. William began to negotiate a foreign marriage for one of his children : the chroniclers' statements are clearly incorrect, but Robertson's conjecture that the proposed match was between Prince Alexander and the heiress of Flanders seems probable, and would explain John's alarm, as a Scoto-Flemish alliance, much more the passing of Flanders to the Scots Crown, would have been extremely inconvenient. On a trumped-up excuse that William had no right to marry his heir without leave of the overlord of his English fiefs, he took the army of foreign mercenaries who were now his main support and marched to the Border.

Neither John nor William could afford a war. They met to discuss terms, but before anything could be settled, William again was seriously ill. A truce was made until he should recover. When he had done so he held a Council at Stirling. The lords pressed for war and sent John an ultimatum : but William, who by now was nearly seventy and a broken man, was in a mood to accept any sort of terms rather than the war which might very possibly dethrone his son. Moreover, John was marching, and William's mobilisation was slow. He dealt with John in person, and over the head of his Council, and the two agreed. John should raze Tweedmouth : but William bought peace for 15,000 merks. It seems that they made a secret agreement also, as to the marriage of William's two elder daughters. What the precise terms were we shall never know : [1] it seems fairly clear that one of the children was to marry John's elder son, Henry, since Alexander II was later given certain English lands as compensation because she had not done so. The two children were given into John's hands : but he did not keep his promise as to their marriage. Princess Margaret, of course, was the nearest heir to her brother, who would very obviously soon succeed, and John probably put off the wedding until he saw further.

The arrangement was intensely unpopular. It saved William an English war (and John remitted half the indemnity) but it set Scotland against him. The South was in a general state of disaffection : the North rose in open revolt, and tried to depose him. Donald Bàn

---

[1] Fordun affirms (on what authority is not known) that the princesses were to be married to John's sons Henry and Richard, but not for nine years, and that it would suffice if one was married, so long as it was to the heir.

MacWilliam, the grandson of Duncan II, who had
been 'out' in the early years of the reign, had left a
son Godfrey, who had been brought up in Ireland and
the Isles.   In 1211 he was invited over, and carried on
a guerilla war in Ross.   Had the insurgents chosen a
MacHeth candidate, they might have roused sufficient
Highland support to dethrone King William : but the
incomer was too much of a stranger.   Even so, the war
went on for more than a year, and drove the old King
to a closer alliance with John.   In February 1212 the
two met at Norham, and made an actual treaty of
alliance, each pledging himself to support the other's
heir :   and John was even given leave to arrange
Alexander's marriage, on condition that the lady should
be suitable to the dignity of the Crown.

With his rear thus to some extent safeguarded,
William went up to deal with the northern menace,
Prince Alexander, whom John had just knighted, going
with him to win his spurs.   The rising was over before
they could take action.   The insurgents surrendered
Godfrey to William Comyn, Earl of Buchan.   Buchan
moved to take his captive to the King, but as Godfrey
set about suicide by starvation, he was hastily beheaded
before he could die, and his head went instead.

1213, the last full year of the reign, brought renewed
tension with England.   John had been forced to make
England a direct fief of the Pope, and had also a fresh
war on his hands in Wales.   His barons planned a civil
one against him, and William, hearing of it, warned
him.   One of the ring-leaders, however, was Eustace de

Vesci, who had married William's illegitimate daughter :
and he fled to the court of his father-in-law, who refused
to extradite him. The result was another angry meeting
at Norham. Again William's serious illness broke off
negotiations : and again there was no war. The next
summer brought fresh trouble with the Earl of Orkney.
William succeeded in asserting his authority, but his
health broke down again. He bade them carry him to
Stirling, where on the 4th December 1214 he died, aged
seventy-two, after almost the longest reign in Scottish
history, and was succeeded by his only son, a boy of
sixteen, now Alexander II.

The civil and domestic side of the reign may be
briefly dealt with. The continual small but threatening civil wars show the disintegration that inevitably
followed a weakening of the moral authority of the
Crown. Yet David I had built powerfully, and the
framework of his structure stood the strain, and even
made certain further developments along its natural
lines. The regularising of land tenures by charter was
now taken for granted as the normal thing. Trial by
jury was the regular process of law, save in Galloway,
where it was only granted if the accused should desire
it. The Great Council in 1180 decided that no courts
of Justice should be held save in the presence of the
Sheriff or his Depute. Regalities—rights of jurisdiction which corresponded in civil matters to the Sheriff's
and in criminal (treason excepted) to those of the
Courts of Justiciary—were now to be confined to the
greater barons and prelates : they made serious inroads

on the Sheriff's jurisdiction. Another Council of 1197 pledged the great barons not to support any breaker of the law, and to take no money for remission of penalty after due sentence.

The main feature of the ecclesiastical history of the reign is the struggle with the English Church, already described. William was rather frequently at odds with his clergy through his intrusion of his own nominees into important benefices, and he does not seem to have been a great benefactor of the Church. His foundation of Arbroath has been mentioned : the only others of importance in this reign are his brother's of Lindores, in Fife, for Benedictines from Kelso ; one by Roland of Galloway at Glenluce, for Cistercians from Melrose ; and one by the Earl of Strathearn at Inchaffray, for Canons Regular from Scone. One of its later abbots blessed an army in the midsummer dawn of the year 1314, and led their Paternoster as they knelt before action.

The most notable civil development is in the burghs, which grew steadily in both numbers and importance. The earliest extant burgh charters are of this reign, and William certainly gave new ones, Glasgow's among them. Hitherto burghal life had scarcely existed north of Tay at most : but now Forfar, Aberdeen, and the towns of the Moray Firth began to rise, and the fact marks a change in the national centre of gravity, which was to have considerable effect on the foreign policy of the next two reigns.

CHAPTER XI

THE KINGS OF PEACE

SEVENTY-TWO YEARS: 1214–1286

'Quha Scotland led in loue and le.'
Popular song of the end of the century.

'In me, as your King, is vested for a time the duty of maintaining the country's honour and integrity.'
George VI on the evening of his coronation.

'PERIODS,' in history, are apt to be rather vague things. What we mean by 'the thirteenth century' in Scotland is a time that runs from the death of William I to that of his great-great-granddaughter Margaret—from 1214, that is, until 1290. This time, for Scotland and for Europe in general, is the full noon-tide of the Middle Ages. The strong new movements of the eleventh century and the twelfth are crystallising into institutions. Its whole note is one of stabilisation, definition, order—order at least on the intellectual plane and as an ideal, for actual life was full enough of war for most parts of Europe. The great national states of the modern world were emerging, in something approximating to their present shape, and with an increasing national consciousness, that went beyond the fief to the nation itself: and the twelfth century revival of the study of law and of its philosophical basis helped to give the

233

new idea the firm skeleton of organised thought concerning its principles. Frederick Barbarossa had made firm the Imperial rule over the ill-mated team of Germany and Italy. Louis VI and Louis VII had made the nebulous and almost nominal power of the French Crown into a real national force, that by the middle of the thirteenth century was to produce a real national kingdom, the strongest element in the politics of Europe. Henry II had done as much for the English, though his huge French dominions that lay as it were between the French Crown and the English one were already bringing about that rivalry that was one of the chief and most disastrous elements in the history of the later Middle Ages. In Scotland, even earlier, David I had made a national monarchy, recognised as such, whose territory was not yet coterminous with that of modern Scotland, but which none the less was an organised Scots kingdom. The old *regnum*, the United States of Christendom, was gone for good : it had never since Charlemagne been more than a political ideal, but now the ideal itself had disappeared. It had revived, indeed, towards the end of the twelfth century, in the hands of Henry VI, who had made himself overlord from the Tweed to the South of Italy, and had formed a dream of rule that included not only Western Europe but the Eastern Empire. But in 1197 he died, and the checked forces asserted themselves once more.

There was still a unity that transcended these, whose power sprang not from the *regnum* but from the rival concept of the *sacerdotium*—a unity of common thought

and culture, and, in the broadest sense, of a common
spiritual life.   The forces which directly expressed it
were threefold.   There was chivalry and its associated
culture and art, especially literature, for French was
still an international speech.   There was the international learning, with its corollary in the growth of
the universities, great organised schools, local and
national in framework, but international in speech and
personnel.   And dominating both these, which had
sprung from it, there was the international Church,
which in the first half of the thirteenth century rose to
its greatest power under Innocent III.

The long strife of the *regnum* and the *sacerdotium* had
seemed to be ended in victory for the former.   But
Henry VI, as we have seen, died in 1197, and the next
year brought Innocent's election : and Innocent, a
man of thirty-seven, with enormous vigour, unblemished
character, and great scholarship, especially in law,
revived the theories of Gregory VII.   ' Princes have
power on earth, priests have power in Heaven.   Princes
reign over the body, priests over the soul.   As much as
the soul is worthier than the body, so much worthier
is the priesthood than the monarchy,' or again, ' The
sacerdotium came by divine creation, the *regnum* by
man's device.'   He had more to face than Gregory,
however, for instead of the feeble feudal princes, there
were now strong national kings.   But he did face them,
making and unmaking monarchs, forcing Philip
Augustus of France to take back the Danish wife he
had cast off, forcing a king so remote as John of England

to be his vassal in direct feudal subjection. He raised the temporal power of the Papacy to such a height that a reaction was inevitable. He himself could enforce that power because in him it was backed by a fervent spiritual power. He desired the temporal rule for the sake of the spiritual welfare of Europe, nobly conceived, and he never paltered with that ideal. At a dangerous moment he surrendered the alliance of Philip Augustus rather than betray the principles of Christian marriage and refuse his protection to a wronged and helpless young wife. He led the great Fourth Lateran Council in its efforts to check worldliness in the clergy, to humanise the law, to provide for the wider spread of education. He supported St Francis and St Dominic. But even Innocent had his failures : the Fourth Crusade of 1201, meant to redeem the unsuccess of the Third, never so much as saw the Holy Land : it captured Christian Constantinople instead, and set up there a short-lived Latin state, a purely secular and feudal structure, that fatally weakened the bulwark of the East. In England his support of his vassal John and of royal authority caused him to oppose a national movement against tyranny, and did much to weaken his influence in that country. Moreover, when he died, in 1216, he left successors whose strife with the temporal rulers continued for obviously lower motives. They could not stand. Frederick II, Philip Augustus, were too strong for them. Louis IX, a most devoted son of the Church, and a very real saint, came in conflict with them. At the very end of the century, indeed, the

Papacy was to revive under Boniface VIII (1294-1303), who renewed the claims of Gregory and of Innocent— and used them, by the way, in defence of Scotland. But Boniface was broken by Philip of France, and in 1309 the Pope was a virtual prisoner of the French king, and the attempt to recover freedom again brought the Great Schism of the fourteenth century, that fatally weakened the Church's authority.

Another international force has been mentioned. The great revival of scholarship that had begun with the foundation of the Cluniac order in the tenth century had flourished mightily all through the twelfth, and its machinery showed the general tendency to stabilise and organise and define. As Professor Tout has admirably put it,

> Just as the institution of knighthood had set up a new cosmo-politan principle of union that bound together men of different lands, wealth, and social station in a common brotherhood of arms, so did the establishment of the corporations of doctors and scholars unite the subtlest brains of diverse countries and ranks, in a common professional and social life.

With a common international language, great schools of men from widely separate countries tended to rise wherever there were great teachers. Paris was one such : famed for philosophy and theology, it was the brain-centre of the North. In the South, Bologna was equally famous in law. In the third quarter of the twelfth century the schools of Paris were already organising as a guild of teachers, with power to admit new members on a basis of defined qualifications. Before 1200 Philip Augustus had exempted it from municipal jurisdiction and made it self-governing. By 1250 it was fully organised as a great autonomous teaching corporation. Bologna grew similarly, though as a guild of students, not of teachers. Before the Paris schools were fully organised, a body of teachers and students seceded from them, about the end of the eleven-sixties, and moved to England, where they settled at Oxford. In 1209 Oxford suffered a similar schism, and the seceders founded a school at Cambridge.

Similar processes were going on in other parts of Europe. These *studia generalia* (great open schools accessible to all comers) or *universitates magistrorum* or *scholarium* (corporations of masters or of scholars) were essentially guilds which either by assumed prescription, or later by the grant of a Pope or a sovereign, could regulate admission to the teaching profession. The Middle Ages had a profound dislike of the unqualified man, the amateur. Knight, scholar, tradesman, artisan, alike had to be formally admitted to his calling, after satisfying those who were members already that he had received the necessary training : one can see the very same process surviving yet in the admission of a medical practitioner. The *facultas docendi*, the licence to teach of the recognised university, was internationally acceptable : the typical meaning of it survives, for instance, in the formulae of the Doctor's diploma of the late-mediaeval University of Aberdeen :

Nos Praefectus Vice-Cancellarius Artium Facultatis Decanus et Senatus Academici Secretarius hoc scripto testatum volumus N.

postquam se suosque in *Litteris* (Medicina, etc.) titulos Senatui probasset Gradum Doctoralem in Litteris subjecta prius publicae Professorum et Examinatorum Censurae Dissertatione seu Thesi Inaugurali solennibusque rite peractis consecutum esse Eique amplissimam potestatem in Litteris ubique gentium legendi docendi commentandi concessam aliaque omnia privilegia quae hic aut usquam alibi ad Doctoralem apicem evectis concedi solent. Cujus rei quo major esset fides Nos sigillo communi Academiae appenso chirographa apposuimus.[1]

These universities show learning detaching itself from the monastic or cathedral school, for their clerks, *clerici*, were no longer necessarily even in minor orders : the word begins to separate from *clergy* and denote merely someone who is literate. The secularisation grew more marked. The scholar, untrammelled by any discipline outside his class-room and fired by the general rowdiness of massed youth, could be disreputable as an individual—there were plenty of Villons in that earlier age—and corporately a menace to civic peace. And he did not confine his studies to the douce curriculum laid down by his bishop : he adventured after the learning of the heathen, especially of the great Saracen schools in Spain, where Averroes had died in 1198 and Maimonides in 1204. From the Saracens, Aristotle returned to Europe, brought by

---

[1] *Doctor*, of course, is literally a teacher. The *bachelor* (like the knight bachelor) was the aspirant, half-way to a higher grade : the word, probably, was originally slang, like our *bajan* (béjaune, bec jaune, greenhorn) for Low Latin *baccalarius* is a farm-hand. The *master* was the recognised scholar, with a right to teach, and like the knight was *Dominus* or *Sir*. The *doctor* was the teacher who had proved himself capable of sustaining his thesis or proposition in open and often fiery debate with his peers, and as his scarlet gown still testifies, was a considerable personage : in the academic world he corresponded to the knight banneret in the military.

the Archbishop Raymond of Toledo and our own
Michael Scott, to dominate all the learning of the time.
His formal logic shaped all its scholarship, giving a
new bone, so to speak, to theology, where the Godhead
was conceived as Essential Reason. But the Spanish
schools, both Arabic and Jewish, were powerful
stimulants also of heresy, and the south of Europe was
very strongly affected by the materialistic pantheism
of Averroes.

The wave of heresy was one of the causes of the
coming of a new kind of religious order, the friars.
The new learning was to colour their general outlook,
and the struggle of the Pope with the lay power to give
them something equivalent to the position earlier held
by Cluny. The orders reformed or created in the
eleventh and twelfth centuries had to some extent
suffered the nemesis of their popularity, and grown
wealthy and consequently corrupt. Various attempts
were made to restore them to their original spirit : but
to Dominic de Guzman, born in 1170 at Osma in
Spain, to Giovanni Bernadone, called Francisco, born
in 1182 at Assisi in Italy, there came the idea of a new
kind of monk. It was Francis who first saw the spiritual
power of sheer poverty, of a body of men who would
possess absolutely nothing, not only individually but
corporately, beyond the rough woollen frock that
covered them, who would live on the casual charity
of the street. Soon after 1200 he gathered a band of
companions. In 1210 Innocent recognised them as
a new order, and by 1223 they had increased so much

that Honorius had to give them a constitution. By
1226, when Francis died, the grey frock of these Lesser
Brethren, the *Fratres Minores* or Friars Minor, was
familiar through all Christendom and beyond, and
since for long they kept their combination of rigid
poverty and fearless devotion with a joyous faith that
won them the name of God's Jesters, they soon became
a great missionary force. Dominic's order was differently based. The Friars Preachers, Blackfriars,
Dominicans, were founded in 1216 as a mission against
the heresies of the South, their first inspiration being
the Canons Regular, or monks who could do the work
of parish priests. In 1220 they added St Francis's
principle of utter poverty. Both orders were essentially
missionary. The fact brought the Dominicans in
charge of the organised Inquisition into heresy that
was in time to win an evil name : and it gave to both
great interest in scholarship. So early as 1221 the
Dominicans at St Jacques in Paris (Jacobins) were
founding a great school of theology, and it very soon
had a Franciscan rival. The culmination of Scholastic
philosophy is the *Summa Theologiae* of the Dominican
St Thomas Aquinas (1225-74) which represents the
completest application of the principles of Aristotle
to the Creed, while the Franciscan Roger Bacon
(d. 1294) is one of the chief founders of modern
science.

The friars won a universal favour. It gave them
power, and the temptations of power. It gave them
wealth, and the temptations of wealth. They were to

Q

suffer, like most other orders, from the moral decay of
the fourteenth century, the age of the Great Schism
and the Black Death. But through the whole of the
thirteenth century they were to be a force that brought
new life.[1]

The passionate scholarship of the universities, the
spiritual fervour of the friars, were paralleled by
flaming life in the arts. It was an age of the most
splendid building. There had been that already in
the eleventh century, but the French discovery of the
pointed arch had given it a new and brilliant strength.
The choir of Notre Dame comes in 1194. Chartres
was begun in that year, Reims in 1211. These glorious
buildings drew to them other arts, especially those of
sculpture and staining glass. The statues of Chartres
have a noble beauty that neither Greece nor Egypt
ever bettered, and the glass of the age has the colours
of Paradise. Painting in the more general sense begins,
for modern Europe, with Cimabue, born about 1240.
Alongside architecture and the sculpture associated
with it, the major art of the time was literature. Here,
Latin apart (and there is superb stuff in that) the
hegemony of France was as marked as in building.
The *chansons de geste*, the great epics of old wars, were
still in being, but were giving place to the *romances*,
also long narratives full of adventures, but with the

[1] There were other mendicant orders, chief among them the
Carmelites, founded in 1219 in the Holy Land, and to be a great
school of intellectual mystics, who included St Teresa of Avila and
St John of the Cross. All three of the chief ones soon had their
women's branches.

interest now in psychology rather than in action : to
borrow a metaphor from the stud-book, they are by
the Provençal lyric out of the *chansons de geste*. Other
vernaculars were beginning to imitate them, though
haltingly, and Celtic influence swept down from the
North to meet, in France, the Provençal and the
Eastern : already by the mid-twelfth century Geoffrey
of Monmouth was laying (in Latin, not French) the
foundation of the great Arthurian Legend, a cycle of
literature common to all Europe, in an enormous
international structure that embodied the very core of
chivalric tradition and of its underlying mystical values.
The abstract doctrine of chivalric love was crystallised
early in the thirteenth century by Guillaume de Lorris
in the allegorical *Roman de la Rose*, which with its
satiric pendant the *Contre-rose* added later by Jean de
Meung, profoundly affected all later mediaeval literature and a good deal of Renaissance. The Provençal
lyric of the Troubadours went down with the sup-
pression of the Albigensian Heresy that filled the
South : but its North French pupils of the late twelfth
and early thirteenth century carried on the inspiration,
and it spread into Germany and Italy, where it founded
brilliant schools of vernacular lyric. The latter was to
give his early training to the greatest figure in all
mediaeval letters and one of the dozen greatest of the
world's, Dante Alighieri, who was born in 1265, a
couple of years after the battle of Largs, and whose
first work belong to the early 'eighties, the last years of
the period covered by this book. The year when he

met Beatrice by the Arno was that in which our Robert
Bruce was born.

For Scotland, the three-quarter century that followed
after the death of William I was covered by the reigns
of the Kings of Peace, and saw a return to the steady
process of consolidation and development that had
marked the earlier half of the twelfth century. The
peace, to be sure, was relative : to the wistful eyes that
looked back from the dreadful years about 1300, from
the grim war for national existence that did not end
till 1328, from the other, as terrible and less glorious,
in the ghastly minority of David II—to these, it seemed
a golden age of rest. In fact, there were certain civil
disturbances : but these were mild in comparison with,
say, the Douglas Wars under James II, and a flicker
to those of the sixteenth or seventeenth centuries.
Foreign war occurred also, but threatening rather than
serious, and in its issues importantly successful.
There was never enough disturbance to hamper progress, and Alexander II and his son were both devoted
and intelligent rulers, with the ideals of the best of the
Old Stewarts, of James I, James II, James IV, and
with better luck. Both were true national leaders, so
accepted. The quality we call leadership consists in
the power to stir men's best imaginations, to give them
faith in these and in themselves, to make them love
something greater than themselves, and embody their
dream of it in a personage whom they can trust to seek
it at their head and with further vision. David I and

all the three kings called Alexander had that quality :
and the country answered them. Before the third
quarter of the century was ended the long slow process
of consolidation, begun so long ago as 843, had come
to an end, and Scotland was in being as a nation, at
once fully herself and fully a part of Europe, with her
heterogeneous elements fusing together, and capable,
when a leader arose once more, of united resistance to
colossal odds . . . for what we have been studying
through this book is the evolution of the Scotland of
Bruce.

Alexander was young yet, no more than sixteen, a
red-haired lad, clear-headed and strong-willed, with
far more sense of responsibility than his father in
youth, and far more force than his father at any time.
He had, notably, that gift for personal contact, for
making men like him, that was a part of the genius
of James IV. His nobles, Gaelic, Norman, Angle and
British, came to serve him faithfully. His Church was
ready, for his sake, to defy the Pope, and like David I
he was a King of the Commons : the Latin verses
Fordun quotes of him call him *pax plebis*, *dux miserorum*,
peace to the folk, the leader of the poor. Many kings
have earned less worthy epithets.

Two days after his father's death he was crowned at
Scone, seven great earls being present—Fife, Strathearn, Athol, Angus, Menteith, Buchan, and Dunbar.
Not all the kingdom accepted him as yet, for next
summer brought the usual northern rising in favour of
the rival line—indeed, of both rival lines, for their

representatives seem to have conjoined, as its heads
were Donald Bàn, apparently a brother of the last
MacWilliam claimant, the Godfrey who had been
killed in 1212, and one Kenneth MacHeth, whose
relationships are not clear, but who was probably one
of the House of Lulach, perhaps a son of the Donald
captured in 1156. They brought Irish allies, but even
so the rising seems to have been a feeble business, and
it was put down at once by the Earl of Ross, Fearchar
Mac-an-t-Sagairt.[1] Both leaders were killed, and their
heads sent to the King.

There was war in the south too—not a war with
England but an English war. England by now was in
an appalling condition. In 1214 John had tried to
recover his father's lost French dominions, but Philip
Augustus's victory at Bouvines had made it impossible,
and he had returned to face the wrath of his unlucky
kingdom, where his misgovernment had done more
to unite the Norman ruling caste (who were now cut
off from France) and the Saxon masses than anything
that had happened since the Conquest. Church,
barons, townsfolk, countryfolk, all loathed him, for
adequate reasons, and the cup was full. Early in 1215
his barons presented their demands. He put them by,
and in May they made war on him : by June they had
forced him to swear to their Great Charter, which
seemed an effective bridle on his power. But John
appealed to his overlord Innocent III, and Innocent,

---

[1] It is not known who Fearchar was. Presumably he had his
earldom from King William.

ignorant of the ins and outs of the struggle, felt himself bound to maintain the principle of royal authority and to support his vassal : he absolved John from an oath made under constraint. It meant war, and war on a large scale, for John had used his plunder to gather an army of foreign mercenaries—*ructarii et alii satellites* Fordun calls them, which may be translated as rowdy hangers-on. His lords appealed to the Kings of France and Scotland. Alexander promised support, and in October 1215 he crossed the Border with a useful army. The barons of Northumberland, remembering his grandfather's good rule, came and did him homage : those of Yorkshire, the old opponents of his father and great-grandfather, followed suit, and those further south greeted him as a welcome ally. (Indeed, all through his reign, as the English chroniclers make clear, he was as well liked in England as at home.) John was furious : he swore ' to beat the red fox-cub from his earth,' and by mid-winter he had marched north with all his foreign riders, burning whatever towns of Northern England or Southern Scotland he could get into his hands. Berwick and Roxburgh were sacked, Haddington and Dunbar, with all the ' frightfulness ' congenial to the Plantagenet temper at its worst : he is said to have brought up Jewish torturers and to have started the burning of Berwick with his own hand. Alexander fell back, too slowly to save these towns, and waited for him in the Pentlands, covering Edinburgh : but John's own ravages defeated him. He had stripped the country so bare that his

army was starving, and he had to retreat, sacking
Coldinghame Priory, while the Scots followed him into
Cumberland, and the wild men of the West took
bloody reprisals, Holmcultram going the way of
Coldinghame.

The English lords, in default of any heir but John's
son, a child, offered the Crown of England to Louis
of France, the son of Philip Augustus. In May he
landed with a force in Kent, and most of the English
barons did him homage. Alexander advanced in July
and took Carlisle, then, joined by the English barons
as he passed, marched on through the whole length
of England to Dover, sacking the lands of the few
royalists, all save their churches and religious houses,
but careful to spare those whose lords were out against
John, and storming Lincoln, the royalists' chief
strength. French, Scots, and English occupied London
together, and Louis, Alexander, and the English
barons pledged themselves not to make any peace with
John except collectively, while Alexander did homage
to Louis for his English fiefs.

John tried to cut off the Scots on their way home,
by breaking down the bridges over the Trent, the great
river that divides England much as our Forth does
Scotland. But in October he became gravely ill—
whether from poison, gluttony, or emotion—and died
at Newark. It changed the whole political situation.
The English barons preferred a French prince to John,
but even so their followers were less willing. Now the
lawful King was a small boy of nine, who was not

capable of tyranny. There was an instant collapse of
the insurrection. The Earl of Pembroke, who was
Marshal of England, crowned the child at Gloucester,
young Henry doing homage for England as the Pope's
vassal. A council of barons appointed Pembroke as
Regent, holding their pact as to collective peace to be
automatically dissolved by John's death. Alexander,
indeed, had returned to Scotland. Louis was still in
the South of England with an army, and disposed to
press his claim to the fulfilment of the English promises
that had brought him from France. In May of 1217
his English allies turned on him, the Pope's Legate
excommunicating all his supporters, and Alexander
as well. Louis fought, but was defeated heavily at
Lincoln, while his fleet was destroyed by John's
Justiciar, Hubert de Burgh. Alexander had moved
again to join his allies, but learning they did not need
him he withdrew, and in early autumn Louis and
Pembroke made peace, a clause in the treaty extending
the peace to Scotland if Alexander would return his
conquests. He had entered the war as the ally of the
English popular party, and all that he had taken was
Carlisle : he therefore returned the town, recognised
Henry, and in December his English fiefs were restored
to him, and he was released from his excommunication.
That last had left inconvenient consequences, as the
Scots prelates had refused to recognise it, and insisted
on giving him the Sacrament : the result of their
defiance was an interdict, and the Scots Church could
not win reconciliation with the Papal See without a

handsome contribution to papal funds, on which someone expressed himself in Latin verse that is very much
more pointed than polite.

A couple of years later, Alexander's next male heir
and the actual holder of the English fiefs, his uncle
David, died. Two of David's three sons were already
dead : the third, John, was a young lad, who succeeded
not only to his father's possessions but in time to the
English earldoms of Chester and Lincoln. This son
was now the only male representative of the dynasty,
in the direct male line, save the King himself : he
married a daughter of Llewellyn of Wales, and died,
childless, in 1237. Alexander had three sisters, however, all unmarried and two of them in English hands :
John of Huntingdon had four : the descendants of two
out of these four, though with very different degrees
of glory, were in time to be John and Robert, Kings
of Scots.

The rapprochement between Alexander and young
Henry brought discussion of the agreement made by
their fathers. Alexander appealed to the new Pope,
Honorius III, who confirmed the independence of the
Scots Church, and appointed his Legate, Cardinal
Pandolf, to arbitrate. In June 1220 Alexander met
Pandolf, with Segrave, King Henry's representative,
at York. It was agreed that the Scots princesses
should be married within the year ' to our honour and
that of the said King of Scots,' or if not, should be
sent back again to their brother ; and Alexander undertook to marry Henry's sister Joan, if the English were

able to get hold of her, or otherwise her sister Isabella.[1] Joan was recovered, with some difficulty—the Pope, in fact, had to intervene—and on the 19th June 1221 Alexander married her at York, his eldest sister Margaret being married at the same time to Hubert de Burgh, now virtually Regent of England. Princess Isobel was not married till four years later, her bridegroom being Roger Bigod, Earl of Norfolk.

The stabilising of relations with England allowed Alexander time for other affairs. All through the previous century the country had been harried at intervals by civil wars in the North and West, which were the legacy both of the Norse invasions and of the dynastic struggles of the eleventh. The central point of the foreign policy of David I and his grandsons had been to increase the Crown revenues and safeguard the Border by maintaining a hold on the great North English fiefs. Alexander II, as he grew to manhood, gave a new orientation. He looked north and west, desiring to bring once more under Scottish rule the Isles, so long lost to the Northmen, and the original Scotia, or Argyle. The Crown had kept a loose suzerainty over this last, but it was rather a dependency than a part of the kingdom, and though the power in the Isles was returning to Celtic hands rather than Norse,

---

[1] John on accession had divorced his wife and married Isabelle d'Angoulême, who was betrothed to Hugh de Lusignan, Comte de la Marche. The rejected fiancé was consoled with a promise of their eldest daughter, the said Joan, who was duly sent to him as a baby, to be brought up in his household. She was still in his hands, but on John's death his widow had returned to her old pledge, and was now Hugh's wife.

Somerled, in the previous century, had been a powerful rebel and a very active danger, that might have been fatal in an English war.

The division of Somerled's possessions at his death had weakened his house. Argyle had gone to Somerled II, son of his eldest son. The Isles were divided between Somerled I's sons Dougal, Ronald, and Angus, all three being called Kings, while Rognvald, their cousin, son of Godfred Olafson, held the title of King of Man and the Isles. In the resulting feuds, Angus and his sons were killed and his line extinguished. The descendants of Dougal were to be the MacDougalls of Argyle and Lorne, of Ronald the MacDonalds. The MacDougalls were soon to go down in Bruce's Wars, the MacDonalds to become the Lords of the Isles, who for long were half-independent potentates, very often allied with Scotland's enemies, though later still, after James IV had reconciled the Isles, the clan became constant supporters of the Stewarts.

Now Somerled's descendants stirred up trouble. It is by no means clear how it began. We know that in 1220 Alexander had to take an army north against one Donald MacNeil, and this may have had something to do with it : but we know nothing of Donald, nor who he was. In 1221, on his way home from his wedding, the King raised a fresh army in the South, and took it by sea to Argyle. It was late in the year, and a storm drove back his fleet. He went again in May, and marched through the country. It was rather a demonstration than a campaign. Those chiefs who

had been rebellious in the past fled and were forfeited :
some others were fined. The forfeited lands were
given to royal supporters : but Somerled's house
were left in possession, as the King's vassals. The
province was brought into the general national
system, legal and ecclesiastical, being made a sheriff-
dom, while a new bishopric was created for it, with
its seat at Lismore.

The matter was hardly settled when there was a
disturbance in the North. The Bishop of Caithness
had increased his teinds. His flock appealed to the
Earl, and as he would do nothing, took the law, and
the Bishop, into their own hands. They stoned him
and burnt his palace over his corpse. The rising was
against him, not against the Crown, but it broke the
King's Peace, and Alexander went north, fined the
Earl, forfeited half his earldom, and dealt very firmly
with the actual culprits.

It may possibly be as a result of this that there was
the threat of a rising in the West, headed by a dis-
possessed laird of Bute, with for figurehead one
Gillescop, the heir of the descendants of Duncan II.
The revolt fell flat, and Gillescop was executed at
Forfar, his infant daughter being also put to death.
(This last action is singularly unlike what we know of
Alexander : but as we know nothing of the details, a
local magnate may have been responsible : the house
of Duncan had caused four generations of civil wars.)
Another rising in Moray in 1228 burnt a good deal of
Inverness, but was put down by the Earl of Buchan,

one of the great Norman house of Comyn, who had
married the heiress of the old Gaelic line.

The settlement of Argyle had left that province a
definite part of Scotland, no longer a vague buffer-
state between Scots and Norse territory. (The House
of Somerled held the Isles from Norway, and Kintyre
was counted as being part of the Isles.) The west and
north coasts were now effectually guarded. The Earl
of Caithness was dead, and his earldom had gone to a
brother of the Earl of Angus, Sutherland being divided
from it to make a new earldom. Ross was in the hands
of the powerful Earl Fearchar, a strong supporter of
the Crown, who also had grants of forfeited land in
Argyle. The Lords of Lorne and Argyle had sworn
allegiance, and were on unfriendly terms with the
King of Man. Bute and Arran had gone to the High
Steward, who, holding Renfrew, was master of the
Clyde. Galloway was under Roland and his son Alan,
Carrick under Roland's cousin Duncan, all loyal to the
Crown. There was a continuous barrier now against
Irish attacks in support of pretenders to the throne,
and also against any invasion from Norway.

Norway recognised the fact. In 1230 King Hakon
urged Olaf of Man to capture the Sudreys, the South
Isles, and lent him a fleet to do it. There ensued some
wild episodes of raid and murder, but the affair died
down, and is only important as warning for stronger
attacks in the next reign.

Besides these movements towards political definition
and organisation, the 'twenties brought an ecclesiastical

one as well. In 1225 Honorius III formulated what
for over two hundred years was to be the peculiar
constitution of the Scots Church. She had been
handicapped, in concerted national action, by the fact
that no one but an Archbishop or the Pope's Legate
could call a Provincial Council. Honorius therefore
gave leave to the Scots prelates to hold such a Council
or Synod without a Legate, and a constitution was
provided for it. The bishops, abbots, and priors were
to meet annually, electing a Conservator Statutorum
who should act as Moderator, and hold his office till
the following year. The scheme may possibly have
been Alexander's own, for he greatly disliked the inter-
vention of foreign ecclesiastics. When in 1237 a
Legate wished to visit the kingdom, the King is
recorded by Matthew Paris as having told him that no
Legate had ever been there before (which, if he said it,
was very far from true, as they both must have known)
and that the inhabitants of his kingdom were *indomiti
et silvestres homines, humanum sanguinem sitientes*, wild
and savage men who thirsted for human gore, and whose
ongoings he could not undertake to control. The
Legate had possibly heard of the Bishop of Caithness,
and he decided not to make his visit : when Alexander
later allowed him to enter, he kept very carefully to
south of Forth.

All through the 'twenties, which were more or less
the King's twenties also, relations with England continued most amicable. That country was settling down
under the strong regency of Alexander's brother-in-

law, Hubert de Burgh, Earl of Kent. But the young
Henry was approaching such manhood as he ever was
to possess, and he was much under the influence of
the Poitevin Peter des Roches, Bishop of Winchester,
who hated De Burgh. In 1231 there was a breach
between Henry and the Regent. Princess Marjorie,
Alexander's youngest sister, had grown up, and was
very beautiful. Henry, already Alexander's brother-
in-law, desired to marry her. The anti-Burgh faction
saw their chance. The Earl of Pembroke (who possibly
wanted to marry her himself—he did marry her four
years later, at all events) objected that the match was
impolitic, as her elder sister was wife of Henry's
subject. Hints were apparently dropped too that De
Burgh had designs on the Scots throne, for Alexander's
marriage had proved childless, and the only male of
the dynasty save Alexander himself was the also childless John of Huntingdon. The match was not made,
and Henry—though not until 1236, after the Princess
had married Gilbert of Pembroke—married a daughter
of the Count of Provence : but Henry's relations with
De Burgh were not bettered, and those with his subjects
were also growing stormy, for Des Roches brought in
a swarm of hungry Poitevins, and Henry himself, who
now was into his twenties, was proving fickle, weak,
and extravagant, with no sense of responsibility as
ruler.

The peace continued, but it grew more brittle.
Henry had carried on a desultory war for the recovery
of the lost French lands. It was completely unsuccess-

ful, and he began to turn his eyes on Scotland. In
1234 he was tempted further by a disturbance in
Galloway, though it was not a rising against the Crown,
but, as in the Caithness affair, a breach of the peace
through local complications. Alan of Galloway died
in that year, and left no son. (He was a cousin by
marriage of the King's, for his wife had been Earl
David's eldest daughter.) He did leave three daughters,
Helen, wife of Roger de Quincy Earl of Winchester
(who became in her right the Constable of Scotland),
Christina, wife of the Earl of Albemarle, and Devorgilla, wife of a noble of Picardy, John Baliol, who had
also lands in England. By the common succession law,
the three ladies were co-heiresses of the province. Its
people strongly disliked the idea of partition, and
begged Alexander to take it as lapsed to the Crown.
It was not a male fief, however, and this was quite
illegal. He would not. They therefore invited
Thomas, a natural brother of the three ladies, to take
it over. He was married to a daughter of the late King
of Man, and had no difficulty in raising a force to
support him. In the summer of 1235 Alexander had
to take an army to Galloway, and there was a serious
action. The royal army got itself into a bog, and had
not the Highlanders of the Earl of Ross, who were used
to bogs, taken Thomas's men in flank, Alexander's
troops might have been badly defeated. They won,
however, and the revolt collapsed. Thomas fled to
Ireland : the local leaders arrived in the King's camp
next morning with halters round their necks . . . and

R

the province had hardly been restored to peace before it rose again, more seriously. Thomas returned, with his chief supporter Gilroy, and Hugh de Lacy, Earl of Ulster, the father of Alan of Galloway's first wife : the three swore blood-brotherhood, and having landed, burnt their ships to cut off the possibility of retreat. In spite of this desperate prelude, the attack came to nothing. The Bishop of Galloway, the Abbot of Melrose, and the Earl of Dunbar negotiated with the insurgent leaders. Thomas surrendered, and was imprisoned, and the luckless Irish, cut off from return, were massacred by the citizens of Glasgow, two of their leaders being torn by wild horses in order to discourage a repetition.

Henry, urged on by the Bishop of Winchester, took advantage of his brother-in-law's apparent embarrassment, and began to intrigue against him with his own overlord the Pope—not Honorius now but Gregory IX, who knew much less about Scotland. The information presented to His Holiness was rather carefully manipulated, the Treaties of Norham and Northampton of the preceding reign being telescoped with the Treaty of Falaise, while that of Canterbury was tactfully ignored. Gregory, pronouncing on the information given him, bade Alexander do homage to Henry for Scotland, and supported the old claim of York to control the Scots Church. Alexander, naturally, was annoyed. In the last few years he had helped his impecunious brother-in-law with handsome gifts of money (though he was careful to specify that they were not to be taken as a precedent) and he had carefully remained neutral during Henry's struggle with his barons. Now he was roused. In 1236 he counter-claimed the northern provinces of England, and married his sister Marjorie to the Earl of Pembroke, who was head of the English anti-royal party.

The Kings met at Newcastle. Alexander, in vigorous terms, claimed the northern counties as held by his grandfather Henry, pointed out John's non-performance of the bargain for which he had accepted 15,000 merks—or the half, for he had remitted the second instalment—and the breach of agreement over his sisters' marriages, and called on the northern barons to support him. Apparently they were willing to do this, and the breach of a promise to marry Margaret to Henry seems to have been admitted. The English barons at least supported Alexander against their own King, demanding satisfaction for him. Henry dared not begin a war without their support, and Alexander did not want one : he had only put forward his claim as a check to Henry's. The two Kings parted in peace, and at a Council held at York next year, both agreed to abandon their claims, and Alexander was offered and accepted lands worth £200 a year in the northern counties, at the annual rental of a hunting hawk. He was not to hold the castles, but received an impressive collection of other rights :

terras et homines dictarum terrarum cum omnibus libertatibus et libris consuetudinibus et quietandiis suis in bosco et plano, in pratis et pasturis, in aquis et molendinis, in viis et semitis, in stagnis et vivariis, in mariscis et piscariis, cum Sok et Sak, Tholl et Theam,

Infangenethef, Utfangenethef, Hamsoken, Grithbrek, Blodwit, Fyghtwyt, Ferdwit, Hengwit, Leyrwyt, Flemenesfrith, murdro et latrocinio, Forstall, infra tempus et extra tempus, et in omnibus locis, with a list of eighteen taxes, besides tolls.[1]

The dispute being thus amicably settled, the Kings went home, Queen Joan going with her sister-in-law on pilgrimage to Canterbury. Alexander never saw his wife again : she died in the South of England the next March (1238) and was buried in the nuns' church at Tarrant Crawford. Few Queens in history have a quieter grave, for the abbey and all its buildings have disappeared, and she lies unmarked in a hidden valley of Dorset, with a stream going gently through pasture under trees. Her death both left and solved a succession problem. Alexander was rising forty, and had no children. His three sisters were all married to English nobles, but perhaps rather fortunately, only one of them had a child, a girl who died young. His cousin, John of Huntingdon, Chester, and Lincoln, had died the year before. John's son had predeceased him, and the King was the only man of the house in the male line. John's sisters, who came next in the succession after the King's, were all married, however, and all of them had issue. The eldest, Margaret, had married Alan of Galloway : her son was dead, her daughters the Countess of Albemarle, who had only daughters, and Devorgilla, Lady Baliol, who had as yet no children. The second sister, Isobel, had married Robert Bruce, Lord of Annandale, the third, Ada, the English Lord

[1] Taxation, in Scotland, was still considered to be an emergency measure.

Hastings : and both had sons. The son of Isobel and Robert Bruce was thus the senior male after the King. Alexander, in Council at Scone, named him his heir if he himself should have no heirs of his body, thus blocking the claims of his English brothers-in-law. Then he set about finding himself a second wife. He seems to have thought of a sister of Henry's Queen and the Queen of France, for there are traces of negotiations. If they were ever seriously conducted, they fell through, however, and in 1239 he married a French lady of great beauty, Marie, daughter of the great Sieur de Coucy who had come to the English war in 1217. On the 4th September 1241 the claims of the English brothers-in-law were definitely superseded by the birth of a son, who was to be Alexander III.

The French marriage made the King much less popular in England, for Henry's inglorious French wars had continued, with a conspicuous absence of success. Alexander, however, had stayed firmly neutral, and when Henry went in person to the war, he left Alexander to guard the English marches, and betrothed his small daughter to the baby Prince of Scotland. Alexander carefully fulfilled the trust : but the Anglo-French war went on without success, ending in 1243 with Henry's formal surrender of Normandy and all his other fiefs north of the Loire—the patrimony of his house and of the Norman kings. It worsened English tempers, and inclined the English barons to consider a Scots war as a possible means of recovering prestige : and while Henry was still in France there was an 'incident' which very nearly caused one to explode.

In 1242 'all the knights of Scotland' were gathered at Haddington for a great tournament. Among them was Walter Bisset, of a Scoto-Norman house of the North-east, and the young Earl of Athol, nephew of Alan of Galloway. These two had a family feud between them to start with, and in the jousting Athol bore down Bisset. His lodging was burnt that night and he within it, and the Earl of Dunbar charged Bisset with the murder, and declared that William Bisset of Aboyne, head of the name, was art and part in it. Aboyne protested his innocence, and bade his own chaplain excommunicate the murderers, and the Queen herself gave him an alibi, for on the day of the murder she herself had been coming south under his escort. None the less John of Badenoch, the Red Comyn, and his uncle the Earl of Menteith raided Bisset's lands, as friends of the murdered man.

Alexander strongly objected to private war. He called the assailants to heel, and tried Walter Bisset at Forfar. Walter declined a jury, and claimed wager of battle. It went against him, and Alexander banished his family, sparing their lives on condition they took an oath to fight against the enemies of the Cross. (Public opinion was so hot against them that he had to smuggle them secretly out of the kingdom.) The oath weighed lightly, or they gave it an individual interpretation. Walter's nephew John, who was held to be the actual murderer, went to Ireland, where

De Burgh gave him lands in Ulster. Walter went to England, with a grievance, and made the most of the ill-feeling roused there by the French marriage. He stirred up Henry to that claim of suzerainty over Scotland that, treaties or no treaties, was for centuries yet to be a regular prelude to English attacks upon the Scottish kingdom:[1] he also accused Alexander of resetting an English fugitive, Geoffrey Marsh. Henry listened, and let himself be persuaded. He asked the Count of Flanders (his wife's uncle) to lend a fleet, called up twenty Irish chiefs, and took the whole force of England to Newcastle.

Alexander was, not unnaturally, angry. He swore that Henry had no kind of right over so much as an inch of Scottish soil : and an equally angry kingdom flocked to his banner, raised at Caddenlee, not far from where Gala Water joins the Tweed. Matthew Paris, a level-headed Englishman who had not lost his liking for Alexander, and had no illusions over Henry's claim, found that army impressive. There were few knights compared to Henry's great force of them : but the Scots, as later, relied upon their foot, a most unusual principle at the time. The Scots spearman was not mere stuffing for a gap, but a fighter who would stand up to cavalry, who in another couple of genera-tions was to scandalise Europe by charging cavalry, and smashing it, in face of all the accepted rules of war. These men came now as to a crusade, with their priests'

---

[1] It was actually raised, by an eminent English lawyer, in 1705, as a reason against federation of the kingdoms.

support : *omnes unanimi confessi et praedicantium consolatione quia pro patria sua iusti dimicaturi forent animati, mori minime formidabant,* all with one mind (being shriven and encouraged by the comfort of their preachers, because they were justly fighting for their country) did not fear death at all.

They had not to face it either, as it happened. Matthew was not alone in finding them impressive. The King marched them to Ponteland and waited there, inviting the Northern English barons to join him. Henry found that his war had become less popular. His brother Richard, Earl of Cornwall, and the Archbishop of York, opened negotiations. The English claims were reduced to a statement of grievances : Alexander had built castles in Galloway and Lothian, had sheltered an English traitor, and appeared inclined to make an alliance with France. Alexander was ready for war, but he did not want one. He offered to pledge himself to form no alliance with Henry's enemies and not to invade his territory unless he found himself unjustly dealt with. Henry undertook not to make war on Scotland save in self-defence. The question of the castles was left to lie, and the opposing armies went home in peace.

For the rest of the reign there was no threat from England. Under the peaceful regime, Scotland was thriving. The country had recovered from the slack rule of William, and was continuing along the lines of progress laid down by David. The King's Law and the King's Peace were enforced now over the whole of mainland Scotland, and firmly, for Alexander dismissed his Justiciar, one of the most powerful nobles of the kingdom, for not checking the Comyn attack upon the Bissets. The organisation was tightened and defined. The privileges of sanctuary, for instance, were carefully defended from abuse, and another abuse was checked : those lords who had taken advantage of legal fictions to get criminals off from their just punishment and thus acquire useful bands of broken men whose lives hung on obedience without scruple, were dealt with, and vigorously. Within this framework of peace and stability, there was room to thrive, and care was taken for thriving. Very early in the reign, legislation was put in hand for agriculture : there seems to have been an attempt to increase arable as distinct from pastoral land, and a fixed minimum of cultivation was enforced on all tenants. The towns too prospered, and there are traces of new industries. We hear of a very notable ship being built at Inverness in 1249, for the Count of St Pol, a great magnate of Brittany : as he might have been expected to buy his ships from the yards of Southern England or the Low Countries, it suggests that Inverness had a reputation.

Alexander cared also for the spiritual and intellectual well-being of the country, and he was always a steady friend to the Church, which was his in turn, and passionately loyal to Crown and State. The stabilising of its constitution, noted above, must considerably have helped its efficiency. Certainly, there was great activity, and Alexander, like Alexander I and David I, stimulated it by keeping his kingdom in contact with the new religious movements on the Continent. Balmerino Abbey, which he and Queen Ermengarde founded in 1229, was for Benedictines, who were brought from Kelso : but quite near it, at Pluscardine, he himself established a house for Valliscaulians, a new, reformed, branch of the Cistercians. His chief favour, however, was for the new friars. In 1230, only nine years after Dominic's death at Bologna, he brought in the Friars Preachers or Dominicans. They were popular at once, and soon he had settled groups of them at strategic points over the kingdom, on what was obviously a national mission : they had houses at Berwick, Edinburgh, Ayr, Stirling, Perth, Aberdeen, Elgin, and Inverness. In 1231, only five years after Francis's death, he brought Greyfriars also to Berwick and Roxburgh.

His example was followed. The reign brought an outburst of ecclesiastical building surpassing even that under David I. In the North and West local notables founded Valliscaulian houses at Beauly and Ardchattan in Lorne. Fearchar of Ross founded Ferne for the Premonstratensians : it may have been a relic of his share in the Galloway war, for he brought his canons all the way from Whithorn. Duncan Earl of Carrick brought Cluniacs from Paisley to found Crossraguel, and Walter Stewart imported the English double order of St Gilbert of Sempringham—unsuccessfully, as it turned out—to Dalmoulin in Ayrshire.

The churchmen themselves were not backward. Dornoch Cathedral was built and given a constitution by St Gilbert de Moray, who after the murder of the Bishop of Caithness had been sent to pacify that turbulent district, and, being saint and statesman, had admirably succeeded. Elgin Cathedral was also built in this reign, and the noble choir and undercroft of Glasgow, while there was a whole harvest of parish churches. Bishop David of St Andrews alone is recorded as having consecrated a hundred and forty churches, most of them parish ones. Some of these of course may have simply been enlarged, and some of them, such as the nuns' church at North Berwick, are obviously rebuildings. St Giles's, Edinburgh, was one of his consecrations, on the 6th October of 1243.

By the end of his forties Alexander could look on a kingdom at peace and thriving vigorously. His firm dealing had coped with the threat of English war, and he had no reason to anticipate its recurrence : England, indeed, was clearly heading for a civil one, for Henry had followed in his father's footsteps, and his barons were following in those of theirs. The most serious foreign danger was from the turbulent Gall-Gael of the Isles, who might very easily bring in Norway behind them. His growing desire to bring the Isles under control induced him to offer to buy them from Hakon of Norway. Hakon, who knew as well as Alexander that the Isles were an excellent base for invasion of Scotland, replied that he was not in need

of money : and a second embassy had the same
result.

In 1248 Duncan of Argyle, vassal of both Alexander
and Hakon, died, leaving his great fiefs to his son Ewen,
whom an English contemporary describes as *miles
strenuus et elegantissimus*. Alexander was tempted to
what his own time considered the only unjust action
of his reign. He tried to induce Ewen to do him
homage not only for Argyle but for the Sudreys.
Ewen answered that he had done homage for those to
Hakon, and was told that no man could serve two
masters. Ewen declared that he could, if they were
at peace, as Alexander and Hakon were at the time,
and when the King would not listen, offered to resign
his Norse fiefs. Alexander, who wanted them, would
not accept the arrangement. In 1249 he raised a fleet
and took it up the West Coast to the Firth of Lorne.
Ewen refused either to surrender or to fight against
his overlord, and fled to the Lews . . . and no further
action was taken, for while the fleet still lay in the Firth
of Lorne, the King was stricken with a mortal fever.
They landed him on the island of Kerrera, that lies
like a long cloud in the mouth of the Firth, and there
he died upon the 8th of July.

He was barely fifty. His death plunged Scotland
into another minority, for his son was still some weeks
from his eighth birthday. Yet the boy succeeded at
once, without opposition, and so well had his father
builded, or rebuilded, that in spite of serious dangers
in his boyhood, the structure held firm until he was a

man and could head it, and the steady progress of the
previous reign went on unimpeded, though not, for a
while, untroubled.

Alexander III was brought to Scone to his crowning.
There was dispute. What was for long to be the
regular pattern of the recurrent minorities threatened
already. Some argued that the King could not be
crowned until he had been knighted : it is possible
that Alan Durward the Justiciar, the husband of the
dead king's natural daughter, may have desired the
honour of knighting him. Walter Comyn, Earl of
Menteith, cadet of a very powerful Norman house,[1]
objected to the objection, and the boy was girded with
the royal sword by the Bishop of St Andrews, who
gave him the oath, translating its Latin for him into
French. Then they passed in procession from the
Abbey Kirk, to where under the great Cross within
the kirkyard the Sacred Stone stood covered with silk
and gold—the stone that Fergus had brought long
since from Ireland. On this they enthroned him, like
his predecessors for seven hundred years. The lords
did homage, and an ancient sennachie in a scarlet gown
recited in Gaelic the King's long pedigree, the fourteen

[1] The Comyns were to play a major part in the affairs of the next
three generations. William, son of William the Conqueror's Earl
of Northumberland, Robert de Comines, had been Chancellor to
David I. His nephew had married King Donald Bàn's granddaughter : their son had married the heiress of Buchan, and his
son again, this Walter, the heiress of Menteith. They had now,
besides two earldoms in the family, immense estates in Badenoch
and Tynedale, and there were over thirty knights of the name.

generations back to Alpin, then back again to Fergus son of Erc, nearly eight centuries before that time . . . and back again through cloud to the Princess Scota, daughter of Pharaoh, and Gathelus her husband, son of Cecrops.

The split at the coronation was prophetic. The main notes of the King's thirty-seven years of reign are three-fold : on the one hand there is the continuance, in spite of threats, of progress and the increase of pros-perity, and linked with that the final consolidation, the drawing in beneath the Scottish Crown of all the present territory of Scotland, save the Northern Isles : but on the other hand, there is the first, scarcely ob-served, beginning of what was to be the worst of Scottish dangers, the emergence, among her magnates, of two factions of which the main interest of one lay outside the kingdom—of the National Party and the pro-English one, that ever thereafter have made the fundamental separation that underlies all Scottish politics. The latter have always been a minority : but a minority always in alliance with an England whose population was five to eight times our own, whose position was hard against an open border, and in whose politics since she existed it has generally been a cardinal principle that Scotland must somehow be obliterated. There was, no doubt, an abstract logical case for the union of the two countries into one state : each was already built up of several small ones. But in politics, logic counts less than psychology : and psychologically it was too late. Under the descendants of Malcolm III,

Scotland had become a definite national entity. Under the Plantagenets, England was now another. It would still have been possible to federate the two under one crown, for they were on terms of increasing friendliness, and there was obvious wisdom in close alliance. In time, if the union had come peaceably before the Three Hundred Years' War, even incorporation might have been possible without ill results. But the greed and the violence of Edward I made it impossible : the basic weakness of *machtpolitik* has never been more clearly demonstrated. By 1500, though intrigue with England was a common expedient of disloyal nobles, the two countries were further apart than in 1200 or even 1300. It was not only the memory of long and brutal assaults upon the one side, the shame of constant unsuccessful aggression upon the other, that held them apart by them : their national cultures had developed on different lines. In the twelfth century England was more a Continental country than Scotland : in the thirteenth she was at least equally so. By 1500, after two centuries of disastrous and humiliating French wars, England had turned her back upon the Continent, and her outlook was insular. Scotland, on the contrary, was still an integral part of Europe, and her whole outlook was European. Federation, under one crown, was still feasible, if it should come peaceably, as in fact it did : and when it came the Scots did all in their power to make it successful : had English resentment for the old unsuccess been sunk after 1603, had the Religious Wars not begun once more, the

Union of Crowns might well have had happy results. Political incorporation, with its corollary of social, however, could only come with harm to all that was characteristically Scottish, including much of what was best in Scotland : and if England was to pay for her insistence by a succession of Scots in her high places, the result to Scotland was even less of gain.

It is worth noting—and it shows how the union of Scotland had progressed—that the division of the parties now was not a racial one. Alan Durward's surname is Anglian, but with him was the young Earl of Athol, of the House of Galloway ; the Earl of Dunbar, descended from Malcolm II ; and the Earl of Strathearn, as well as that Robert Bruce of Annandale whom the young King's birth had dispossessed of his heirship, and William de Douglas, of a native house of Strathclyde. The head of the national party was of Norman stock, and his followers included John Baliol and several men who were of Norman descent.

The first public act of the reign was the canonisation of St Margaret, and the transference of her remains to a splendid new shrine adorned with gold and gems : its bare stone base still lies, confronting the weather, in the roofless choir of her abbey kirk at Dunfermline. The ceremony took place on the 19th June of 1250, in the presence of the young King and his mother.

The party divisions among the nobles were not very long in making themselves felt. In 1250 King Henry projected joining Louis IX of France in a crusade. He induced the churches of his own dominions to grant him a tenth of their revenues to defray its cost, and then tried to persuade the Pope to grant him a tenth of the Scottish Church's as well . . . on the grounds that he was overlord of Scotland. The Pope, however, snubbed him heavily, telling him very curtly that he would do nothing *in praejudicium Regiae dignitatis*, derogatory to royal dignity, and that such a grant *in alterius Regno alieni est penitus inauditum*, in the kingdom of another, foreign, monarch was almost unheard of. The Scots crusaders, however, had to appeal to His Holiness for a special bull defending them from Henry's attempted extortions.

The incident caused ill-feeling between the countries, and there were even rumours of possible war. Henry submitted, however, and put in hand the arrangements for the marriage of the boy King and his daughter Margaret, to whom Alexander had been betrothed in his cradle. At Christmas of 1251 the affair took place, very splendidly, at York, the Queen-mother Marie being present with her son and a great retinue of Scots and French. (The splendour was somewhat offset by the bride's scant dowry, 5000 merks, a sum which Henry admitted that he already owed to the bridegroom's father, and which he did his best to avoid paying.) On Christmas Day the boy was knighted by Henry, with twenty other squires of high degree, and next day the children were married in York Minster : Alexander was ten, the Princess a little older. Alexander then did homage to his father-in-law for the English fiefs he had inherited : and Henry tried to

s

trap the child into admitting that the homage should be done for Scotland also. It is probable that his guardians, who knew Henry, had foreseen this very thing, and drilled the boy. He kept his head now, and answered Henry firmly that he had come in peace, at that King's invitation, to marry the Princess, and not to discuss important matters of state, on which he could not speak without his Council. To press him meant a scandal, perhaps a war, and Henry had to let the matter drop.

Even then the wedding did not go peacefully. The English Marshal (the Earl of Norfolk, husband of the King's aunt) claimed Alexander's horse, as his perquisite at the knighting of Henry's vassals. The Scots were annoyed. Alexander had accepted the accolade from his father-in-law, not his feudal superior. There was muttering, and the Earl did not get the horse . . . and then more serious matters came to light, for the Earls of Menteith and Mar then accused Durward, aided by the Abbot of Dunfermline, who was Chancellor, of trying to get the Pope to legitimise his wife, Alexander's half-sister, so as to make his daughter heir to the Crown. Durward's previous attitude had roused suspicion, and there was a stir. Some of the persons concerned fled back to Scotland, and the Abbot had to surrender the Great Seal, which was given to a priest called Gamelin, a very fortunate choice, as it turned out. And Henry sent as a counsellor to the young King an English knight Geoffrey de Langley, who as Keeper of the Royal Forests in England had made himself acutely unpopular, and who proceeded to do the same in Scotland.

Alexander went home, and a new Council was appointed, whose leaders were the Earls of Menteith and Mar and John Baliol—the leaders, that is, of the anti-Durward faction, while the Earl of Buchan, who like Menteith was a Comyn, soon after became one Justiciar, the other being an unidentifiable Fergus, probably a Highland chief. When in August of 1253 Henry sailed for Bordeaux, Alan Durward went with him, and won his favour by service in his wars. That year also saw the beginning of a dispute over the see of St Andrews, which ended in the consecration of Gamelin the Chancellor two years later.

Henry pursued his intrigues. In 1254 he again asked Innocent IV for a grant from the church revenues of Scotland. Innocent refused : but he died very soon thereafter, and his successor Alexander IV yielded the grant, on Henry's promise not to make it a precedent.

The factions were still at odds, and by 1255 were laying down what was to be the regular pattern for the recurrent minorities of the next three and a half centuries—two parties trying to win control of the sovereign, with England intervening as ally of one of them, and endeavouring to make herself mistress of the kingdom. In the summer of that year Henry complained that his daughter was not well treated, marched to the Border at the head of an army, sent an embassy headed by the Earl of Gloucester, and announced his formal protection of Durward's party, by name, against those who had wronged ' our dearest son Alexander ' or the Queen. He then backed this beginning by denouncing the King's Council, the Comyns and their party, as hostile and aggressive, but declared that he meant no injury to the King, and had no intention of trying to break the marriage.

The Scots Council met at Edinburgh, where the King and Queen were, and adjourned to Stirling : and hardly were they out of the city when Alan Durward and the Earl of Dunbar joined Gloucester, seized the Castle by a *coup de main*, garrisoned it, and took the royal children, Gloucester sending to the Queen's father a pitiful complaint that she was forced to live in a castle like a prison, *salubri aere et virore ut iuxta mare penitus destitutum*, almost destitute of verdure and wholesome air, being near the sea, and was not allowed to share her husband's bed. (He was thirteen and she perhaps fourteen.) Gloucester remedied what he could of these complaints, and returned to Henry, who had fallen back. That anxious parent then advanced to Newcastle, loudly announcing that he meant no harm to Alexander, but that in order to give him good advice and to maintain the liberties of his kingdom he intended from fatherly love to talk to him, and sent safe-conducts for both King and Queen.

The Comyn party marched on Edinburgh, but were too late. Alan Durward had brought the children to Roxburgh, and thence to Wark. The Kings had an interview there, and parted in peace, Alexander leaving his young wife with her mother, who was ill. Early in

September Henry came to Roxburgh on a state visit. The Kings went in procession to Kelso Abbey Kirk, and there on the 20th September the boy Alexander was induced to put his seal to what the Melrose Chronicler, and a good many of his contemporaries, described as ' a certain abominable document,' *quoddam nefandissimum scriptum*—a proclamation that gave the government to the Durward party, which, in effect, meant giving it to Henry. The Bishops of Glasgow and Dunblane, the Chancellor Gamelin, Bishop-elect of St Andrews, Mar, the two Comyn earls, and John Baliol were all removed from about the royal person until they should make reparation for their misdeeds : and the whole Durward party were appointed to be the King's guardians for the next seven years, and to govern the whole realm during that time. They were not to be removed without *Henry's* consent, and he named himself Principal Councillor to the King of Scots . . . and forfeited English lands held by John Baliol and another member of the national party.

The Comyns were now out of power. The Bishop of Glasgow, however, insisted, against the wishes of the Regents, on consecrating Gamelin to his see. The Regents tried to get the Pope to prevent him, and were too late. Then they tried to make Gamelin pay a sum of money. He refused, and they outlawed him and seized his revenues, whereon he went to Rome. In the summer of 1256 the King and Queen paid a state visit to England, where they were feasted at London, and Alexander was invested with Huntingdon : and

Henry commanded his own northern nobles to help
his son-in-law against his rebels—i.e. to harry the
Scots national party. Gamelin, by this time, had
reached Rome, and on the 16th December the Pope
wrote to Henry, bidding him reconcile the Regents
and Gamelin, and condemning the formers' ' empty
and pernicious counsels.' Henry refused to do so, but
his own Council forced him to submit.

The young King meanwhile showed signs of growing
up. He was still only fifteen, but was clearly refusing
to rank any more as a child. In February 1257 he
wrote to Henry from Roxburgh, saying that the Comyns
and Mar had been beseeching him for ' a certain form '
concerning the peace of the realm. Explanations were
to be given verbally, so we know no more. But Gamelin
had returned, cleared by the Pope from his opponents'
charges, and with a Papal excommunication for them.
The Council were stubborn, but having been excommunicated, first generally and then by name, they
surrendered. At this point, too, Queen Marie, who
had been for some time abroad and had married John
de Brienne, son of the King of Jerusalem, returned
with her husband, much to Henry's annoyance. Her
sympathies were with the national party : and the
excommunication of Henry's supporters gave a good
excuse for getting her son out of their hands, as it was
obviously unsuitable that the boy should be brought
up by people who were under the ban of the Church.
On the 28th of October Menteith raided Kinross,
took the King from his bed, and carried him off to

Stirling. He also contrived to get hold of the Great Seal, which he gave to William Wishart, Gamelin's Archdeacon.

The Comyn party were again in the saddle, and as a gesture for Henry's benefit they made in March a treaty of alliance with the Welsh, with whom he was at war, by no means successfully. This card played, they invited Durward's party to a conference at Roxburgh, and came there with the King and an army from the Highlands and Galloway. Durward induced them to adjourn to Forfar, but instead of going to meet them fled to England.

Under the influence of the Comyn regents (and probably by no means unwillingly) Alexander, who now was nearly seventeen, began to take a firm tone with his father-in-law. In the summer of 1258 Henry, who had intervened all through on the highest moral grounds of pure affection, had those grounds rather awkwardly cut from under his feet by a letter in which his son-in-law pointed out that it was now more than six years from his wedding, and his wife's dowry had not yet been paid. Henry was apologetic : he was ill, his Treasurer was dead, and he could not do anything until he could appoint a new one, adding meekly *quod si placet, graviter non feratis*, please don't be annoyed. Apparently he decided that it would be as well henceforth to be on peaceful terms with both Scots parties, and sent up an embassy, headed by Simon de Montfort, to mediate between them. In September Alexander came to Melrose, where he met another English em-

bassy, led by the Earl of Hertford, the Earl of Albemarle (who had married Baliol's sister-in-law, Christina
of Galloway) and John Baliol, who of course was an
English lord as well as a Scots one. The King had
left his army at Jedburgh, and suspecting that the
English had planned his abduction (it would not have
been the last English plot of the kind) he adjourned to
that town, where the presence of an army in the Jed-
wood could adequately chaperon discussion. They
spent three weeks there. The episode marks the real
beginning of the King's reign, and a beginning highly
characteristic. By the end of that time, the factions
were reconciled, and a new Council created from both
parties. Queen Marie and her husband were upon it,
then four men from each side—the two Comyn earls,
with Mar and Gamelin, and from the other party
Durward, the Steward, Robert de Meyners, and
Gilbert de Hay : and the Earl of Buchan was made
Justiciar. Menteith died soon after, officially by a
fall from his horse, according to rumour poisoned by
his wife, who married an inconspicuous English knight,
and was forfeited of her share of the earldom, which
went to her sister's husband, the Steward's brother.
Menteith had done his work, however. Henry's
intrigues had been parried, the King was near manhood,
and promising well to be both man and king : soon he
would take the realm in his own hands. And indeed
thereafter, for the twenty-eight years Alexander was
to rule, there was steady peace and unity within
Scotland. Durward lived for another twenty years,

but during that time he remained the King's faithful servant.

Alexander III, Alexander the Peaceable, grew up in many ways very like his father. He had a noble presence and great charm, united with no less force of character. Even his enemies loved him, says Fordun : but he had so much innate authority that a man would have hanged himself if the King bade him. His strength came from clear vision and self-control : *iuste dictus est rex, eo quod recte se rexit et suos.* Much of the love he won depended on trust, and the trust on his uncompromising justice to high and low, *jus unicuique tribuens,* giving each his own. The Lanercost Chronicler accuses him of looseness with women : but the Chronicler of that time is intensely and spitefully hostile to the Scots royal house, and there is no sign anywhere of any illegitimate child of the King's. He was never tried as a soldier, a fact which he owed to his skill in government : but his one serious war, though with little fighting, had important issues, and virtually completed the shaping of Scotland.

Henry, apparently, had not given up his hopes, even after the diplomatic defeat of Jedburgh. In 1259, on the news of Menteith's death (which perhaps had roused them) he sent up an ambassador to the Regents. The mission was secret : whatever it may have been, they were annoyed. There were some very discreet negotiations. Alexander was invited to England to discuss unspecified matters of importance, and did

not go, sending instead a letter which in terms carefully
vague offers Henry satisfaction on the guarantee (again
unspecified) that he had given. Alan Durward was one
of the embassy who bore it, but Buchan and the
Chancellor were the others. Robertson thinks—and
it is very likely—that what Henry may have been
attempting to do was to win Alexander as ally against
his own barons, who had just forced from him the
Provisions of Oxford. Certainly when the English
civil war did break out, in earnest, in 1264, a Scots
contingent fought for Henry at Lewes : and according
to Boniface VIII in 1300, Henry did ask Scots aid, and
was extremely careful to specify that it was as a favour,
not as a feudal duty.

In the autumn of 1260 Alexander and the Queen did
visit England. He wished to see his fief of Huntingdon,
to claim the lands his father had held in Tynedale, and
to press for the Queen's dowry, which was still unpaid.
When they were once fairly over the Border, the Queen
informed him that she was expecting a child : she was
devoted to her own family, and wanting her baby to
be born among them had concealed her condition.
There was some alarm, for Alexander and the Scots
knew Henry by now, and the child would be the immediate heir to the throne. Alexander allowed his
wife to have her way, and left her to spend the winter
with her mother, but before he left her he took the
precaution of making Henry swear upon his soul that
the Queen should be free to go home forty days after
the birth, and that if either her husband or she should

die, the child should be given to certain lords of Scotland, *sine dilatione qualibet et difficultate, vel cujuscumque contradictionis obstaculo*, without delay, opposition, or argument.

The child was born at Windsor, on the 28th February 1261, a daughter, christened Margaret after her mother. And the visit seems to have caused a real rapprochement : the King was nearly twenty, and Henry either liked him or realised that he could not safely oppose him now, or both : at least he ceased to intrigue, and for the rest of the reign there was peace and genuine friendliness with England.

Alexander now was the real head of the state. Relations with England being successfully quieted, he followed his father's policy, and looked north and west. In the summer of 1261 he sent an embassy to Norway, perhaps to renew the attempt to purchase the Isles. At this time it would seem that the Earl of Ross and others of Alexander's northern vassals had made private wars on Hakon's in the Isles : and Hakon detained the ambassadors and claimed satisfaction. Alexander, at this time, was demanding the last 1000 merks of his wife's dowry : Henry could only raise 500 merks (which he declared pathetically was all the money he possessed) so in lieu of the balance he intervened as mediator. Hakon answered that he meant to keep peace with Scotland, but in 1262 his vassals again complained of raids by their Scots neighbours, and he decided on war with Alexander.

Through that winter and spring he made vast pre-

parations. In July 1263 he sailed at last with the finest
fleet that ever had left Norway, a hundred ships and
his own royal galley, new-built of oak with a gilded
dragon prow. In August they lay in the Orkneys,
shadowed by a ringed eclipse of the sun. The chiefs
of the Isles came and joined him, and did their homage.
Then he sailed south through the Isles. As he lay off
Gigha, Ewen of Argyle came to him. He was Hakon's
vassal for his island lands, but Alexander's for the
Mainland ones, and he would not fight against the
King of Scots. Hakon pressed him, and he denounced
his Norse fealty, which involved, of course, surrendering the Norse fiefs. The stout old Hakon, who knew
a man when he saw him, allowed him to go in safety,
with rich gifts, and Ewen promised to make peace if
he could.

Alexander also had made his preparations, calling
up all the levies of the West, and building ships at
Ayr to watch the coast. Already there were raids, and
Bute was attacked by one Ruari, a laird of the island,
who had been outlawed by Alexander II : he massacred
the garrison of Rothesay. Hakon rounded Kintyre,
sailed up the Firth of Clyde, and lay off Arran. Negotiations were opened. Alexander sent certain friars to
him, and Hakon sent an envoy in return to a town in
Cunningham where the King then was. It seemed for
a while that they might come to terms. Alexander
admitted Hakon's right to the Hebrides, but he claimed
the islands of the Firth of Clyde, Bute, Arran, and the
Cumbraes. The discussion dragged on : it may indeed

have been lengthened purposely, to give the Scots further time for preparations, and allow the weather to break. Hakon grew impatient, and finally sent one Kolbein to the King, telling Alexander to meet him with his army, and either settle the matter, or fight it out.

It was now September. The Norsemen's provisions were becoming exhausted, and the weather was threatening. Hakon broke off the discussion, and sent sixty of his ships to raid Loch Long, with Magnus of Man and certain chiefs of the Isles. They dragged ships overland to Loch Lomond, and plundered the whole country as far as Stirling. Alexander's army lay in Cunningham, watching the sky and waiting on the weather. On the last day of the month it blew a gale, and the Norse fleet suffered very heavily. Several vessels were dismasted, and Hakon's flagship, with five anchors out, dragged her moorings and collided with another, while some were driven ashore on the coast by Largs. The coast beacons, laid in readiness, were lighted, and the countrymen came out to attack the wrecks, but were driven off. The gale was moderating, and on the 2nd October Hakon landed a number of men to save the cargoes. A Scots force came down on them : it was hardly an army, as the army had the whole Ayrshire coast to watch. There was a body of knights, who of course were more quickly moved than infantry, and with them what seems to have been the local levy. The King, apparently, was not present, and they were led by Alexander the Steward. The Norse insisted on Hakon going back to his ship, and stood by the wrecks, and there was a wild fight then upon the shore. The gale rose again, and no Norse reinforcements could land. The Norsemen, outnumbered, put up a gallant fight until the darkness : it was already late in the afternoon.

The end was a victory for the Steward's men. Largs was a skirmish rather than a battle : it was won by the weather before the fighting began. But in its issues it had great importance, for it ended what had been a most threatening war. Hakon set fire to the wrecks and sailed away. The Irish invited him to come south as their ally against England, but he was short of provisions and the winds were foul. He sailed back through the Isles, much harried by stormy weather, and came to the Orkneys to winter there in Kirkwall, where in November he fell gravely ill. He lay there while they read to him from the Sagas, and on the 15th of December he died. Till spring he lay in state in Kirkwall Cathedral, and then they bore him home to his grave in Bergen.

It is said that the day when the news of Hakon's death reached Alexander was also that which saw the birth of his son : a Prince of Scotland, called Alexander also, was born at Jedburgh on the 21st of January 1264. Soon after, the chiefs of the Orkneys asked for terms. The Scottish answer was unfavourable, and in the summer Magnus, the new King of Norway, sent ambassadors to make peace. Alexander was not unwilling, but his terms were harder than they at first would grant.

He had already set about pacifying the Hebrides : Alan Durward and the Earls of Mar and Buchan had carried the business out, with a heavy hand. Proposals were also made for an expedition against Man, but Magnus of Man came to Alexander at Dumfries and made a treaty : he would hold Man as Alexander's vassal, and send ten ships whenever they were required, if the King would defend him against reprisals by Norway. He died the next year, and the island passed under the Scottish Crown.

In 1265 Alexander re-opened the negotiations, sending up (as the Melrose Chronicler tells with pride) one Reginald, a most eloquent monk of Melrose. Moved by Reginald's eloquence, or by the fact that Alexander was now in *de facto* possession, Magnus agreed to sell, and by a treaty made at Perth on the 2nd of July 1266 defined the terms. Save for the ecclesiastical jurisdiction of the Archbishop of Drontheim over their bishop, Magnus resigned all claim upon the Isles, in consideration of 4000 merks, and a subsidy of 100 merks a year. The Hebrides were to be under Scots Law, but those inhabitants who wished to leave should be free to do so with their goods and gear, and all who had fought against Scotland should be amnestied. The Isles thus returned to be part of Scotland again, and except for Orkney and Shetland, which were not Scots for another two hundred years, and for Berwick and Man, lost to England during the Three Hundred Years' War, the boundaries of the kingdom were as now.

While the affair was still in progress, war had broken

out in England between Henry and his barons. As was said above, a Scots force (which included John Baliol and Robert Bruce) fought for Henry at Lewes in May 1264, and suffered heavily : the Scots lords were captured, as was Henry himself, and Simon de Montfort imprisoned them at Dover. In August of the next year, however, Henry's son Edward defeated and killed Montfort at Evesham by the Severn, and some little time thereafter this same Prince Edward, who was to know Scotland better before he died and be one of the forces that went to shape her spirit, came to visit his sister the Queen at Haddington. They say he was greatly charmed with his niece and nephew.

1266 brought a good deal of ecclesiastical trouble, and the threat of worse. Henry, as was said already, had managed during his son-in-law's minority to lay hands on some part of the Scots Church's revenues. It had been distinctly stated at the time that the grant was not to be a precedent : but in 1266 his overlord the Pope sent Cardinal de' Fieschi to arbitrate between Henry and his contumacious barons : and the Cardinal thereupon wrote to the Scots prelates demanding a subsidy towards his expenses, of four merks from each parish kirk and six from cathedrals. The King put his foot down and forbade the extortion, and his clergy made him a gift of 2000 merks, to defray the cost of an appeal to the Pope, while as a sort of solatium to Fieschi they sent him a gift of sixpence for every merk he had demanded from them : a merk, by the way, is thirteen shillings and fourpence.

Unfortunately, Alexander soon thereafter found himself in the unusual position of being at loggerheads with his clergy himself. One Sir John de Dunmore, an old supporter of the Comyn party, had a quarrel with the Canons of St Andrews. They excommunicated him. The King took up his cause. Bishop Gamelin, who had always been the King's loyal supporter, thereon excommunicated all Sir John's backers, politely excepting, however, the King and Queen. The clergy appealed to the Pope's Legate, who was still in England, and he made to come north, when Sir John discreetly saved the situation by submitting. Alexander forbade the Legate to enter the kingdom, and it is pleasant to add that he thought no worse of Bishop Gamelin for withstanding him. Trouble was not over, however. The Pope and the Legate were both strongly pro-English : when the latter called a Council of the two English provinces to London in 1268 he demanded the attendance of the Scots prelates. They declined : they did in fact send a deputation, but only with a sort of watching brief . . . not uncalled for, as another crusade, the last, was in preparation, and the Cardinal induced the Pope to grant Henry the tenths of *both* Churches for it. The Scots clergy refused, declaring that they had to equip their own crusaders, and the Pope had to give way. Many Scots in fact went on that last venture under St Louis of France, and many died, among them the Earl of Athol, before Tunis, and Adam Earl of Carrick, who died at Acre and left the young wife through

T

whom he held the earldom to marry again and bear a notable son.

In November of 1272 King Henry died. His son Edward was on the Crusade in Palestine, and was not crowned till August of 1274. Alexander and Margaret went to the coronation, in great splendour, for the Kings of Scots at this time were very wealthy. Alexander seems to have doubted his brother-in-law, for before he would accept the invitation he was at pains to get a clear statement from him that his coming implied no sort of vassalage. It was Margaret's last visit to her native country, for on the next 26th of February she died at Cupar, leaving besides Princess Margaret, just fourteen, and Prince Alexander, who was turned eleven, a baby, Prince David, not quite two years old. Though in her childhood she had, perhaps unconsciously, made trouble between her father and her husband, she had helped, as she grew up, to keep good relations between Alexander and her family, by whom she seems to have been much beloved. Until the succession was jeopardised nine years later, the King made no attempt to marry again.

Relations with England continued to be good. When in September of 1275 there was a revolt in Man, led by a bastard son of its late King, the leaders of the force that put it down were John Comyn of Badenoch and an English baron. In 1277, however, there was tension. The Justiciar of Lothian had held a court at Tweedmouth, on the English side of the river. Edward complained, and Alexander offered a commission to settle the precise line of the March. The matter dragged on into 1279, and in 1278 Edward allowed an ominous glimpse of his mind. Alexander had never done homage for his English fiefs, but in autumn of that year he proposed to come south and do so. Edward shows, in a letter to one of his bishops, that he was trying to convince himself that the King's homage would be done for Scotland. They met at Tewkesbury : Edward would not accept the homage at the time, saying that he wished to have his Council about him, and it was therefore done later at Westminster. Now, there are two records of the ceremony. The English one bears an impossible date : it is the day when the homage *was to have been done*, but we know (from Edward himself) that it had not been done at a time nearly three weeks later : and on the day assigned to it in the record we know that Edward was not near the place. Moreover, the actual terms of the homage itself have been written in on top of an erasure. They represent Alexander as doing homage for ' all the lands I hold of the King of England,' with no phrase of definition or exception. But the Register of Dunfermline gives a very full account of the ceremony. It took place upon the 28th October. Alexander did homage for the English lands, ' reserving my kingdom,' whereon the Bishop of Norwich declared that Edward's right to homage for Scotland was also reserved, and Alexander answered, loudly and clearly, ' To homage for my kingdom none has right, save God alone, and to God alone will I give it.' And when the Earl of

Carrick, Robert Bruce, the son of old Robert Bruce of Annandale, rose to take the customary oath for his master, Alexander added, after he had spoken, ' For the lands I hold of you in the Kingdom of England.' The situation was thus very clearly stated, and peace lasted for another decade and more. But already there was a thought in Edward's mind. . . .

Indeed, the stage was being set, though invisibly yet, for the great drama of so few years later. Its personages, in fact, were appearing already : King Edward himself was to play a leading part. In 1268 John Baliol had died, and the head of his house was his son and Devorgilla's, a lethargic young man, the heir to Galloway. In 1274 the nephew of Bishop Wishart of St Andrews, Robert Wishart, was consecrated Bishop of Glasgow. In 1271 the young Bruce who swore the oath of King Alexander had come home to Annandale from the Crusade : travelling one day in Carrick he met a hunt, and among its riders was Marjorie Countess of Carrick, young and a widow. Bruce was not a man of great energy, it would seem, but he had a most decorative presence—*egregius miles, iuvenis speciosissimus*. The Countess lost her heart to him at sight, and insisted, apparently rather against his will, on taking him home with her to Turnberry. She was a ward of the Crown, and the greatest heiress in Scotland, but a fortnight later the two of them were married, without the formality of the King's consent. Alexander was angry at first, but pardoned them. Robert Bruce became in his wife's right Earl of Carrick. In 1274 their eldest son was born, and called Robert after the custom of his house : he soon had acquired a number of brothers and sisters, but there was no sign that three of them would wear crowns of three different countries, that three would die upon a foreign scaffold, and two more suffer years of painful prison. And when the small Robert was born a boy called William was playing about the Renfrewshire house of his father, a country laird and vassal of the Stewarts, whose name was Sir Malcolm Wallace of Elderslie.

But their stormy destinies showed no cloud as yet. Indeed, the country by about 1280 seemed more secure than she had ever been. England and Norway seemed to have settled to friendship, to be further sealed in the latter case by a marriage. The lords were loyal vassals to the King, and his firm peace kept them from war with one another. The country loved him : the people had known him for long now, for he was nearly forty, and they throve under his rule as under his father's, with

> sons [wealth] of ale and brede,
> Off wyne and wax, off gamyn and gle.

It has often been remarked that the constitutional developments of mediaeval Scotland are slight and uninteresting, as indeed they are : we have no Provisions of Oxford or Magna Charta. The reason is in the characters of the Kings. Stephen of England, Henry II, John, and Henry III, even Richard I, who was not ungenerous, make a poor show as kings beside David, the Alexanders, even Malcolm IV. The Crown,

to the small folk, as later under the Stewarts, was not
tyranny but a defence against tyranny : while those
lords who found their privilege lopped by a king were
Scots, and worked more directly than in England :
instead of changing the general law of the country in
order to make opposition to him legal, they merely
revolted without preliminaries. None the less, some
sort of legislative assembly was developing by now. Its
germ was David I's Council of great vassals and the
Officers of State. By William's time it was known as
the Curia Regis, and seems to have been composed of
prelates, earls, and barons. A foreigner, Jordan de
Fantosme, uses the phrase *plenier parlement* of it, and
in English documents the word *parlement* is used for
the assemblies of 1284 and 1290. The word, however,
is barely specialising out of its original sense of (a
meeting for) discussion. It does not appear in Scots
records till 1293, though then the context suggests it
is not a new one. Thanks to the wholesale destruction
of records previous to 1300, this is all that we can say
with certainty. It does not seem to have been till
Bruce's time that the burghs were represented on this
body, though there are earlier references to a *com-
munitas* which appears to be distinct from lords and
prelates.

We know that in this reign as in that before it the
King's law ran with firmness through the country.
Every year Alexander went through his kingdom with
his Justiciar, being met by the Sheriff at the border of
each shire. Within this firm framework of adminis-

tration both trade and agriculture had scope to flourish. We know that temporal lands were worth twice as much and church lands half as much again as they were to be no more than a life-time later. By this time the customs of Berwick, the principal entrepôt for foreign trade, were worth £2000 a year,[1] those of all England being then worth about £8000 : an Englishman calls it a second Alexandria. Fifteen other towns had sufficient foreign trade to require authorities who could grant a *cocket* or customs clearance certificate : they included burghs as far north as Cromarty and Dingwall.

The Church too flourished, though there were few new foundations, for the last reign had made so many that none were needed. There is only one great abbey of this time, Devorgilla's Dulce Cor, Sweetheart Abbey, by the Solway, built in 1275 to hold her husband's heart.

Strong castles were growing, with room in them for a spacious way of living. The old wooden castle on its motte gave way to great stone ones, groups of towers joined by curtain walls. Little is left of them : Robert Bruce razed a hundred and thirty-seven, in order to leave no foothold for the invader : but Kildrummie, built by St Gilbert of Moray, and Bothwell, show at least what the greater ones were like.

Of the other arts of the time we know very little. No doubt the tradition of music still endured, and the

---

[1] In 1305 they were worth under £120.

thirteenth century yields at least names and traces of a literature in the various languages. We know that an elaborate literary tradition persisted in Gaelic, but we do not know what of its remains are Scots, though the Irish epics were certainly known in Scotland. The Glenmasan MS. of *Deirdre* belongs to 1238, and shows that there were Scots versions of some of them, and early in the century Muireadach Albannach, Murdo the Scotsman, was writing religious verse. French literature was certainly read, if not written. Barbour makes Robert Bruce illustrate an argument by quoting in passing from the ' matter of Rome,' the classical romances, and in another place tells how he read to his men from the tale of *Fierabras* to pass the time : and a Picard poet, one Guillaume le Clerc, made a French *Roman de Fergus*, whose hero, an Arthurian knight, is son to Somerled and whose setting is for part of the tale the Mearns : it is dedicated to Alan of Galloway, of a Celtic house. Among Latin writers certain Scots of this age had a European reputation that lasted long, though they are scholars rather than men of letters. The mathematical treatises of Johannes de Sacrobosco, John Hollybush, were edited in the sixteenth century by no less a man than Melancthon. The most famous was the mathematician and astronomer Michael Scott, who taught at Oxford, Paris, and Toledo, brought Aristotle back to Europe again, and was a notable figure at the brilliant Sicilian court of the Emperor Frederick II, *Stupor Mundi*. In pure letters the most famous name

is that of Thomas Lermont, Thomas the Rhymer of
Ercildoune, Earlston in Lauderdale. We do not know
if his work was French or English : from his district,
and time, it may have been the latter. He gave to the
great structure of the Arthurian Legend a famous
version of the Tristram story, known and praised in
Germany : an English poet of the next generation
(Thomas seems to have outlived Alexander III) calls
it the greatest of all *gestes*. What is thought to be the
earliest of the English metrical romances purports to
be based on it, or may even be a southernised version
of it. Certain other anonymous romances, which are
clearly Scots, may perhaps belong to this time : it is
not easy to fix their dates very surely.

Education prospered : besides the schools of the
Church the burgh grammar-schools were growing up.
That of Ayr dates from the beginning of the century,
and that of Aberdeen, still something of an outpost,
was founded some time before 1262. There was still
no university in Scotland : Scots scholars travelled as
far as those of Spain and Italy, but the growing fame
of Oxford, its accessibility, and the friendship with
England, made it specially popular, and in 1262
Devorgilla and her husband John Baliol founded a
college there for Scottish students.

The peace and welfare were soon to be so shattered
that we have only glimpses of their details. But from
all that we know, the Scotland of 1280, though not
rich, was not far from being the best-governed country
in Europe.

For some years—for a decade yet—the peace was to last. The incident of the homage, in 1278, is the first mutter of the coming storm, and might have passed off as so many other previous threats had passed. In the midsummer of 1281 the first rim of the shadow touched that brightness. The young Prince David died : he was eight years old, and John of Fordun, looking back, sees in his death *initium dolorum Scotiae futurorum*, the beginning of the coming sorrows of Scotland, and cries, *Heu, proh dolor, O Scotia! Quoniam si cognovisses et tu futuros luctuum dies et lachrymarum*, ' Woe to thee, Scotland, for if thou hadst known how many days of sorrows and of tears were to fall on thee.' Those days were soon to come now. Yet a prince and a princess of Scotland both were left, and growing up to manhood and womanhood. Within the next eighteen months they had both been married, and their marriages brought new allies to the kingdom. In August 1281 the peace with Norway (which never, indeed, was to be broken thereafter) was cemented by the wedding of Princess Margaret to the young Eirik II, who had just succeeded his father. Her dowry of 14,000 merks, *novae et usualis monetae*, reveals the wealth of the Crown, by contrast with her mother's 5000, paid with such difficulty and reluctance. Next year at Roxburgh, on the 15th November, Prince Alexander married another Margaret, the daughter of the Count of Flanders, a grandson of the Emperor of the East : and Flanders was the market of Northern Europe.

Next year the shadow began to grow and spread.

In the spring of 1283, it would seem in April, Queen
Margaret of Norway bore a daughter and died. For
long that year her brother, too, was ill. He recovered
for a while, and then relapsed. At the New Year he
lay at Lindores Abbey, his mind wandering in the
delirium of his fever : then on the 27th January, six
days after his twentieth birthday, he spoke clearly, and
foretold that next day the sun of Scotland would set.
Next day he died : his young wife had borne no child,
and the only possible heir to King Alexander, nearer
in blood than the great-grandson of his great-uncle,
was his baby granddaughter, Margaret, Princess of
Norway.

On the 5th of February 1284, a week after his son's
death, the King called his great vassals into Council at
Scone—thirteen earls, eleven prelates, and twenty-five
lords : and they recognised Princess Margaret as his
heir. Reading the names, one feels the curtain shake
for the next act. Robert Bruce, the Lord of Annandale,
is there, the same who forty-six years previously had
seen a similar settlement on himself. Next him in the
list is James the High Steward of Scotland, who had
recently succeeded to his father, and whose grandson
was to bear the Scottish Crown. Next him, John
Baliol, who bore it also above an Empty Jacket ; then
John Comyn of Badenoch and William Soulis : and
among the earls is Robert Bruce's son, the Earl of
Carrick, father already of another Robert, who by this
time was nearly ten years old.

It was clear, however, that the King must marry.

He was only forty-two, in full vigour yet, with the promise of many years of brilliant reign. He chose, like his father, a second wife from France, Yolette, the daughter of the great Comte de Dreux : and to Scotland's sorrow, she was very lovely. He married her in the great abbey kirk of Jedburgh, on the 14th October of 1285, with much pomp and splendour. But there was a masque at the royal feast that followed, a dance of armed men : and a strange and ghostly figure, like Death himself, whom no man had bidden, was seen to dance among them. There were wild thunderstorms, unseasonably, and a whisper ran about Scotland through that winter that the Day of Judgment was very near at hand.

Yet all seemed well. His bride's beauty made the King her eager lover. The kingdom continued in its thriving estate . . . until March the next year. On the 19th of that month the King held a Council in Edinburgh Castle. The business was done : he ate and drank and jested with one of his courtiers about the rumour of the Day of Judgment, for the night was wild storm : they would feel it, high on that rock. Then, against all men's will, he would ride to join the Queen, who was at Kinghorn across the Firth of Forth. The master of the Queen's Ferry begged him to stay : he crossed, in great danger but safely, and from Inverkeithing he rode on, with only three of his gentlemen and two guides. In the dark and storm they lost their way near the cliff, and were separated. The King's horse missed footing. In the morning they found

Alexander dead on the shore. The sovereign of the Scotland strong kings had made was a baby girl, not yet three, at the court of Norway.

The child Queen's nominal reign lasted four years, whose detailed story is told in another volume. Old Robert Bruce endeavoured to seize the Crown, but gave up the attempt, and still the peace endured. There was almost a federation of Scotland and England, that so long had lived at peace with one another. Sound and careful arrangements were made to secure its success, without harm to the welfare of either country. Then the child died before she had seen her kingdom. There was no certain heir, but many claimants : and as nearest sovereign, head of a friendly nation, kin to the dead King and Queen, Edward of England was called to arbitrate, and the Three Hundred Years' War launched on its course.

Three times within the length of a single lifetime was Scotland leaderless, and three times stamped down in apparently final conquest. And three times, as soon as she could find a leader, she flung off her assailants, at odds of five to one, rose from the dead, and became a free country once more. She owes that glory to Wallace, his pupil Bruce, and the younger men who in turn were fired by their spirit : but she owes it also to those generations who through long centuries built up a Scotland that could greatly follow greatness as it arose.

BIBLIOGRAPHY

Sources and Early Historians

The Acts of the Parliament of Scotland.

T. Rymer. *Foedera.*

J. Bain. *Calendar of Documents relating to Scotland.*

A. Lawrie. *Early Scottish Charters.*

C. Innes. *National Manuscripts of Scotland.*

F. Palgrave. *Documents an d Records illustrating the History of Scotland.*

J. Stevenson. *Illustrations of Early Scottish History.*

D. Patrick. *Statutes of the Scottish Church.*

A. O. Anderson. *Sources of Early Scottish History.*

Gildas. *De Excidio Britanniae.*

Adamnan. *Life of St Columba.*

William of Glasgow. *Carmen de morte Sumerledi.*

Chronica de Mailros.

Chronica Regum.

Chronicle of the Picts.

Chronicle of Dalriata.

Chronicon Coenobii S. Crucis.

Duan Albannach.

John of Fordun and W. Bower. *Scotichronicon.*

Annals of Ulster.

Annals of Tighernach.

Book of Armagh.

Book of Leinster.

A. O. Anderson. *Scottish History from English Chronicles.*

Anglo-Saxon Chronicle.

Ailred. *Vita Niniani. Eulogium Davidis. Relatio de Standardo.*

Æthelward. *Chronica.*

Annals of Durham.

Annals of Lindisfarne.

Bede. *Chronicon. Historia Ecclesiastica.*
Benedict of Peterborough. *Gesta Henrici II.*
Chronicon de Lanercost.
Eadmer. *Historia.*
Florence of Worcester. *Chronicon.*
Gesta Stephani.
Henry of Huntingdon. *Historia Anglorum.*
Roger Hoveden. *Chronica.*
Jordan de Fantosme. *Chronique de la Guerre.*
Nennius. *Historia Brittonum.*
Matthew Paris. *Chronica Majora. Historia Anglorum.*
Symeon of Durham. *Historia Dunelmensis Ecclesiae. Historia Regum.*
N. Trivet. *Annales.*
Turgot. *Vita S. Margaritae.*
Walter of Hemingburgh. *Chronicon de Gestis Regum Angliae.*
William of Malmesbury. *Gesta Regum Angliae. Historia Novella.*
Annales Cambriae.
Fagrskinna.
Grettis Saga.
Olaf Tryggvison's Saga.
Orkneyinga Saga.
St Olaf's Saga.
Saxo Grammaticus. *Gesta Danorum.*
Heimskringla.
Tacitus. *Agricola.*

MODERN HISTORIANS

J. Hill Burton. *History of Scotland.*
A. Bellesheim. *History of the Catholic Church in Scotland.*
G. Grub. *Ecclesiastical History of Scotland.*
J. Cunningham. *Church History of Scotland.*
W. C. Mackenzie. *The Highlands and Isles of Scotland.*
E. W. Robertson. *Scotland under the Early Kings.*
Cosmo Innes. *Scotland in the Middle Ages.*
V. Gordon Childe. *The Pre-history of Scotland.*
R. Munro. *Pre-historic Scotland.*
A. Black Scott. *St Ninian.*
A. Boyd Smith. *The Pictish Church and Nation.*

W. Douglas Simpson. *The Celtic Church in Scotland. The Historic St Columba.*

J. Dowden. *The Celtic Church in Scotland.*

R. L. Bremner. *The Norsemen in Albann.*

A. W. Brøgger. *Ancient Emigrants.*

J. Johnstone. *The Norwegian Account of King Haco's Expedition.*

J. Fergusson. *Alexander III.*

M. F. Moore. *The Lands of the Scots Kings in England.*

J. MacKinnon and J. A. R. MacKinnon. *Constitutional History of Scotland.*

I. F. Grant. *Economic History of Scotland. Social and Economic Development of Scotland before 1603.*

R. W. Billings. *Baronial and Ecclesiastical Architecture of Scotland.*

D. MacGibbon and T. Ross. *Castellated and Domestic Architecture of Scotland. Ecclesiastical Architecture of Scotland.*

J. Stirling-Maxwell. *Shrines and Homes of Scotland.*

W. M. Mackenzie. *The Mediaeval Castle in Scotland.*

C. Oman. *The Art of War in the Middle Ages.*

H. Waddell. *The Wandering Scholars.*

ENGLAND

R. H. Hodgkin. *History of the Anglo-Saxons.*

J. H. Ramsay. *The Foundations of England. The Angevin Empire.*

IRELAND

A. S. Green. *History of the Irish to 1014.*

E. Curtis. *History of Mediaeval Ireland, 1110-1513.*

S. Gwynn. *A History of Ireland.*

NORWAY

Knut Gjerset. *History of the Norwegian People.*

FRANCE

E. Lavisse. *Histoire de France.*

F. P. R. Guizot. *Histoire de la civilisation en France.*

EUROPE

C. Oman. *The Dark Ages.*
T. F. Tout. *The Empire and the Papacy.*
The Cambridge Mediaeval History.
As an introductory survey, the relevant chapters of C. S. Terry's
Short History of Europe: Mediaeval may be read, or two
small but excellent books in Messrs Benn's Sixpenny Library,
M. Cary's *History of Western Europe*, A.D. *1-455*, and Claude
Jenkins' *Mediaeval European History*, *455-1453.*

U

INDEX

In this index, names including a surname are entered under the prænomen when the surname is personal to the individual and under the surname when this latter is an hereditary family name : thus Ragnar Lodvarson, but Wishart, William.

307

By Agnes Mure Mackenzie, M.A., D.Litt.

*The five volumes which follow form collectively a general
history of Scotland from earliest times until 1748.*

THE FOUNDATIONS OF SCOTLAND
FROM THE EARLIEST TIMES TO 1286   12s. 6d.

ROBERT BRUCE KING OF SCOTS   5s.

"Bruce was one of the last of the real heroes; for to be a hero,
in that sense, one must be the representative of some race or
religion, the chosen champion of a whole people."—The late
G. K. CHESTERTON, *broadcasting*.

"This book will take its place as the standard biography for this
generation."—*The Times*.

THE RISE OF THE STEWARTS
1329–1513
With frontispiece of James IV.   5s.

"*The Rise of the Stewarts* is an admirable work and ought to do
much to adjust the popularly distorted view of Scottish history.
It is written with a fine feeling for words and a true sense of the
past."—MORAY MCLAREN in the *Spectator*.

THE SCOTLAND OF QUEEN MARY
AND THE RELIGIOUS WARS, 1513–1638
With frontispiece of Mary.   12s. 6d.

THE PASSING OF THE STEWARTS: 1639–1748
With frontispiece of Claverhouse.   12s. 6d.

"Her work as a whole is so well documented, and her outlook so
balanced, that even her most provocative judgments are not to
be challenged without consideration."—*Observer*.

***

W. & R. CHAMBERS, LTD.: LONDON & EDINBURGH

WILLIAM WALLACE
GUARDIAN OF SCOTLAND

by JAMES FERGUSSON   5s.

"He (the author) has handled the facts with concision, clarity and a scrupulous care; but the book is very far from being dry, for he has brought to their exposition a sense of both human and political values that enables him to make their meaning plain, and a turn for lucid and straightforward prose, lit and pointed by well-chosen quotations from his sources."—*Times Literary Supplement.*

ALEXANDER THE THIRD
KING OF SCOTLAND

by JAMES FERGUSSON

With frontispiece of Dunfermline Abbey. 5s.

"Mr Fergusson has dealt admirably with his subject, bringing out not only the reign's significance but the attractive character of the King.... His narrative is clear and full but not overloaded, and told in a prose that has pleasant echoes of Berners."—*Times Literary Supplement.*

SHRINES AND HOMES OF SCOTLAND

by SIR JOHN STIRLING-MAXWELL, K.T.

Second Edition. With 200 illustrations.

10s. 6d.

This is a book with a human appeal. Sir John Stirling-Maxwell looks at Scots buildings with an appreciative understanding of the mind of those who built them, and a scholar's knowledge about the people who worshipped and lived in them.

"If it were only for its splendid collection of photographs, this record of what survives from Scotland's early architecture deserves to be treasured by all her sons."—*Observer.*

"This is the best short history of Scottish architecture yet published."—*Spectator.*

W. & R. CHAMBERS, LTD.: LONDON & EDINBURGH